Ninja Tools and Weapons

Ninja Tools and Weapons

Michel Farivar, MD

White Cat Publications, LLC.
2013

Ninja Tools and Weapons

Edited by Charles P. Zaglanis

FIRST EDITION
ISBN-10: 0984692096
ISBN-13: 978-0-9846920-9-5
Published May 2013

Published by White Cat Publications, LLC.
33080 Industrial Road, Suite 101
Livonia, MI 48150
www.whitecatpublications.com

Cover design by Scott Wilson
Interior design by Vasha Lewkowicz

"To every martial artist who has felt time collapse in the search to connect with their ancestors."

Contents

Historical Periods of Japan (AD)

Nara 710–794

Heian 794–1185

Kamakura 1185–1333

Nambokucho 1333–1396

Muromachi 1396–1568

Aizuchi-Momyama 1568–1596

Edo (Tokugawa) 1596–1780

Bakumatsu (late Edo) 1780–1877

Meiji, Taisho, Early Showa 1877–1945

Late Showa to Heisei 1945-Present

Forward

If a teacher's accomplishment can be gauged by his best student, then Grandmaster Robert Law of the Geijin Ryu has accomplished a great deal in his life. In Michel Farivar, he has shown the world what the modern art of Ninjutsu is all about.

Like other great martial artists, Grandmaster Law is a living dynamic and his ever evolving Geijin Ryu Ninjutsu is the proof of his creative genius. He did not create this art, but every master has to contribute something to it; and merely keeping it alive and moving forward demands a creative intelligence. In the nearly thirty years that I have known him, his mastery of combat techniques has never ceased to amaze me. He is the most physically capable man that I have ever known. When he was nearly 80 years old, I personally watched him carry a tree on one shoulder for over three miles, and half of that journey was uphill. Once when I went to visit him, he was restraining two 200 pound Rottweilers with both their leashes held in one hand. When the two massive animals saw me, they lurched forward, their mouths snapping, showing teeth that made me want to turn and run. Surely no man could hold these two monstrous dogs with only one hand. But Grandmaster Law did. I saw his massive forearm muscles tense, saw them sharpen with the strain, but the grandmaster never used more than that one hand and, despite their rage, the powerful Rottweilers were unable to cause him to move so much as an inch.

But there is more to Dr. Farivar's teacher.

He is passionate and brilliant, angry and peace loving, and a man of action who often prefers stillness. I have seen him so angry he hit a heavy weight bag hard enough it actually split in two, and I have seen him cry at movies. He is grandmaster of a supremely deadly art but happens to be funnier than a primetime stand-up comic. He is suspicious of everyone but loyal to his family and his students. Grandmaster Robert Law lives and loves life to its fullest. He is not a stereotype. He does not wear martial arts uniforms strapped in by a black belt with gold stripes. He himself is the validation of his physical prowess and there is none like him.

For that matter, Grandmaster Law has no use at all for lineages.

"There's only one way you can tell who a guy is," he told me once. "It's by what they do. If you need to see scrolls to see if an art is Ninja, you're crazy. Think about it—would a real Ninja have a piece of paper that said he was a Ninja? That's how you can tell if a guy is fake. They start talking about their lineage and crap like that and it's like joining a cult. Use your brain—what kind of a spy has a paper saying he's a spy? What kind of assassin has a paper saying he's an assassin? These schools that got papers saying they're real Ninjutsu are just looking for saps so they can get their money."

And yes, that is the way Grandmaster Robert Law actually talks. As a member of Mensa for over forty years, though, I can honestly say that he is the most intelligent, unconventional, and brilliantly competent martial artist I have ever had the pleasure to meet, and I have met many.

When I was told that I needed back surgery after prednisone injections into my spine were unsuccessful; when I couldn't stand straight and my leg ached and felt numb at the same time, I thought I had no alternative. Two different doctors told me the same story. My discs needed to be fused. There were no alternatives and the potential results were iffy. I called Grandmaster Law and explained that I wouldn't be able to visit him in a few days as I'd planned. He was conducting one of his Training Summits and I was going to interview him for an article I was writing.

He asked if I could find a way to get there. If I could get to the Summit, he said, he would look at my back and see what he could do. Sometimes it helps if you move some things around, he said. I thanked him and said I'd try to make the Summit, but wasn't sure if I could. Driving was painful for me. The pain would start before I had even been on the road for 10 minutes.

I mentioned the possibility that the Grandmaster could help my back to my doctor.

"Don't do it," he said.

He didn't need to say anything else. Don't let anyone mess with your spine who isn't a medical professional.

The pain got worse. Surgery or let Grandmaster Law manipulate my back? Those were my options.

I made it to the Summit a day late. It was a five hour drive with a good back, but the pain, even with the medications I was on, meant that I stopped every forty-five minutes to get out and walk around. By the time I arrived in the middle of Ontario, I felt like I'd been on the road for weeks, not days. If I didn't ask him to help with my back, at least I could spend a half day with him, conduct the interview, and suffer through a long, long trip back.

Surgery I understood. Back manipulation? That was a different matter. I didn't even understand what was involved, how it might help or make it worse. Grandmaster Law wasn't and isn't a doctor. But sciatica pain is sometimes nagging and sometimes debilitating. I decided to ask him for his help. Really, though, I didn't have to because when he saw me coming across the field dragging my leg, he told me, "You look like shit. Lay down and let me see what I can do. You get no guarantees and I'm not a doctor. You got that?"

I did. He would try and help, but he wasn't acting in a medical capacity so if I ended up crippled it was my problem. Those were the rules. He'd try to help, but if I got hurt in the process I shouldn't bother suing him. If you think that sounds coldhearted, consider that he worked on my back for five minutes and I have not had a problem since and it's been five years.

It wasn't a miracle cure and Grandmaster Law isn't a psychic healer. It was the application of his art's knowledge of the human body with his skilled hands. My back has never bothered me since, and I will be grateful to him for the rest of my life.

The grandmaster has very few students, because he expects them to be serious about the art. If they're not, he doesn't need them and pushes them away. He told me that the way he looks at it, the techniques of the Geijin Ryu are too valuable to pass on to idiots. The general public's understanding of Ninja and the art of Ninjutsu is drawn from comic books and movies. Throwing stars and dark wraparound hoods, smoke bombs and split toed shoes called tabi. The death touch, mystic hand symbols and super swords that cut through titanium. The Ninja cult of feudal Japan with a little anime thrown in. Grandmaster Law has no patience for such things. Even less than for those who claim Ninja lineage.

Over the years he and I have talked about this problem. What is Ninjutsu in the modern sense of the word? Is it relevant to us now or is it a caricatured legend like Camelot? Is Ninjutsu the art of espionage, or martial techniques, or assassination? I asked these questions because Ninjutsu is a worldwide empire of Ninjutsu franchises for some schools. They are like re-enactors reliving past glories of other men and women while their arts stagnate. Surely the art is more than that. Surely it should live and grow.

"It's about the mind," he told me. "That's where power comes from. It's the mind that makes the tools that get the job done. It's the tools become the weapons of the art. You get that?" he asked. "This art's about the mind. From there you get the tools and from there the weapons and the ways you got to use them. And there's always something new. That's why I don't name techniques. You call it a technique and it has a beginning and end and things aren't like that. The world keeps moving and so do we."

The mind makes the tools and the tools are the weapons. And the mind devises the strategies to use them.

So it was no surprise to me that Grandmaster Law would choose Dr. Farivar as his successor. Dr. Farivar is a physician and a psychiatrist. A man who understands both the body and the mind. He is an accomplished artist and writer. And he is a man who never quits. He is relentless in his pursuit of knowledge and devoted to mastering the challenges he takes up.

Grandmaster Law is both a brutal and brilliant teacher, and, as I've already said, he quickly sorts out those who will not last. Dr. Farivar did more than last. Through fierce determination and commitment, he achieved the blessing of the grandmaster that the art of Geijin Ryu would pass to him as its next grandmaster.

This book, *Ninja Tools and Weapons*, shows the wisdom of Grandmaster Law's choice. Dr. Farivar has focused in on the lynchpin of the Ninja art, which was their refined ability to create unique weapons and tools to accomplish their goals. His careful research and disciplined analysis of the information he uncovered make for compelling reading because Dr. Farivar's study of Ninja tools and weapons unveils aspects of the Ninja mind that have been addressed nowhere else.

He reveals the origins of the art and explains how the development of the mindset that created the staggering array of Ninja weaponry as we know it today. When Grandmaster Law trained Dr. Farivar, he did not train him with swords and other classical martial arts weapons. Instead, Dr. Farivar learned to use screwdrivers, credit cards, computer cords and crowbars. He learned to use the edges of desks and buildings as weapons. While students of other martial arts trained wearing school uniforms and in bare feet, Grandmaster Law trained Dr. Farivar and his other students wearing street clothes.

There were no beginner and advanced techniques; no artificial conceptual separations were allowed. Dr. Farivar was trained in the dark, in the woods and mountains. The training was harsh and always demanding because Grandmaster Law's unwavering standard was physical mastery. Many arts teach students one or two techniques per class. Grandmaster Law never allowed repetition of techniques. Instead, he put Dr. Farivar and the other students through fifty to two hundred techniques in a day.

At first glance, Dr. Farivar and Grandmaster Law could not be more different. Dr. Farivar is soft spoken, thoughtful, and deliberate. Grandmaster Law is loud and forceful, bigger than life. But you can see the similarities in their eyes. Both are men of penetrating intelligence. Dr. Farivar speaks multiple languages, is university educated and a natural born scholar. Grandmaster Law is educated in a different way. His knowledge of the combat arts, woodcraft, and an almost endless variety of trades is formidable. Both men's eyes reveal an intensity and focus that is intimidating.

The drawings in this book are done by Dr. Farivar, who is a gifted artist. I have a copy of his masterful rendition of Fudo hanging in my laboratory. Grandmaster Law's woodworking is an art in itself, and his carved demon masks belong in a gallery.

Both men believe that Ninjutsu is an empowering art whose time has come to share its benefits with the world. Dr. Farivar's background as a clinical psychiatrist gives him the insight to reveal its benefits for health and strength to the rest of us. By this book, he honors not only his teacher, Grandmaster Law, but the rest of us as well by giving us a new perspective on the endless possibilities for growth intrinsic in the true Ninja tradition.

It is my pleasure to publish this book by Dr. Farivar, honoring with its publication the lifelong devotion to the art by his teacher Grandmaster Robert Law. By choosing Dr. Farivar as his successor, he has helped move our understanding of the Ninja art forward, as you will learn by reading this book.

Ferrel D. Moore
May 2013

Who Were the Ninja?

Above all else, the Ninja were feared.

Their judgment was swift, their vengeance final.

To commoners and Samuari alike, they were nearly mythical beings. They were dark magicians—assassins for hire from whom no one was safe. They struck in the night like deadly shadows. Their stealth and lethality caused debilitating fear to clench the hearts of their enemies.

No one was safe from the Ninja.

They were thought of as both supranatural and supernatural beings, whose knowledge and physical prowess were legendary.

Yet commoners had little to fear from the Ninja. Their true enemies were Samuari and oppressive government overlords. The Ninja worked as hired assassins and spies for these over-privileged individuals. Operating through intermediaries, they took money from one overlord to wreak havoc on the other, then disappeared until contracted again by one side or the other.

Ninja were both the ultimate weapon and the ultimate mystery.

What was the source of their power? In a society where access to weapons was brutally controlled, in an authoritarian world where tyrants ruled through sheer military might, how could such people survive? Hunted by those who feared them, how could they achieve the ability to strike with impunity against those they accepted as targets while remaining invisible to those who pursued them?

To understand the mind and life of the Ninja more completely, we must also question their morality: Were they really without values? Did human life have so little meaning to them that they would literally kill anyone, anywhere for money?

So compelling is this potent combination of myth and mystery that even today, five hundred years later, we still grope blindly through the shadowed mists that engulf their history and struggle to grasp the secrets of their power.

The hundreds of years intervening frustrate our attempts to understand them, but unraveling the mystery of these shadow warriors is made possible by studying the two threads that bind both the mythos and the reality of the Ninja together. To accomplish this, we must reveal and sympathetically understand the beliefs and methods of these legendary people; it is from the union of these two elements of their psyche that all the power and substance of their popular legend was born.

Nowhere is the synergistic union more clearly displayed for our study than in the Ninja's creation and double-edged utilization of their tools. From the usage and transmutation of daily implements into weapons of survival in the face of seemingly insurmountable odds, we will divine the intertwining of their beliefs and their methods into a platform for personal power unlike any the world had ever seen. We will explore this in great detail, because each tool systematically puts into place another piece of this intricate puzzle to ultimately reveal a clear picture of the mind and methods of the legendary Ninja.

The first step in our journey of discovery begins with learning who the Ninja were and where they came from. From the origins of their people will flow the origins of their beliefs.

✳✳✳

In spite of how much has already been written about the Ninja, much about them remains mysterious, and the existence of contemporary, derivative schools continues to be regarded with skepticism by many martial arts scholars.

Common stereotypes of the Ninja usually range from casting them as epic heroes to casting them as soulless mercenaries. In many historical accounts, they are conspicuous by their absence. In others, their legacy is documented in a more or less sporadic manner throughout Japanese history. Early military strategy writings in China and Japan occasionally mention using "spies." Ninja were indeed spies, though probably not the only group working in that capacity. Although the popular reputation of the Ninja is very strongly rooted in their legendary prowess in the art of espionage, over time it has come to encompass much more.

Written Japanese records go back at least 1500 years, and further still in China. Donn Draeger and Robert Smith in their book Comprehensive Asian Fighting Arts point to the earliest known references to Ninjutsu dating from the reign of Empress *Suiko* 593-628 AD. They indicate that the name "Shinobi" was given to a warrior *Otomo no Saijin* and memorialized in writing for his work supporting prince *Shotoku Taishi* during that period. Additional mentions occur, according to Draeger and Smith, during the Heian period. This establishes that Ninja were firmly integrated into military operations by the time of the Gempei War during the years 1180-1185. References to the Ninja as spies, saboteurs, and assassins were recorded by Samurai or their chroniclers.

In general, Ninja families and groups did not keep written records of their exploits or their lineages. Much like the secret societies and many martial arts schools in China, traditions were passed on orally. As an interesting side note, we should observe that the very existence of the princess or empress Suiko and several other Imperial figures predating Shotoku Taishi are postulated by some to have not even existed as actual Imperial rulers. They were instead inserted during the writing or editing of the *Nihon Shoki* to justify the Imperial reign of Shotoku (18, pgs 44-46). Controversy over the content and meaning of historical records is typical. In fact, it becomes readily evident that those who wrote these documents most likely had agendas of their own. The potential for such bias should always be kept in mind when examining portrayals of historical events.

In the introduction to the Shoninki, it says that the first open revelation of the already established Ninja art was during the Gempei war. Minamoto no Yoshitsune was said to have "selected valiant warriors to employ during the battle as Shinobi" (22, p. 28). This passage, however, is quite vague. It could easily be interpreted to mean that Yoshitsune merely selected bushi (warriors) to act as Shinobi. In other words, they may not have been professional Shinobi/Ninja. The mythology surrounding Yoshitsune includes the belief that he himself was a trained Shinobi, something that so far we have never been able to independently verify.

Schools of martial arts that include Ninjutsu methods in their curricula have old written and illustrated records of the arts that date back no more than 100-300 years. Yet it is claimed by several authors, without any clear historical justification, that the arts originated back well into the first millennium. It is, in fact, stated in the shoninki and commonly taught to students of Ninjutsu today that Ninjutsu is actually that old. One of the interesting things we learn from Ninjutsu records recently available to us (besides the fact that they are relatively recent when compared to the art's purported age) is that they show virtually no combative techniques. Instead they showcase Ninja tools, some weapons, strategy, and stealth methodologies. The records of such schools that do show fighting techniques are taken from the Samurai arts they taught.

The name "Ninja" is apparently not one that Shinobi assigned themselves. It is a popular name given them by mainstream Japanese society around 1600 AD. It is commonly assumed that the early Ninja (prior to at least 1500 AD) were not known as "Ninja." They were instead known by a variety of names. Some of the more common names such as *Shinobi-(no)-mono*, *Shinobi* (for short); *Monomi* and "Ninja" are still used today. No one seems to know exactly how old these names are. So far, none of the source material available to Westerners that I have reviewed has clearly indicated a comprehensive term they would have used for themselves. "Shinobi" would have likely been the most proper and widespread name.

Stephen Turbull's book *Ninja* indicates that prior to the popular expression "Ninja," the Shinobi were likely referred to by names relating to the specific functions they performed (16). This is consistent with our current belief that it depended to some extent on who was having the conversation. Non-Ninja likely simply called them spies (*kanchoo, suppa, onmitsu*) or scouts (*teisatsu*), or even by cruder terms like *rappa* and *kusa*. Mr. Turnbull indicated that kusa means, "sniffing and listening." In fact, Kusa simply means, "grass," which seems to be a possible reference to hiding in the grass and invisibility. I have also heard it used to describe imbedded espionage agents, which like blades of grass are indistinguishable from one another (i.e. commoners) and are many. Rappa can be translated as "disheveled waves" according to Draeger. Did the term "wave" refer to a warrior in the sense that it does with the term ronin? And in this case can the descriptor "disheveled" indicate someone lowly as would be a ragged beggar? The actual kanji will need to be studied to accurately translate this term. If and when the kanji become available, the type of warrior referred to and the context in which it was used can shed light on this issue.

In fact, our understanding is that these terms were used in different places by different people to denote specific groups performing various activities associated with Ninjutsu, all of whom were Shinobi of some kind or another. According to Stephen Turbull, the term "rappa" was used in the Kanto region and refers to local rogue warrior elements that were likely bandits. These people had local knowledge and unorthodox skills that made them useful to warlords who therefore employed and supported them. The name "kusa" was reportedly used in the province of Kai and describes unmounted warriors that waited to ambush enemies at night, especially scouts from enemy encampments. They worked directly in the service of generals during times of war (16).

Other names such as *nosaru*, or "mountain monkeys," seem to refer to wild people who lived in the mountains, were likely undocumented, and ideal for committing untraceable anonymous acts.

There are a number of other names by which Ninja were known and therefore the art of Ninjutsu itself also went by various names. Ninja themselves probably did not use these names or even the word "Ninja" early on in their history. They are believed to have referred to themselves simply as Shinobi, or by their family or clan name. Thus, for example, the Iga Ninja group would simply call themselves *Iga shu* ("Iga Men" or "Men of Iga"). What is known about this terminology is only what is left behind in the chronicles written by those Samurai families who kept such records and what has been found in the Shoninki. If it were it not for these sources, this information would be completely lost.

The Shoninki was written originally in 1681 by Masazumi Natori (also known as Natori Sanjuro Masatake), a Shinobi of Samurai rank, retainer of the Kishu clan and translated in two separate works by Axel Mazuer and Anthony Cummins. It gives a fairly clear and rational explanation corroborating that the terminology used for Shinobi or Ninja varied with the region, city and/or domain that may have employed them. We see additional terms used such as *Oniwaban, Kurohabaki,* and a number of others. The author of the Shoninki expressed that Ninja, or Shinobi as they are referenced in the text, were to be clearly distinguished from thieves, some of whom performed their activities in the same manner as Ninja and whom he described as having an "art." The differentiating term for these thieves was *nusubito;* it is clear that, according to this author, this term was not to be used when referencing Ninja.

This point is important in revealing that Ninja differentiated themselves into distinguished groups, ranking themselves according to whom they served, the kind of service they provided, and their own internal code of ethical conduct. Grandmaster Law said many times that there were different types of Ninja: some were highly specialized warriors in assassination and night raids, others in espionage, while still others were generalists in most Ninjutsu activities. He also stated that many came to be Ninja from highly varied backgrounds, including criminal families who lived as thieves and bandits. According to Grandmaster Law, these groups were no less important as Ninja in terms of the services they provided and the role they played in society.

So what does the word "Ninja" really mean? The way the Kanji are written in Japanese (and their similar connotations in Chinese) can be interpreted in various ways. The concepts of patience and endurance emerge in the first ideogram, *nin.* However, the names chosen for important things like martial arts and their schools rarely have a singular meaning. We interpret the name "Ninja" as meaning "invisible people" or "invisible person." Conceptually, they are like default explanations of how things happen seemingly without explanation. For example, if an important political person were to die suddenly from unknown causes, this might cause a change in the balance of political power. The populace might develop a sense of unease, wondering if the event were part of some conspiracy, while the causative agent would be the "invisible people." Of course, no one would ever really know the truth, because if the Ninja had anything to do with it, they were sworn to secrecy.

The first kanji, *nin,* a blade over a heart representing patience and endurance, has also been said to refer to concealment and being hidden and might be interpreted to mean a blade hidden in one's heart. A blade over a heart can also be interpreted to indicate subjugation. The blade would represent authority and the heart would be the soul of the person. Another potential meaning is of the sword being the discipline or law of the warrior, with its dominance of the heart or soul. The later character means "person." The idea of concealment is also implied here through the meaning of one who is low. "Low" in this case can mean "commoner," thus possibly having to do with social class, or at least the class among which one is hidden. It is well known that Ninja were often considered to be warriors of low social standing and not legitimate members of the warrior class (known as *bushi*). They were also reputed to practice extreme discipline, necessary for the unsung achievements of their trade. "Low," in a literal sense, can mean low to the ground and concealed. As we shall see later, there is much more that is implied and to be understood about this term and what it means to be "invisible." Axel Mazuer wrote another interesting interpretation: that the heart beneath the blade refers to the fact that the Ninja is one who places himself (his soul and his heart) directly into harm's way, who risks his life in ways such as going into the territory of the enemy.

What is Ninjutsu?

Ninjutsu as it is known in the West has come a long way from how it was first portrayed to us in the early 1980s. Once the subject of B grade TV serials, even lousier movies, and of course, a whole cohort of comic books, it has somehow, slowly, gained a place among the martial arts practiced in Western nations. Notably, this evolution was paralleled years earlier in Japan, where many decades after the fall of the Samurai class and its feudal government a revival of interest in the martial arts occurred. In spite of the obvious nostalgia, it was clear to the Japanese by this time that there was no turning back to the old ways.

The revival also appears to have been a collective reaction of the Japanese populace to the erosion and loss of their cultural heritage in the rush to modernize and compete with Western nations. In the years leading up to World War II, Japan sought to strengthen its sense of identity by promoting all that was uniquely Japanese. Few things are closer to the core esthetic of the Japanese culture than their proud warrior heritage. It is an ancient and respected symbol of the Japanese assertion of itself against the great magnetic influence of China. The conjured image of the Ninja, revitalized along with their Samurai warrior counterparts, provided a mystical and phantasmal connection with the deep mystery and secrets of the past. The enduring and alluring dark power of these seemingly lost souls still captivate us today.

After World War II, equipped with little core knowledge of real Ninjutsu, Japanese media created romanticized films, manga (comics), and novels about the Ninja. This renewed vigor in the aftermath of the war occurred as the Japanese explored, and excelled at, promoting their culture to the world. This eventually resulted in a more open and honest interest in the historical Ninja. The intrigues of cold war espionage added new dimensions of interest in Ninjutsu. It was the needed stimulus to initiate a real search into understanding the Ninja for who they really were. There may even have been, in some quarters, an imperative sense to reinvent or re-contextualize the Ninja as a model for the modern spy. Scholars and martial artists came forward to report their knowledge of Ninjutsu. Some, like Seiko Fujita, had surfaced prior to the war. They were taken seriously by the Japanese government and by their martial arts contemporaries. Some, like Seiko Fujita himself, may have discreetly taught some Ninjutsu methods and strategy to the military schools. Others claimed to have used their knowledge and experience during the war and lived to tell the tale. Still others are said to have sold their secrets to the Americans and the Soviets, perhaps true to the Ninja practice of selling their services to the highest bidder. Those who operated in this way never went public. I'm told their activities continued quietly in the shadowy realm of spies and organized crime. Perhaps this is where they felt most at home.

As foreigners made inroads into Japanese culture and martial arts, they managed to get themselves initiated and trained to higher degrees of proficiency. Finally some of them found Ninjutsu. In other cases, Ninja families left Japan and settled in other nations, bringing their skills with them. Eventually these were taught to a handful of non-Japanese or people of mixed ethnicity. Not content to keep the art to themselves, Westerners went public with their knowledge and promoted it to enhance their prestige and profit by it. A few tried to keep it honest and serious, practicing in the traditional manner of hard work and combative relevance. Others, seeing a great opportunity to make money, promoted themselves even while possessing limited skills. They sold tiny morsels of Ninja knowledge to an eager public and ushered in the "Ninja Boom" of the 1980s.

This phase eventually passed. No-holds-barred martial arts competitions began later. A new era was ushered in by MMA (Mixed Martial Arts) and the UFC. These became today's new and different martial arts craze.

Although many practitioners now cringe at the exaggerated portrayals of Ninja during the "boom" days, some must still acknowledge that they wound up learning Ninjutsu, at least in part, due to the hype. We understand so much more today than we did back then. Many people now interested in the Ninja arts yearn to understand the true Ninja ways, but do they know why? Those who do, hopefully, are asking themselves how these arts benefit people today. Hopefully we are not done exploring this subject. It still retains the power to excite our imaginations like so many other timeless icons of the warrior world: Spartans, Gladiators, The Knights Templar, Shaolin Monks, the Samurai, Mongols, and the Indian braves among others.

The arts that comprise greater Ninjutsu evolved over centuries; the earlier forms of the art became more elaborate, broad, and inclusive with time. Not all groups that contributed to the formation of Ninja society and their arts were completely secretive. Although most were warriors of some kind, some groups were religious, while others belonged to various trades.

Warrior history in Japan indicates that, as early as the 7th century AD (well before the development of Samurai clans and the much later creation of the social caste system in the 16th century), the Japanese followed social models set by the Chinese for the conscription and training of armies. Although there were individuals and families who specialized in martial arts, it was not at all unusual for commoners to bear arms for battle and to be trained in fighting skills. In fact, looking at social models of organization and stratification according to rank and trade within the governance of later 8th century clans, it was expected that commoners, like their conscripted counterparts in China, would act as foot soldiers when war broke out (12, 23).

These historical precedents establish that martial arts were not considered to be the sole privilege of warrior families. Since, as we shall see later, Ninja could be either commoners or Samurai, it follows that the development of Ninjutsu had to predate the caste system that was imposed by Toyotomi Hideyoshi in the 16th century, which dictated (among other things) that only Samurai were allowed to wear two swords (Daisho) and train in the warrior arts.

The Chinese had probably developed sophisticated systems of martial arts even earlier than the 4th century AD. These were most often kept secret, since they provided power, status, and a livelihood to those who kept such traditions. Japanese warriors also guarded their arts from rival groups and martial society in general for the same reasons. Historically, the most complex and effective martial arts have been shrouded in secrecy.

Early Chinese martial arts had no formal written documentation. Their histories were passed on orally. Yet we know of their existence from other sources. In particular, the Shaolin temple kept detailed written histories. Shaolin martial arts were being developed as early as the 5th century AD. Persons who contributed documentation of techniques and strategies were often accepted into the temple because of their highly developed skills. These contributors remained as monks at the temple and deepened their studies of martial arts with the Shaolin. Some eventually left and taught elsewhere.

It is therefore clear that martial arts had been in development well before the 5th century AD. Certainly the necessity for training in combative arts had been around in China for millennia. We know that China's history goes back approximately 7000 years, and much of it was marked by nearly constant warfare of some kind.

We are fairly certain that most of the fighting arts found in Japanese systems either have their earliest origins in Chinese martial arts or were very heavily influenced by them. It is quite probable that the migration of such skills occurred repeatedly over the centuries and likely went in both directions. The fundamentals of complete martial systems in China are also found in their Japanese counterparts. The most successful martial systems were those with great diversity in their curricula. Such systems fostered the development of what is called a martial generalist.

For unarmed combative studies, complete systems have four basic categories: a striking art using the arms and hands, a kicking and sweeping dimension, a grappling system and a method for seizing and controlling enemies (8). Comprehensive classical Jujutsu or Taijutsu systems honor these categories. Nearly all of them, whether Chinese or Japanese, also include the study of *atemi* and *kyusho*, which were the arts of finding and using or striking the vulnerable points of the body in combat. Their techniques found expression in all four categories. A study of the development of koryu bujutsu and jujutsu indicates that many systems branched and evolved from comprehensive systems to more specialized systems over time.

To some traditionalists, specialization in a subset of skills from a broader system often reflects a regrettable degree of loss from what was originally available. That is in some ways a valid perspective, if the sacrifice of methods no longer felt to be useful is not followed by the acquisition of new skills needed to maintain combative relevance. This point should be noted as we later visit the contextual importance of Ninjutsu and its weapon's systems for today's martial artist.

It is also common to refer to martial systems as being "complete" when they contain a well-rounded curriculum of weapons training. Historically, this meant training in arts that were important for the battlefield, especially as it pertained to the warring states period in Japan. The arts involved included *kenjutsu* (with different kind of swords and under different conditions), *bojutsu* (often with staffs of varying lengths), *sojutsu* (spear), *naginatajutsu* (naginata) and *jujutsu* with kumiuchi, which included *yoroi* or *katchu* kumiuchi, and later *suhada* or *heifuku kumiuchi* (5). Many koryu bujutsu schools had sub-specializations that were in some ways signature arts; such arts might include *kusarigama, shuriken, tessen* and perhaps the *kakushibuki*.

Ninjutsu is considered a complete system, encompassing the four pillars of empty hand fighting systems and also the standard weapons of the general warrior. They also trained in martial skills particular to the Ninja. These were the skills relevant to espionage, sabotage, scouting, guerilla warfare and strategy, assassination, capture and interrogation, and bodyguard activities. In this sense, Ninja were martial generalists with added specializations. For this reason, many schools of Ninjutsu did not spend a great deal of time refining general battlefield skills they were unlikely to use. They also did not reach the level of expertise in these methods that Samurai did. Instead, the main purpose of such training was to reach a level of competence that helped them survive and to practice their own special tricks and tactics against warriors skilled at using these weapons.

It is well known that Ninja society was highly secretive and controlled. There are many reasons for this, but above all it was necessary as a matter of survival. In fact, most martial systems, even if their exponents were publically known and demonstrated their skills openly, retained secret teachings. It took a long time for a master to trust a student enough to allow them to learn the higher-level methods. In fact, granting access to *hiden* or "secret teachings" continues to be part of the grading system of some koryu schools and in a number of traditional WuShu as well. According to Grandmaster Law, efforts directed at prevailing over their enemies meant that the Ninja would send spies when possible to train in the dojos of other martial arts; it is likely that they were in contact with Chinese martial systems as well, which is something that will be discussed further below.

Practitioners of other martial systems who observe Ninjutsu fighting skills will often comment on similarities with their own arts. This is not a coincidence and it likely led to the conjecture that Ninjutsu is merely a collection of other arts. We will see below that this was not actually the case. Nevertheless, Master Kawakami of the *Ban-ke* Shinobi-no-den and curator of the Koka Ninja museum stated at his first ever conference in the United States (2009) that Ninja trained in whatever bujutsu system was available to them and learned their fighting skills in Samurai systems.

Perhaps he was implying that Ninja did not have any true martial systems of their own. Statements variously attributed to other prominent authorities in the bujutsu and researchers into Ninjutsu have also implied that Ninja did not have their own martial systems and that, with the exception of specialized tools, Ninja had no weapons that were uniquely identified with their own art. Historical texts available (ninpiden, etc.), some going back to the 16th century, lack any clear reference to the Ninja having their own martial arts, which they further distinguish from so-called "war arts." War Arts, as we understand them in our school, include activities such as espionage, scouting, infiltration, and others.

The limitation of such research, as important and revealing as it is, lies in the fact that Samurai produced and kept these records for their own use. We believe this is why the records do not contain information about Ninja fighting skills. All the information the Samurai were able to obtain was what they were exposed to or that which was provided to them by Ninja groups. Further, these are the only remaining records available to the public. It is our belief that Samurai had more such information, but that much or most of it has been deliberately kept hidden or lost over time.

Please note, a Samurai schooled in the non-combative arts of Ninjutsu could have functioned in the capacity of a Shinobi, utilizing his own bugei if the need for combat arose. Such a warrior would still identify first and primarily as a Samurai and not as a Ninja. This sort of warrior would be different than those whose primary function was to be Ninja and for whom being Samurai would have been nothing more than a disguise. This is a very important point to remember as it has implications on the distinction between Samurai Bugei, hybrid systems, and the patrimony of more specific Ninja groups. We shall see why the theory that Ninja had no unique combative systems of their own and the explanation that they trained in whatever systems were available are not sufficient to account for their historical exploits.

In defining the Ninja it becomes clear that it has to be done contextually. We know from the limited historical sources and from what is taught in Ninjutsu schools today that Ninja engaged in covert activities for which they were paid or rewarded. It follows that the martial arts they practiced and refined were modified and suited to the functions associated with these activities. Many of the martial arts as practiced in the Samurai bugei were not well suited to the work of the Ninja. If a practitioner's primary function was to be Ninja, it would be counterproductive to spend a great deal of time perfecting his skill with battlefield weapons he might rarely use. Opinions on this issue hinge to some extent on whether a person believes that all Ninja were, in fact, Samurai or not.

Certainly, as Samurai, they would have access to then current Samurai bugei —but lacking this status, they would not have the privilege or right to learn martial arts in the manner the Samurai did. Resolving this problem can be approached in different ways. Having a good working understanding of Samurai arts, morality, and codes of conduct was important, since some of what Ninja did were things that a proud Samurai would not. At other times, Ninja lived as Samurai and/or fought against them, requiring that they have a good understanding of their enemy's strengths and weaknesses. An examination of actual techniques is also helpful, as long as we keep in mind that many of today's martial arts, with the possible exception of most koryu schools, practice a modern and somewhat modified version of the original arts. So when we examine techniques from different systems, we should be careful to focus on their fundamental strategies and approaches along with certain preserved technical practices. Contrasting the history of these warriors, their conduct, and their fighting methods will reveal areas of overlap and also key areas of differentiation.

In considering the various factors associated with the origins and practices of martial schools, it should be noted that different schools of martial arts have varying degrees of affiliation and influence from major Eastern religious or spiritual groups. Some concentrate more on ethics, others on enlightenment, still others on the development of personal power. The prevailing religious influences in Japan during the consolidation of Ninjutsu into a unique entity were Buddhism, Shintoism and Confucianism. Confucianism is largely regarded as the basis for the ethical teachings associated with martial arts practice. Having some form of ethical code is typically necessary for any society of warriors; without it, they would over time lose their identity and purpose and either deteriorate or eventually be destroyed.

Like all other major martial systems, the Ninja had codes, rules and ethics. Just as with many of today's religions, some of these ancient rules and codes cannot be applied literally without violating laws and the rights of others. Much of the disdain held for Ninja by other warriors was based on the false belief that Ninja had no codes or honor, or that Ninja were not believed to value what is good in society. To some extent these views were justified, except for the fact that the Ninja were typically hired by people to do what their codes and values could not or would not allow them to do personally. The hypocrisy is evident. Nevertheless, it recognizes that ideology can fail and that the Ninja fulfilled a necessary role in society. The ethics of our entire world are still evolving, so to understand any historical group, the examination must be done taking into account some understanding of the culture, ethics and values of their time.

I have read an opinion of one exponent of the koryu martial arts, whom I will leave unnamed, who actually goes so far as to state that unless a modern practitioner also practices Shinto, or at least develops a profound understanding of it, they cannot truly call themselves koryu practitioners. Given that the origins of the Samurai warrior traditions formed in large part under the auspices of the ancient Japanese nobility with service and heritage within those power structures, and the fact that those structures endorsed Shinto (Buddhism gaining influence only later) as their national religion, this view has some merit. Officiating at Shinto ceremonies, for example, was one way in which warriors of the 10th century were recognized and honored as part of noble society (12).

However, many warriors came from other lines. This included provincial warriors who were not aristocratic, peasant warriors and warriors later in the service of Buddhist monasteries. Though all of these groups were not considered true bushi, they practiced ancient martial arts and did not necessarily support any pure vision of Shinto. If their arts or elements of their arts survived into the 19th century, would they not be considered koryu? I don't support any specific view on this subject, nor do I in any way consider myself an expert on these matters. I do, however, think it is important to state that, for a number of reasons, the martial arts representing Ninjutsu today, while perhaps having ancient roots, should not be considered koryu arts in the proper sense.

Ninjutsu evolved in an environment of brutal oppression, which made it necessary for them to exist and operate in the shadows as a secret society. Although ancient rulers in Japan, China, and Korea studied the Chinese classics of philosophy, religion, and ethics, and many strove to apply the principles to governance, they were no different than our politicians today. The urge to conduct themselves in self-serving ways was always tempting.

Unlike today's politicians, however, these rulers had much more autocratic executive power and were very rarely held accountable for crimes against their own people. Another difference worth noting is that ancient rulers expected to hold onto their power until death. They expected to be able to pass on their title to family members or at least a designee of their choice. They were also at serious risk of being killed before the end of their natural lives. This risk increased in proportion to their greed and bloodthirsty acts. Today's politicians typically live out their natural lives in comfort and only very rarely face any serious consequences for their corruption. They are also more adept at committing acts of greed without being noticed, and therefore do not usually need to resort to actual use of force to accomplish their goals.

The Chinese, showing a more enlightened and advanced understanding of society, were the first people to actually create a university with exams to become government administrators. In so doing they demonstrated a clear effort to rise above the ignorance that surrounded them and to enter into a new age.

The Japanese followed many aspects of the Chinese example with the founding of the Yamato court, and the development of a respectable aristocratic society. This effort reflected a substantial shift in societal values drawn in many respects from those in China. Prior to the creation of an aristocratic ruling class, Far East Asian societies were ruled by local strongmen supported by their private armies. Leaders were respected in proportion to their direct power and influence. During the Sui Dynasty (589-618 AD), a change took place where the ruling parties began to hold education and wisdom in esteem above that of martial skill, valor, and military power. Since that time in China, the scholar was held in higher regard than the warrior. This remains unchanged to the present day.

In Japan, the Imperial court held the same values as the Chinese scholars regarding government. They, however, lost executive power with the creation of the bakufu in 1183. The title of shogun was changed to mean "the great general given absolute military rule of all civilized lands." For the centuries leading up to these events, professional warrior families were making inroads into political power. This was especially true as they were appointed to governorships in the provinces where they often served as tax collectors. It was also true where they served as military and logistical support to help tax collectors enforce the tax system imposed upon the populace. Prior to the office of shogun as defined above, military aristocrats were already well established.

The desire by the ruling warrior society to acquire the respectability and spiritual substance of the Imperial court by paying lip service to the emperor, learning courtly etiquette, and the study of the Chinese classics (among many other things), were what was promulgated as the model for the warrior and eventually enshrined into their codes. Despite these ongoing efforts, and the fact that they became a ruling elite in their own right, the system of local strongmen with private armies prevailed for centuries in all territories outside the direct reach of Imperial capital and bakufu armies. Thus, in Japan, the ideal became that the warrior should also be a scholar.

The Ninja lived in this complex world of power and influence with all of its dangers and opportunities. They understood the strange balance between secrecy and freedom. Being public meant being at the mercy of the whims of ambitious tribal leaders. You could not, however, be overthrown, conscripted, or even required to pay taxes if the government had no idea who you were, how many were in your family, or where you lived. Living this type of life meant that you would have been obligated to exist on the fringes of society.

Next, the Ninja understood that security rested not only in secrecy, but also in making oneself indispensable (as a group) to their societal superiors, and sometimes even to their enemies. In this way, Ninja society existed in a kind of symbiotic relationship with the powerful forces around them, and often survived otherwise lethal allegiances with failing factions.

Finally, and deriving from the previous point, the Ninja understood that spy organizations wield great power because information can have as much influence as armies. Naturally, the governing powers might have wanted to destroy Ninja groups that held compromising intelligence that could be sold to enemies, and this only reinforced the Ninja's need for secrecy.

In this way, these "invisible people" facilitated and profited from change and political struggle in a society at odds with itself. In the process, they guaranteed their own niche for survival. It is practically an example of Darwinian natural selection at work, and therein lays one of the great spiritual underpinnings of Ninjutsu culture.

The Ninja always considered themselves part of the natural world; they also viewed everyone and everything the same way. They long ago understood that, while men are guided by their ethics, which are determined by their values, those values were only sustainable and logical when they followed natural laws. They rejected religious influences that might be contradictory to the process of natural balance, which in itself was believed to be divine.

Buddhism, which for many of its followers strives towards natural balance, inner serenity, and the abolition of attachment and greed (which in their view bred violence), was accepted by Ninja as being consistent with their own ethos. This ethos says that because man only lives a short time, he cannot truly own or possess things in the world. That possession both creates and destroys something, whether that "thing" is a material object of the world or another living being. The Ninja ethos also says, because in order to live, one must kill or destroy other things, an individual may, for example, choose to destroy plants more than animals but the destruction itself is an inescapable fact of living. Like birth and death, a human being's existence is limited, and one truly lives by finding the harmony within duality.

How could the Ninja live by a warrior credo and still be accepting or supportive of a Buddhist doctrine that essentially espouses pacifism? It lies in the postulated conflict or inner tension between what is good for oneself and one's community, versus humanity in the greater sense. Grandmaster Law frequently explained that values were personally driven, and that a person will act according to what he or she truly prioritizes. In a reductionist sense it really depends on whether an individual actually believes that what is good for society is also good for them. Thus, even a person who espouses a generally passive religious ideology will likely fight, depending on how they interpret which is the greater good. There are, of course, individuals who will not fight under any circumstances; this choice is exactly consistent with Buddhist practice.

It should be stated that, beyond studying religion and philosophy for the purpose of being at peace with one's own living conditions, Ninja analyzed the prevailing philosophies, religions, characters and personalities of people in an effort to make predictions about their behavior. Having such abilities was critical in deciding how to act when the Ninja intended to influence the behavior of another person or group through some kind of action.

Rulers attempting to unify a nation under their own banner may have felt that, once unification was achieved, there would be an end to open conflagration; this was of course good for them as individuals, for their families, and for their community. In a sense this perspective was true, even if it seems like an excuse for megalomania —and it certainly seemed to turn out that way with the Tokugawa bakufu taking near total power in 1615AD. Any honest modern politician, however, will tell you that peace is brokered at a price and you have to decide whether that price is one you can live with, or at least that the majority of the people can live with.

During a significant part of their history, the Buddhist monastic community in Japan maintained militant elements. Such Buddhists, unlike the "martyrs" of Middle Eastern based religions, were not guaranteed a place in paradise for their acts. Instead they sacrificed their individual karma for repeated rounds of reincarnation in order to defend their temples against the influences of the ruling aristocracy and tribal strongmen and, ironically, each other. We will see later, however, that cloistered and ordained members of the aristocracy and their warriors continued to pursue their political agendas even while operating through the auspices of Japan's greatest temples and monasteries. The use of martial arts by the monastic community was justified in principle as being defensive and peaceful in its overall aims, even though historically that was not typically the case.

It is tempting but inaccurate to liken Japanese militant Buddhism to the example that had already been set by Shaolin in China. In fact, as Dr. Yang defines the terms in Chinese in his book, *The Essence of Shaolin White Crane Martial Power and Qigong*: the word for martial skills "*WuShu*" means the skill to stop and prevent violence. The word "*Wu*" is made up of two other words "*Zhi*" meaning to stop, cease or end and "*Ge*" meaning spear or lance (replace with "weapon" in the meaning) and "Shu" references techniques or skills, thus implying that the responsible and ethical application of martial arts was peaceful and therefore it was not necessarily contradictory to the practice of Buddhism.

The Ninja felt and understood the imperative need to study and master martial arts because, quite simply, their lives depended on it; like other warriors of their day, they believed that man's proclivity to make war on his fellow man is innate and will never be eliminated. The only way to reign in the drive to fight was through the judicious use of martial arts. It is a mystery as to whether these beliefs are true, but certainly they are supported by humanity's unending history of violent conflict interspersed with eras of peace. These interstitial periods of reduced conflict were supported by strong militaries that discouraged challenges.

It is important also to consider that martial arts societies across the Far East understood the benefits of Buddhist psychology on the practice of martial arts and their mastery. I have heard martial artists claim that the practice of martial training can be used in a manner like meditation; even advocating that it is more powerful than meditation in that it helps achieves insight faster than traditional seated meditation, especially when there is a brush with death. Some traditional systems report that some of their adherents, if not their founders, achieved enlightenment through the practice of martial arts (5).

The Ninja's contemporaries practiced martial arts in an atmosphere dominated by the influence of Zen Buddhism (4). Just as for Ninja, these warriors tackled the apparent contradiction of being Buddhists while simultaneously living a warrior credo.

In fact, the Samurai credo of Bushido, which is highly moralistic and adheres mainly to the ideals of Confucianism, combined with a nihilistic Buddhist fatalism, became steeped in the issues of violence and bloodshed. Some would even describe it as a "cult of death." It was thus heavily focused on the subject of honor and respect for ancestors, as is inherent in Confucian ideals.

The warrior credo of the Ninja held honor as a construct not to be openly demonstrated or displayed but upheld while hidden within oneself. Some material relating to this matter states that a Ninja must at all cost live, though they may endure great shame (22). Ninja did not concern themselves with making public displays of loyalty and filial piety. Their respect for their ancestors was demonstrated by adhering to the ideals and skills handed down to them over the centuries. Due to the demands of secrecy, however, their displays were disguised and simply never known to anyone but the Ninja closest to them.

In contrast to Confucian ideals, Ninja did not generally respect the authority of government and are reputed to have lacked loyalty to others outside their own inner circles. The Ninja credo possessed an analytical and anatomic pragmatism that can be chilling in its admonition to achieve the mission by any means necessary short of destroying their own communities. It followed and valued the ways of the natural world, and saw justice within that paradigm. It accepted the reality of suffering, struggle, and death, and sought salvation through the path of transcendental wisdom. It regarded the laws of nature as overriding those of man and human institutions. The Ninja culture embraced such concepts as: the taking of a life as justified if it saves the lives of many others, or the idea that in war the moral imperative is absent because the roots of conflict are based in unethical premises.

Ninja adhering to Buddhism believed in reincarnation and the cycle of karma and, as in the rest of the Far East, they eventually accepted the assimilation of Buddhism with Taoist and Confucian influenced thought. Also, because they were Japanese—a people who had enshrined and elevated their ancient animistic religion to a national identity—there was integration with Shinto. This assimilation was part of the great flowering of spiritual expression in the Far East. Unfortunately, it did not substantially curb the warlike ways of the people to any significant degree.

Ninja culture viewed death as a part of a life-giving regenerative cycle guided by karma. Having understood the basic inevitability of life and death conflict, Ninja viewed combat as essential to survival in a society constantly at war. For them, Buddhism provided a spiritual framework wherein they could find serenity amid profound injustice and chaos. This framework was a personal refuge where even a hardened warrior could find solace.

Ninja were warriors and commoners who neither aspired to nobility nor regarded themselves as subhuman or inferior in any way to other people just because of the way in which they lived their lives. They essentially rejected the idea that some people are by title, status, or birth superior to one another. Instead, the ideal was that one's destiny was something to be seized and actualized, whether born in poverty or riches. At the same time, they recognized that one's will was no match for the forces of the world. Destiny could be like a tiny cork floating on a rushing river: though it is subjected to strong currents that cannot be resisted, it can be guided a little at a time to a more desirable place. That said, they did not regard all people as equal in either opportunity or ability. People were understood to be born with their own unique circumstances. It was what they did with them that made the difference.

Grandmaster Law made it a point to have his students understand that Ninja paid attention to personal character and development; they are believed to have ranked their leaders based on personal qualities and abilities rather than by inherited title, which was the norm throughout most of the rest of society at that time. This selection process was intended to ensure that leaders with the necessary strengths and qualities important for the survival of their relatively small groups were chosen.

Ninjutsu as an art is very broad and encompasses many fields. Master Kawakami correctly characterized them as "life arts." Grandmaster Law would talk about Ninjutsu as a way of seeing the world, of thinking and of doing.

The reason Ninjutsu has this character is because it is not merely a method of waging a certain type of warfare. Those who practiced the Ninja art had to have a deep understanding of how people think and live their lives. For Ninja to blend in with people of all sorts, they needed to tune in quickly to the common ground that exists with everyone and to not emphasize differences unless they were plying alliances. Well-developed skills of observation and empathy permitted them to "feel" others and utilize their skills for mimicry to expertly blend and become "invisible" in the populace. Ninja felt that this practice also enriched their lives on a personal level.

Many of those who contributed to the art of Ninjutsu lived, worked, and died among the common people. Much of its practical character and odd array of weapons existed due to this fact and that many Ninja weapons were simply derivatives of everyday working tools.

In order to understand who the Ninja were, it is necessary to review not only some of the evolution of the ideological and political context in which Ninjutsu developed as we have done briefly above, but also to examine those elements that came together to contribute to and constitute the actual art itself. Before Japan came to be ruled by the Samurai as a class unto their own there were different kinds of warriors, of which the classical Bushi was one representation. Bushi means a "man of arms." From before the time of the Nara period starting in 710 AD, the numeric majority of fighting men called upon to do battle were probably conscripted farmers and lay people. The ascendancy of the aristocracy and the creation of the Imperial court based on the Chinese example led to the evolution of full-time warriors specialized in the combative arts.

In his book *Heavenly Warriors: The Evolution of Japan's Military 500-1300,* William Wayne Farris outlines the evidence supporting what is known about these events. In the early years of the new Imperial Yamato court (500-645 AD), the country was largely under the control of the aforementioned local strongmen and their armies. The Imperial court recruited armies of their own, specialized soldiers called *Toneri*. Many of these warriors originated from Eastern Honshu and the Kanto region (Eastern Provinces) where specialization in the martial arts flourished. These warriors excelled in mounted warfare, archery, mounted swordsmanship, and use of the spear like their contemporaries fighting on the Northern plains of China. Mastery of these combative arts was the hallmark of the first professional class of warriors in the service of the Imperial court, who were among the direct forbears to the Samurai.

Other sources converging and contributing to the origin of the Samurai had to do with men of arms who were either landowners or those in the service of landowners. They later acted as enforcers who guarded and ensured the collection of taxes for local lawmakers and tribal rulers. These warriors were referred to as *Kompei* or "strong fellows," which had a generic connotation meaning *a man skilled in the use of martial arts*. The centuries prior to the ascendancy of the Samurai sees the growing influence of these men for the enforcement of rule throughout the hierarchy of government. They acted in police, military and private militia capacities. These groups were clearly those that influenced the origins of the first Samurai as they later came to be known. They were warriors in service and this is at the core of the Samurai warrior ethos. In fact, the word Samurai is defined as "one who serves."

Warriors from the days of the early enforcers of order, the Toneri, the Kompei and then the Samurai, were persons who specialized in fighting primarily in open battles and skirmish. They gradually rose in status as they acquired power through the exploits of service and with their increasing levels of education. These were people who seemed to have ambitiously sought recognition and status.

One interesting point of view about the origins of fighting men in Japan suggests that martial arts were most actively developing in the Eastern Provinces or Kanto region during this period. It was said to be a lawless area that could not be easily dominatedand was described as a place for rogues and bandits. Its reputation caused it to become a region to dominate and exploit as a resource for the recruitment of fighting men. The Japanese Imperial court focused on doing this after the fall of their allies in Korea and in anticipation of an invasion from China. They desperately needed an elite fighting force.

Like their enemies across the seas, they too would also have needed professional spies. It does not seem reasonable that they would have used proud fighters specializing in mounted warfare for the purpose of espionage. Such spies would have to be trained to dress and act like commoners, warriors, and aristocrats alike. They had to be able to blend in anywhere, whether at the higher circles of government or amongst the lowliest laborers.

In one view, the development of Ninjutsu began with the importation of spying methods already well-established in China. It is reasonable to assume that this took place in parallel with the rise of martial culture in Japan. Chinese texts on military strategy speak clearly about their use of spies, but do not distinguish whether these spies were a separate and specialized group in their own right (1). Again, it is a reasonable assumption that some were part of such a specialized group where the skills and intricacies of their art were sequestered and enhanced with each passing generation. It is counterintuitive to think that those in power were recruiting and training spies from ordinary men *de novo*, only as they were needed, without establishing an actual methodology and platform on which to build their expertise.

The direct application of Chinese methods in Japan has always led to their eventual transformation into something more suited to Japanese culture. To this day, Japan is widely recognized as a place where outside ideas are accepted and transformed (frequently improved upon as well) to suit their own needs. It might be useful to think of this dynamic as a limited analogy, where China would represent Europe and Japan would represent North America.

Espionage is highly sensitive to the culture in which it operates. In such a context, spies with training adapted to working in China would need to adapt to working in Japan. As with the martial arts, imported Chinese methods of warfare were quickly acculturated. Grandmaster Law taught that the core strategy of Ninja espionage and martial arts is Chinese, but that local Japanese influences led to a transformation to a more uniquely Japanese form approximately 1500 years ago. This dates it somewhere around 500 AD. This general context, even if not completely accurate, is interesting because it does coincide with the rise of the Imperial government in Japan, which was strongly influenced by China and had a practical requirement for espionage experience.

Like America, Japan was a frontier with an imperative to suppress a native population and to reign in rogue strongmen dedicated to constructing and defending their own independent fiefdoms. Spies operating with Chinese methods in Japan must have felt the need to recruit people knowledgeable about their enemies in an effort to develop an effective spy network. We believe that it was at this time that Ninjutsu really had its start in Japan and gradually became the integrated family of arts that encompass Japanese Ninjutsu as we understand it today.

Cultural Origins of the Ninja

To understand how Ninjutsu is uniquely Japanese we must take a closer look at the contemporaries of these early spies as they were adapting to their new territories and the demands of their leaders—the very people whom they would have operated for and against. In this environment they would find and recruit individuals with the right skill set to employ and train in espionage and the other covert services that eventually were brought together into the art of Ninjutsu. As in later times, early Shinobi or Ninja needed to be especially capable in the fighting arts. It is reasonable to assume that they would have started by using martial arts that were already part of the original Chinese systems of espionage brought to Japan. As with the changes needed to adapt espionage methods, the associated fighting arts would need modification. This must have required the input and influence of accomplished fighters already active in the area.

With such a strong emphasis on fighting ability, finding fighters from among the local warriors, official or not, was probably a good place to begin. In the previous chapter, it was noted that there were a variety of different types of fighting men that had contributed to the general martial culture of Japan and in particular the evolution of the Samurai. Any or all of these groups probably influenced the development of Ninjutsu to some degree. In some cases, the influence would have occurred in response to fighting against such warriors, in others it would have been through direct exchange of martial study. But it gets more complicated than that. The warriors who were employed by country strongmen in the earliest colonization of Japan participated in the suppression of Japan's aboriginal people. This process continued well after the rise of the Imperial court and into the 9th century using professional armies in the service of the Emperor sent to the pre-colonized Northern provinces. The colonization of the remaining territories in Japan was an enormous political event with strong repercussions on the rest of Japanese society (12).

In our school of Ninjutsu, the belief is held that some of the first guerilla warfare seen in Japan was that between colonizers of Manchurian ethnic origin and the aboriginal people of the archipelago. These aboriginal people were later called *Ezo* or *Emishi* (a term used after 1200) and it is actively being debated whether they were essentially the same stock as those who are now known as the Ainu. An alternative view holds that aboriginals living on Honshu were also Manchurian in origin like their colonizers, but from an earlier migration and therefore distinct from the Ainu. The term Ezo continued to be used as a name for the Ainu for centuries.

Just as occurred with the earliest settlers in the United States, many of these early colonizers learned the ways of the people they sought to dominate. In the United States the *mountain men* of the West and the *hill people* of Appalachia developed their own unique cultures based in part on native influences. We believe that the experience of these warriors with mountain and remote warfare was one of the stronger influences on the development of Ninjutsu. In fighting against and learning from the aboriginal people they would have acquired skills, particularly when learning to thrive in remote country away from outsiders, refining survival skills in the Japanese native lands and the use of guerilla tactics involving stealth and evasion with emphasis on the use of darkness and the natural elements.

In fact, the derogatory name *nosaru* (mountain monkeys) used to describe Ninja resonates well with the descriptions given by colonizers in the regions of Northeastern Honshu of the Emishi people where most of this early conflict took place. Especially considering that the colonizers then, and for centuries to come, regarded these people as sub-human or animal and thus would have had no qualms about calling them monkeys. Mr. Farris, in his book *Heavenly Warriors*, gives a telling description of the enduring guerilla wars that took place there between the years 774-812 AD. Early attempts to colonize Northern lands at first met little resistance, but eventually escalated into a prolonged and bloody conflagration. Professional bushi from respected warrior families and experienced foot soldiers suffered humiliating defeats at the hands of these Northern "barbarians" who were typically outnumbered in some cases by as much as eight to one.

Early settlers were quite afraid of them, describing them as bloodthirsty savages, without social order, and both wild and promiscuous. They were felt to be untrustworthy, wearing furs, carrying concealed weapons, facile and agile in the wilderness, able to hide and disappear, striking when least expected and disappearing when pursued. Bushi facing them in battle described them as consummate warriors, their leaders worth a thousand of the colonizers' men. The wars carried out against them bankrupted the coffers of the aristocracy.

Eventually, by force of numbers, the aboriginal people were pacified and subjugated, but not without the colonizers receiving help from aboriginals that had turned against their own people to serve the Imperial court. With major aboriginal defeats occurring in 792-793 AD, the court relocated cooperative Emishi to Western Honshu domains, giving them surnames, titles, and hiring them as guards and mercenaries.

Western Honshu is the region of Japan closest to Korea, and it could be considered that picking this locality was intentional and perhaps designed to have these people act as a tough barrier against any ambitious Korean or Chinese military forays into Japan. It is also contiguous but not clearly part of the traditional so-called homelands of Ninjutsu of the neighboring Central-Western region. These events clearly demonstrate the probability of intimate contact between Japanese warrior –and by extension covert operatives or Ninja—and native people skilled in guerilla warfare tactics, the hunting and fishing by which the Emishi originally lived, and their astounding skill as warriors. Besides the similarity of these societal dynamics to the examples given earlier with the colonization of North America, there is the striking, if at times derogatory, congruence between how these people were described and how the historical Ninja were viewed. The quasi-aristocratic bushi would have regarded defeated Emishi with a mixture of disdain and fearful respect, the same type of feeling expressed towards Ninja. Thus if any exchange took place between the fighting practices of Emishi warriors and Japanese fighting men, it was likely to have been among the lower ranking groups, the strata where we find the Ninja. Classical bushi also would not have a strong interest in learning the guerilla tactics and fighting skills of the Emishi as they would not be the ones using them, but Shinobi or Ninja would have found these very relevant and useful. Those who employed them would also have seen an advantage in having their Ninja trained in these native skills. It seems reasonable that having observed the devastating effect the Emishi fighting groups had on noble Japanese warriors who used systems based on Chinese models could have led to the conclusion that they would be similarly effective against fighters from China and Korea.

This history further indicates that highly developed fighting skills and strategy of a unique kind were present in Japan before the rise of classical bushi in warfare. It has been further asserted that these early wars between native aboriginal people and bushi changed the way the classical bushi fought and strategized, moving away from the Chinese based models they ascribed to previously.

Where the Emishi learned their fighting skills seems uncertain at this point, but it appears that they had an undocumented and possibly even poorly systematized fighting art, whose name, if it was indeed named, is now unknown. I could find no indication of how old their arts are, but it is known that these people inhabited the Japanese archipelago for millennia. If it is true that their skills had an influence on the fighting arts already used by bushi, and that fighters connected with aboriginal arts were recruited into more conventional military systems for their abilities as trackers, scouts, spies and guerilla tacticians, then it follows that early pre-Ninjutsu systems would have been strongly influenced in their development by these events. As such, the previously existing Chinese systems of espionage with their associated martial arts would have been modified to a form more uniquely adapted to Japan and what would later become known as Ninjutsu. Thus we have a postulated influence from these aboriginal wars on both the conventional bushi warrior and especially the enhancement of a separate and unique group who would eventually distinguish themselves as Shinobi or Ninja.

It isn't clear whether unassimilated warriors of Emishi and possibly mixed origins left without a home after the wars had anything to do with the groups of bandits and pirates that continued to exist in more remote areas of the country. But it is our understanding that early Ninja families thrived in these environments where they felt free from the influence of imperial and governmental forces imposing taxes and rules. Their residing in such an environment would then have necessitated trusted go-betweens acting on their behalf negotiating allegiances and operations for them as a source of revenue and guarantees against future incursions and aggression. Thus by the time powerful noble samurai houses had evolved, there already existed these warriors experienced in unconventional warfare ready to practice intimidating guerilla tactics against any enemy. Given their lowly status such people may well have existed on the fringe as so called lawless "bandits" refusing to be tamed and controlled by the forces of social order. In their unending struggle with professional warriors they used hand-to-hand skills in the form of martial arts that would have helped them to protect their way of life.

It can be postulated that these early warriors, would have continued to add to their martial arts skills over time. Like their covert Chinese forebears, they were building a uniquely Japanese system with ever-greater degrees of sophistication that would make them indispensable to warfare in Japan. Careful observation of the martial arts of Ninjutsu would suggest their skills were preserved from fighting systems originating in China with a steady ongoing process of modification.

It appears likely that these warriors used staff, sword, knife, spear, and the bow. It is, however, weapons like the shoge and shuko that diverge from the usual array of weapons seen in most conventional martial arts of the time. While similar weapons using ropes like the shoge, and claw weapons like the shuko were present in China, we shall see that certain characteristics could indicate other potential origins. In fact, it is possible that the weapons in China and Japan sharing these similarities have a common origin that is older than that recorded in the collective memory of existing martial lineages. It must be emphasized that the arsenal of weapons found in Ninjutsu is especially suited for the type of work which was their real strength and niche—scouting, infiltration, covert attacks, sabotage and silent killing in the night.

As will be discussed further on, another influence on the origin of the Ninja were the so-called traveling gypsy-like performers known as *Kugutsu*. These people are felt to have contributed to the acting skills, psychological methods of manipulation, sleight of hand, trickery and other attributes associated with the Ninja spy. They may have also contributed the characteristic dark clad outfit popularly associated with the Ninja; the *shozoku* (Fig. 43).

There is also the important postulated influence of the yamabushi (Fig. 1) connected with Ninja lore. Some of the more advanced fighting skills seen in Ninjutsu martial culture and the religion of the Ninja are believed to have been at least in part contributed by the Yamabushi, mountain priests or ascetics. They would certainly have added to the Ninjas' training, enhancing their ability to endure starvation, cold, deprivation, pain and loneliness. The Yamabushi are known for their practices of endurance, subjecting their bodies and minds to extreme conditions. They are believed to be at the spiritual heart of Ninjutsu, since the endurance training was not only a matter of preparing for survival in harsh conditions but also a form of spiritual practice. The religion, ethics and credo of the Ninja appear to have been heavily influenced by this group.

Interestingly, a number of traditional Samurai Bugei also claim the same spiritual linkage and state their origin as coming from the Yamabushi at least for some of their insightful developments in the use of standard weaponry (5, 14). In many cases, these stories sound like pure myth, and in fact they may be, or perhaps they are embellishments an underlying truth.

Consider, for example, one of the oldest martial traditions known and documented in Japan—the case of the Takenouchi, Ryu, described in *Classical Fighting Arts of Japan* by Serge Mol (p. 100). The main founder, Hisamori Takenouchi, is said to have encountered a seven foot tall, gray haired Yamabushi in the mountains of Sannomiya, who taught him what he coined as the *torite gokajo*, or "five methods for handily overwhelming an enemy," followed by instruction in *kogusoku* a method of combat involving the short sword.

There are other similar myths and examples of bushi becoming enlightened or divinely inspired and founding new schools after praying to gods like *Fudo-Myo O* and *Marishiten*.

As with the case of the Ninja, I have heard certain contemporary sources, persons interested and purporting to have some expertise on the history of Japanese martial culture, maintain that the Yamabushi had no knowledge and traditions of martial arts. I take issue with that viewpoint. While it would be naïve to assume that all Yamabushi had involvement in martial arts, it is not at all unreasonable to consider that many did. Why would the myths regarding the origin of Japanese martial styles be attributed to Yamabushi, if in reality they had no link to martial schools? It would also be quite strange for members of this religious community to be openly bearing arms as they did and engaging in a limited number of armed

Fig. 1: A Yamabushi; typically they will have long hair, but will often cut it in the hot summer months.

conflicts without knowing how to use weapons. It has been documented by numerous sources that Yamabushi did train in the martial arts, and that they had intimate connections to the Ninja community. Some Ninja are said to have been Yamabushi, though the reverse was certainly not always the case (19).

In fact, in his memoirs, Seiko Fujita (1899-1968), alleged by some to have been the last representative of the Koga Ninja, spoke to his early experiences living among the Yamabushi and learning some of their martial arts (10). He also described interesting parallels between the Yamabushi way of life and the practices of the Ninja. A number of things that Seiko Fujita claimed are very hard to believe, especially for anyone with a scientific and medical background, and probably need to be considered cautiously. It is possible that the reliability of his accounts of the Yamabushi were at least in part fictitious. That stated, much of what he wrote describes exactly what they are observed to be doing to this very day and it is at least consistent with accounts in large part with material from other sources.

The Kanji for Yamabushi actually indicates they were considered primarily priests and ascetics before warriors and translates as *those who lie* (int: live) *on the mountain*. The Yamabushi attended temples, but spent a great deal of time living in the mountain wilderness. Their prime method of spiritual practice was the religious pilgrimage combined with extremely rigorous ascetic rituals. They regard the mountains as holy places in part because so many of them form natural geological mandalas.

Yamabushi continue their spiritual and ascetic practices to this day. Their temples are popular tourist attractions, and books have been written on their ways. It is reported in Japanese history texts that the Yamabushi were secretive and had an extensive underground communications network operating through mountain temples and highland paths that made them an ideal group for Ninja society to inhabit (19). It could be the Ninja's presence in the Yamabushi sect that is the basis for the misleading belief that Ninja society was a form of cult. The Ninja had ties with other religious communities as well and were no more a cult than the Samurai. The Ninja were not a cult, but rather a distinct cultural community of warriors whose integrated beliefs have been taken from more than one spiritual tradition and blended together. Religion was neither the sole nor primary practice of the Ninja, any more than it was for the Samurai. The Ninja kept many of the precepts found in the greater martial arts culture in addition to many uniquely their own, again demonstrating their mentality of keeping what was useful and rejecting what did not fit their needs and purpose.

It would be interesting to discover whether or not there is any connection between the Yamabushi and the Emishi. Such a linkage would help tie together these influences on the development of Ninjutsu, especially in light of the at least superficial resemblance between these people and the Yamabushi regarding dress and survival in the wilderness. So far, I have not found any evidence to support this idea, though it is innately appealing. Perhaps at some point in the future this will come to light as either being possible or completely unreasonable.

We should clarify here that the Yamabushi are distinct from the militant monastic community known as the Sohei (Fig. 2). Sohei were sometimes also called *Yamahoshii* (warriors from the mountain). The Sohei (literally: "warrior-monks")

Fig. 2: The classical image of the Sohei complete with the monk's cowl, robes over the yoroi, the geta and naginata. This illustration is based on a popular photograph taken in the 19th century of an actor dressed as a Sohei. This image has been challenged by some as historically inaccurate

were armed forces that defended the interests of powerful Buddhist temples most actively during the Heian and early Kamakura periods (794 to 1185AD). The Sohei persisted for a considerable time, but their political power began to dwindle after the establishment of the shogunate at the beginning of the Kamakura period (1185 to 1333 AD). By the 14th century they effectively lost most of their ability to influence the Imperial court and the bakufu. Occasionally, the monks and armies acting on the behalf of monks and priests of noble lineage were referred to as "yamabushi" when they originated from the temples under the control of the Enryakuji at mount Hiei located to the Northeast of the city of Kyoto. Kyoto had become the new capital city in the beginning of the Heian period after Nara lost this status at the end of the Nara period. There is an extensive narrative on the history of the monastic communities martial activities written by Mikael S. Adolphson called *The Teeth and Claws of the Buddha: Monastic Warriors and Sohei in Japanese History*.

In the extremely political environment of these religious communities, with their nearly constant conflict (both military and non-military), one can only wonder how much involvement of spies there must have been. The very short tenure of many court nobles and their appointees within the temples, some with very suspicious deaths, hint at the use of assassins as well. The author does not speak in detail about these activities, and there seems to be no clear indication that the would-be assassins were Ninja, although they certainly were candidates for this role.

We know from this work that monks, priests, and monastic administrators with noble and warrior family connections used the military influence of the temples to further their political interests and the defense of their status. Since noble families and their warrior supporters as well as the military strongmen in the provinces used Ninja, it follows that Ninja activities took place within the political infighting associated with the monastic complexes of central Japan in a region known as the *Kinai*. The Sohei continued to be problematic and sought after for support, both spiritually and militarily, for several centuries. The monastic complexes of mount Hiei were crushed militarily under an onslaught by Oda Nobunaga and were finally totally dismantled and defeated by the forces of Toyotomi Hideyoshi in 1585.

The spiritual influences and practices of groups like the Yamabushi, the Buddhist monastic community, Shinto and the native people of Japan all value a life of practical simplicity, a strong connection to the natural world and a pragmatic understanding of life. The mysteries associated with these practices and their alleged benefits on mental and physical health are one aspect of the allure of the Ninja culture. The direction taken by the Ninja community to fill the need for professional scouts, spies, commandos, captors, interrogators and assassins placed them in a niche that both demanded and resulted in developing a unique perspective on the human condition. The expression of these beliefs and that wisdom can be viewed from different perspectives. The Ninja's modifications of weapons and skills to fit their operational needs led to its wide array of sometimes strange and unusual weapons, which are highly interesting in their own right. On closer examination, reflecting on the weapons Ninja chose to study helps us understand something about how their special position in the world influences the Ninja perspective. It is also important to appreciate how this understanding is expressed in concrete terms and how this perspective is relevant to anyone interested in martial arts today. It highlights and clarifies the nature of practical utilitarian conflict strategies and the psychology of success in combat.

✳✳✳

It could therefore be asked, what is the allure of such an obscure art to people living today? Further, in what manner does Ninjutsu remain relevant? Ninjutsu encompasses a broad set of arts; a person could study Ninja religious beliefs, their strategy, their combative and medical knowledge, their weapons, and their cultural and historical influence. Many people practice martial arts for spiritual and philosophical expression. Ultimately people pursue martial arts for personal reasons, some of which are unrealistic or rooted in fantasy, where it is really not much more than a past-time or hobby with certain benefits. If you ask a person who has chosen to pursue a profession that others would consider undesirable they will often profess a rationale for their choice that is meaningful to them, even if others may have trouble appreciating it. People compelled to study Ninjutsu often share this perspective to some extent, because Ninjutsu is one of those gray areas of the martial arts, on the fringe between myth and reality.

Many people today are gravitating towards a serious exploration of traditional or classical martial arts. Having been exposed to sport-like Budo from Japan, Okinawa, and a fairly conservative repertoire of WuShu styles from China, Westerners are realizing that there is much more to these arts than they initially realized. Decades ago, very few Westerners had the opportunity to learn such arts in greater depth. Pioneers such as Donn Draeger and Charles Gruzanski opened up some traditions. Yet, even for knowledgeable and experienced martial artists, the mystery of the Ninja has remained an enduring and tantalizing secret in martial arts society. Ninjutsu provides a desired series of arts in part due to the popularity of Ninja legends. Even though most people now could scarcely find a use for many of the military arts in Ninjutsu, quite a few of those that remain are still quite relevant to us today.

Thus it becomes important to understand what is unique about Ninjutsu. One of the many ways in which Ninjutsu is truly unique among the martial arts has to do with how they thought. This can be examined and approached in many different ways. But few of these, as a process, have practical relevance to people today. Persons interested in gleaning something about the Ninja mind and who want to make it live within them should look at the tools and weapons they used. These are the consummate expression of the Ninja trade and identity and are probably one of the best platforms to study the mysteries of Ninjutsu.

Consistent with earlier assertions that Ninja trained in Samurai bugei and did not have their own specific martial arts, it has been oft stated, as fact, including by highly respected sources on the classical fighting arts of Japan—that Ninja were Samurai specially trained for the many tasks they were required to perform. As we progress, hopefully it will become clear why not all Ninja could fit that description, even if it was true for a substantial number of them.

There are for example some technical differences between typical Samurai martial methods and those found in Ninjutsu. Although a warrior could adapt and change his style of fighting according to the task and situation, this ability called for an increase in the amount of training required to have competence in Samurai fighting styles without betraying the presence of his knowledge of alternative skills. For example, the Samurai often used wider based *kamae* (stances) than the Ninja. These wider stances were designed to accommodate techniques performed while wearing *Yoroi* (armor) and using longer battlefield weapons such as pole arms and longer swords. Ninja methods that were developed outside the sphere of Samurai Bugei influence did not have this aspect. Ninjutsu fighting postures tended to emphasize smaller and tighter circles of movement. Another methodological example is the unique rolling techniques used in Ninjutsu. These are performed in such a manner that they do not allow the head, spinal column or knees to touch the ground. They are very quiet, smooth and controlled. While they can be performed while wearing a sword and even carrying polearms, these weapons certainly increase the level of difficulty and risk. I have never seen these roles practiced in any traditional Samurai bugei. Roles of this kind were created to suit Ninja tactics and were designed to be used in a different context than those of the open battlefield.

Much of what is known about Ninjutsu today comes from the written sources mentioned earlier. Texts, chronicles and old *densho* (teaching scrolls of martial schools) are the main sources available to scholars for a modern reconstruction of the historical Ninja. The reliability of these sources varies, and they are assumed to have errors, misstatements and probably intentional falsehoods within them. Such disinformation served the purposes of those who composed them. Original written sources mentioning Ninjutsu are rare and the majority of them come from the Edo and Meiji periods. It should be reiterated that it was the Samurai who kept such records, and it was by contrast, contrary to Ninja practice to keep written records of their families, accomplishments and techniques.

Some koryu schools keep written texts of only their lower and middle rank curricula. They reserve the highest teachings to be transmitted only orally. (5). It appears that it was only when the arts began to fall into general disuse that there was motivation to memorialize what remained, by Samurai who were concerned that the legacy of the old martial ways including the Ninja, would be lost forever.

Within our own school, the understanding is that many skills of the past were simply abandoned, primarily because they became obsolete. It is also in part for this reason that Ninjutsu is not a koryu art. The koryu schools of martial arts do add new skills to a certain extent, but a large part of their focus is to maintain the legacy of the ancient arts practiced by the Samurai and to preserve them in their original battle-tested form. Modern Ninjutsu would ideally keep only what is considered to be combatively relevant, while understanding the caveat that an art lost due to disuse might one day regain its importance.

One of the purposes of keeping historical records (and sometimes twisting the truth in them) is because these records later become the basis of "facts" that support those with political and other aspirations. Pointing to historical documentation as the unambiguous source of anyone's "right" to claim a certain title, own land or demand respect is highly effective when there are no other historical sources to contradict them. Prestige is not merely an issue of pride; in many ways prestige is power, influence and money.

We further propose that Ninja groups of Samurai rank and title were distinct by degrees from those without such status. Ninja of Samurai rank still lived by the Samurai codes of ethics. They possessed some Ninjutsu skills, tactics and practices, but were also strongly influenced and bound by their Samurai values. Their martial arts essentially had to be hybrid systems. The difference in culture between hybrid Samurai-Ninja schools and those that were only Ninja is apparent in their martial arts.

Grandmaster Law stated that Ninja of samurai rank acted as go-betweens for Samurai clans seeking to hire secretive Ninja to execute tasks they themselves were either forbidden, or unable to do. Ninja without Samurai rank and status, were not as limited and could do what was unthinkable for any Samurai. It is tempting to consider what has been reported about the command structure of Ninja society as further indication of this stratification in social rank.

Mr. Draeger and Smith explained the system as follows: the so-called *Jonin* (upper-men) were the face of the Ninja to their potential employers. These men appeared to preside over several others called *Chunin* (middle-men), whose identity was kept hidden. The *Chunin* then planned and gave directives for operations to Genin (lower-men) who carried out the orders.

Grandmaster Law further explains that the Genin typically did not hold Samurai rank, and not all Chunin did either. Our Ninja group is said to have been a Chunin-Genin group. We believe that the well-known Iga and Koka groups were Samurai in large part and acted as go betweens to the more secretive non-Samurai groups. This is not to suggest that they did not themselves take on tasks and engage in warfare, but that when certain types of tasks required a person of no social rank or identity, they went to the Genin.

I have heard it debated that when Ninja hired persons, such as farmers and servants, not trained in Ninjutsu to be their eyes and ears, these unskilled persons were also Genin. It seems entirely probable that some people would consider that to be the case since they were, by definition, lower class and so by social rank equal. Such persons, however, were not Ninja.

Ninja would also not trust their identities or risk handing any sensitive information to people of this kind because they were too unreliable. Instead, Ninja had ways of extracting information from people through other means than open barter. Grandmaster Law says that, in keeping with Ninja superstitions surrounding the number nine, there were frequently nine layers between the person in contact with the client and the Ninja operative. Although this sounds impractical and creates communication vulnerabilities, it actually does not require as large a group as might be imagined. In actual fact, not each of the individual go-betweens was involved in the planning. Some acted merely as messengers. The layers were intended to make pursuit through the network difficult and confusing.

This pattern of stratification was something not unique to the Ninja. The idea that the Ninja used this stratification gains indirect credibility if we understand it as something general in the way things were done or taught in matters of social status and a basic construct of societal ranking. It is a well-known fact that such stratification was a basic construct of Japanese society and it was a general descriptor for anything with three designated levels. The human body and even the levels built into the structure of Japanese castles were seen through this lens. For example, the grand chambers or *ohiroma* of some castles had three levels in them called the *gedan*, *chudan* and *jodan* (9). In conventional modern Japanese martial arts these same terms refer to the legs as gedan, the torso and arms as chudan, and the head as jodan. This form of stratification based on the number three is as much symbolic or metaphorical as it is literal.

Mr. Adolphson in his aforementioned work on monastic warriors and Sohei identified this very same pattern in the administration of rank among the clergy (*daishu*) and other staff at Enryakuji, as *joho*, *chuho*, and *geho*, indicating top, middle and lower respectively. The joho were the highest ranking group, composed of another four levels of learned monks and priests, the chuho were administrators and organizational leaders, so-called hall clergy or *doshu*, and attendant clerics within the complex, the lower level, or geho was for the lower classes, menial workers, and residential retainers (*bokan* or *bojin*) who acted in a capacity similar to samurai retainers in service of secular authorities. The geho in fact maintained secular lives within the monastery, having wives and children. All levels were capable of arming themselves and pursuing military agendas. It was, however, the chuho and geho who actually were more likely to be trained in martial arts and to engage in warfare. If this organizational stratification was that ubiquitous and wrapped in superstition, it is virtually a certainty that Ninja groups used some version of it.

It seems that we find this rank structure in the monastic complexes, the noble families and the bakufu of the Kinai, which includes the province of Omi and all of its related martial families, and among the Ninja of that region. This fact points to the depth with which this organizational and conceptual construct was held core to the Japanese way of thinking before the modern era.

Mr. Draeger and Mr. Smith indicate one source of this hierarchical information as coming from Dr. Hatsumi Soke of the Togakure Ryu and eight other traditions. They quote Dr. Hatsumi as stating that the area that in the province of Omi which came to be known as the homeland of Ninjutsu and especially the Iga and Koka families, was settled by *ji-Samurai* (Samurai-farmers, where *ji* denotes earth or soil) who under pressure from government forces and for survival, developed and refined the arts of Ninjutsu with minimal technology. While this explanation may account for part of the social structure of Ninja society, it cannot explain it fully. Further, it may account for the Jonin and some of the Chunin samurai families being set up as go betweens, but probably not the Genin operatives. This account also seems unlikely because it does not consider pre-Kamakura espionage networks, nor can it account for how a group of generally impoverished Samurai farmers with martial skills deriving from Bushi roots developed the networks and broad array of cultural connections and martial practices, seen in Ninjutsu.

It also seems to contradict somewhat the aforementioned idea that Ninjutsu was already a developed system by the 6th century, which is before Samurai had distinguished themselves as a warrior society unto their own.

In source materials I have reviewed, the connection between the ji-Samurai from Omi and the warrior retainers serving the temples shows that ji-Samurai were in fact farmers and warriors who lived in the domains governed by the monasteries and their subsidiary temples and shrines. Ji-Samurai also served any local strongmen who were not directly involved with the monastic community. They fed the people populating these complexes and were recruited to fight in the various battles and skirmishes for their overlords and the monastic communities they served. They were not the professional bushi who served the nobles and large quasi-aristocratic warrior families like the Taira and the Minamoto, whom we are probably used to thinking of as the original forebears to the later Samurai. That these people had something to do with the origins of Ninja society is certainly plausible; in fact, it is probable that Ninja lived among them. What emerges from a good look at the variable expressions of Ninjutsu seen today indicates that some ji-Samurai families developed their own brand of Ninjutsu to serve the needs of their communities.

I would argue in support of Grandmaster Law's view that the various groups had some degree of contact with and learned from each other, but retained differences in their identities and social status. The fact that they were not serving as full-time warriors might explain the opinion given by Master Kawakami that Ninja were Samurai, but not necessarily recognized as such by the governmental authorities within the bakufu. Such a description of circumstances fits well the idea that ji-Samurai and their connections with Ninja society in fact were among the geho in service of the monastic complexes and lowest ranking warriors in the service of local strongmen. Warriors in the service of the monasteries also included Samurai warriors in the joho and chuho level of authority and non-samurai retainers in the geho level. The term Samurai here needs to be used cautiously as well. We see this term used for non-warrior and warrior workers within the monasteries who served as attendants, called variably *hosshi*, and samurai-*hosshi*, the pleural called *hosshiwara*. Based on the diverse nature of the fighting men in the service of the monasteries, it is understandable that not all of them would be considered warrior-Samurai of the same sort as the secular warriors in service of strongmen and the bakufu or the Imperial authorities. Lastly, as we have noted, the ji-Samurai serving the monastic domains had their same counterparts in the service of secular domains of nobles and the professional warrior families. In the end, defining which, if any group of ji-Samurai had ties with Ninja society is vague as this information is unlikely to appear in any official records.

A lot of the ancient martial heritage described above is lost and only relevant to understanding how the Ninja came into being and why they possessed certain characteristics. We as a community, martial artists or not, should not be terribly concerned with the passage of such things into obscurity. The important part of the legacy of past warrior societies, whether Ninja, Samurai, or the many kinds of WuShu, is more in how they thought. If this is understood, then the arts will continue to evolve. We will see what the Ninja shared with contemporary martial arts, and also how they were different. This will help us understand why Ninjutsu simultaneously appears to resemble arts like *Shaolin Chin Na, Ba Qua Chang*, Classical *Jujutsu, Aikido* and Aikijutsu. We will see that many arts continue to influence each other in their efforts to remain culturally and combatively meaningful.

Another way to understand the rather unique psyche of the Ninja is through their use of weapons: not only what they used, but also how they used them, and how and why they developed them in the first place. As the pieces come together, it will become clear how thinking like a Ninja in today's world can be liberating, fascinating and ultimately a very practical thing for protecting oneself, whether in the spheres of personal wellbeing, mental health, physical health, or personal integrity.

Readers will find that much of what is included here is not easily found elsewhere; it will be clearly stated what information is the opinion of the writer and the views inherent in the teachings of our school. Some of it, as has already been shown, will be at odds with conventional thinking and writing on the subject. Rather than viewing this as a problem, the reader is asked to keep an open mind and merely consider some of this material as additional theories and alternative explanations. It will be apparent that much of it is supported at least partially by historical material; wherever possible, efforts were made to refer to historical data or historical authorities to support the proposed theories. The intent of this book is not to act as a definitive work on the obscure history of Ninjutsu and its weapons, but rather to provide insight into the unique way of thinking that makes Ninjutsu important to people to study today. It should be humbly remembered that any historical account, especially an oral one, would be inherently inaccurate. We must, however, look to the future using the tools given us by those that passed before us.

Weapon-No Weapon

Most small arms found in Japan, both ancient and modern, have already been assimilated into the Ninja arts. There is a simple reason for this. The Ninja methods of training are based in a strategy that is the same whether one is empty handed or carrying any kind of object. The state of ready awareness practiced in the art makes the practitioner open to the potential application within any situation, condition or thing. The principle of never locking oneself into a single technique or method leads to the freedom to move at will and match what is demanded by the situation. Therefore, things to consider such as distance, the presence of any object, barrier or opening, things such as windows, doors, walls, furniture, automobiles, etc., all enter into the context of the situation. It follows that the Ninja should be aware of any items that have the potential to be used as a weapon by either himself or his enemies. It should not matter what that item is.

How did Ninja train for this? Most things around us have certain universal properties. There are objects that have the characteristics of sticks, others of ropes, and still others which can cut or release projectiles. Many of these can be attached to or held in the hand, fist, or other part of the body. Many of the tools we use have several of these properties at once. Therefore training involving the use of certain basic tools such as knives, staffs (of various lengths), ropes, chains, and a variety of pointed and/or blunt objects is necessary to express and understand these various elements. When training in Ninjutsu, it is not uncommon to practice scenarios occurring in cars, on public transit, the office, bar, or a restaurant. Modern practitioners of Ninjutsu will train with a pen, a belt, a jacket, bungee cord, or anything that happens to be around.

Grandmaster Law emphasized the formlessness, versatility and rationality of the Ninja's way of thinking, doing and moving. He stated that, in ancient times, these ways were central to the Ninja arts; the value of these characteristics is no less important in the present. This was reflected in all aspects of their lives and especially their work. Ninja rarely donned the now famous "Ninja uniform," or shozoku, which in reality is largely a modern stereotype. When traveling they were in disguise, which usually meant they were dressed in ordinary clothes. As such there is no true universal Ninja attire.

Many Ninja had one or more trades of their own and so they could even travel "as themselves" without rousing suspicion. Typically caution demanded that they conceal their identity and movement. If they were on a mission that might require the use of weapons, they had to choose ones that were either inconspicuous or were an accepted part of the retinue of the person that they were impersonating at the time. We would expect a modern-day Ninja impersonating a landscaper to wear typical work clothes, drive a pick-up truck, and have the tools of his trade with him while in his role.

In their efforts to remain unnoticed and to blend in with others, Ninja would often travel carrying only the most mundane objects. These objects separately were nothing to the casual observer, but could be assembled to make anything from a trap or snare to a lethal poisoned projectile. When the Ninja knew in advance about a situation in which a specific weapon was needed, they would cleverly build it from everyday objects or from scratch and prepare it for the right occasion. Items of this kind were used in such a way that they preserved the element of surprise. Sometimes the "weapon" was something as unusual as an animal. The choice of weapon was also influenced by the strategy and conditions associated with its use, such as the weather or the use of fire, poison, crowds or noise. There were times when the Ninja simply obtained his weapons from among his intended targets, either by using it against an enemy bearing the weapon during an encounter, by theft, or even by killing an unsuspecting person, donning their clothes, and getting the weapons in the process.

Ninja strategy then as now called for the ability to take a weapon from another person, to prevent the taking of a weapon from them, and to retrieve a weapon once taken by the enemy. This is essential in weapons training. According to Grandmaster Law, Ninja who were generalists, and especially those not of Samurai rank, never specialized in only one or two weapons or strategies. Such specialization was counterintuitive to them.

Specialization in fighting and weaponry meant becoming limited, over reliant on the weapon, and thus at risk due to being predictable to enemies. A strong, intuitive enemy would read this weakness in combat and quickly defeat it. This explains why one of the most important features of Ninjutsu is versatility. Students are quickly engaged in ever changing techniques that regularly take them out of the comfort zone of what they know and place them into areas with which they are unfamiliar. This is done to keep the mind keen and to prevent settling into an attitude of complacency. Grandmaster Law would often say there are no real beginner techniques or advanced techniques. Some techniques are more difficult to understand and perform, but they are in fact understood more by the result they achieve and the methods involved than by how difficult they might be to accomplish. Techniques could even be easily adjusted to suit the potential of the practitioner, as the case might be for a person with a handicap or injury. Apart from those circumstances, Ninja methods applied equally well to most people regardless of height, weight, gender, or age.

Though perhaps explicable in other contexts, from direct experience it is known that different people will learn different techniques variably from one another. Some may excel in grappling applications, others in striking, and so on. In this sense, what may seem advanced to one person, may not to their peer. Individuals are expected to make up for deficits and focus on areas of weakness rather than repeat doing what they do well; only in this way could they advance. Because of the wide repertoire of a complete martial art such as Ninjutsu, there is no room for complacency or stagnation. Some arts such as shurikenjutsu, ukemi, and the related methods of acrobatics deteriorate without routine practice. Having a broad technical repertoire meant that Ninja were free to use techniques and tools they felt were best suited to them and the task without hindrance or apprehension.

Ninja did not take a conservative approach to martial arts and were not averse to learning the methods and weapons of others. It did not matter where the methods came from; if they were effective and could be used and incorporated into Ninjutsu, then they were worth learning and improving upon. Ninja did, however, reject certain methods or modified them significantly if they did not blend with the overall core practices and strategies of taijutsu. The Ninja reject the method of blocking in the conventional sense as it is seen, for example, in the art of Karate, due to their perspective that it limits and hinders Ninjutsu technique more than it helps and it offers no strategic advantage; in fact, it keeps the person blocking in harm's way. Similarly, modern Ninjutsu rejects the practice of solo *kata*, "forms," or "patterns," which are a series of pre-arranged combative movements practiced without an opponent, due to the fact that they impart no understanding of distance, timing, or the responses of the enemy's body to the techniques used. One has to have a detailed understanding of what the techniques can actually do before using them with any confidence in battle. Also, without practicing on a partner, a student cannot learn to appreciate the danger involved with certain types of techniques. This appreciation is needed, as it imparts the sensitivity necessary for the practitioner to utilize technique as intended. Lacking sensitivity in this area can result in accidental or unintended injury in training and ineffective combative application.

Through concerted effort to understand the true purpose of a technique, weapon and its strategic application, the Ninja found ways to accept new weapons and methods into their art. In fact, the art has been so refined that this takes surprisingly little effort most of the time to do. Solid practitioners of Ninjutsu can pick up nearly any unfamiliar weapon or tool and use it effectively. When this is done, however, the techniques may not look anything like the way they were used in the art from which they originated. In our own art, the nunchaku is not one of our traditional weapons. Nevertheless, we can use it seamlessly for grappling, choking, throwing, joint-locks and atemi rather than just for striking.

Ninja were trained to use intelligent and principled approaches incorporating all aspects of the mind and body; their own and that of the enemy, as the basis of all fighting strategy. It is not unusual in modern practice of Ninjutsu to perform techniques that were only witnessed once but never trained in, or to do something the practitioner has no recollection of ever learning. This is not accidental, nor is it making things up as you go along. Instead, the mind sees possibility no matter what position the body happens to be in and intuitively finds a technique that will work. It may not always be the best technique, but the success of application will be strongly influenced by experience. In some ways, this process is like using language. After a person has a core mastery of how to spell words, write sentences and use proper grammar, they can proceed to write something they have never written before and usually do so without having to slow down and think about it a long time. This is a very important point to bear in mind when thinking about how the Ninja used and developed weapons, and how these concepts remain important today.

To the Ninja, a weapon is not necessarily an inanimate object. Ninja used animals such as snakes, spiders, dogs, cats, and especially plants and microbes as weapons. The historical Ninja were certainly early practitioners of biological warfare. Plants and microbes were used to concoct poisons, spoil water supplies, and cause epidemics of dysentery in enemy ranks and strongholds. Although they knew nothing of actual microbiology and what we now call the "germ theory of disease," Ninja knew how to contaminate water using disease-laden source materials.

Microbes were also used to poison edged weapons, clothes and even the ropes used in *hojojutsu*. Since Ninja had no special attachment to their weapons as heirlooms and regarded them more as tools, they had no qualms about leaving their blades in buckets containing a mixture of fecal matter and blood or coating them with venom. The result of even a small wound from such a blade could cause a serious infection and necrotic tissue loss that could latently kill the intended victim or disable them to the point that they lost capacity, presented no further threat, or could be easily killed. In such circumstances even if the Ninja themselves were killed or wounded, their objective might still have a better chance of being accomplished if they wounded their target or adversary. In keeping with the understanding that the weapon was a tool and only needed for the task for which it was acquired, a Ninja was likely to discard some weapons after use so they could once again be inconspicuous on their journey home.

Ninjutsu teaches the dual nature of all things and applies that philosophy to the martial and body arts. Having a sophisticated understanding of the body could be used as much to destroy another human being or animal as to heal and rescue them. This was of course true of their use of plants, many of which can poison at higher doses but at lower doses or prepared differently are used medicinally and for survival.

As is the case today, many of the substances used as medicines are, in fact, poisonous at higher doses. Sometimes survival meant a Ninja used his poison against himself in such a dose as to feign illness or death. The same poison could facilitate escaping detection by using it on a difficult captive, not only to silence them, but also to ease their transport if that was required.

Then there was the way to understand multiplicity in the nature of things, and not necessarily only through the lens of polar opposites such as healing and poisoning. This means understanding the many different ways things can be used by exploiting their physical properties and in some cases more subtle aspects like the potential for physiological and psychological influence. The poisoned arrows or blow darts used for hunting were the same ones used in combat. The improvised tool used to cultivate and gather food was the weapon used to kill, capture, torture and defend. This form of creative thinking in which Ninja were trained made them able to beat unfavorable odds and survive situations that would normally kill another person.

Ninjutsu teaches people to be self-sufficient. Ninja had to understand how to control and heal themselves and others. It was of high importance to not have to rely very much on others. The more people a person must rely on, the more precarious becomes their continued existence. Self-reliance as a martial principle is not consistent with the team-like approaches used in conventional military work. Due to the often solitary nature of the Ninja's occupation and meager circumstances related to having to "travel light," everything they did had to minimize effort and maximize efficiency and secrecy. A good example to illustrate this kind of thinking was how they concocted special dietary substances *suikatsugan* and *kikatsugan* that could provide nutrients, energy, and control appetite and thirst on a temporary basis. These were usually tiny pill sized pieces that could be concealed in the folds of their clothing and hair. These aided Ninja who were in hiding and had to remain still for prolonged periods where they might be subjected to starvation and other adverse conditions.

Another fundamental concept was that of fusion and synthesis; seeing, understanding, and operating fluidly in the world. This form of thought is one of their most important legacies. Combining a deep understanding of strategy that held to the principles of duality, multiplicity in purpose, following the natural properties of the mind and body, efficiency, minimal effort, self-reliance and the rejection of artificial limitations are the ways in which Ninja were able to live well as "invisible people." They further cultivated a deep understanding of human behavior so that they could always keep their enemies either over confident or uncomfortable and unbalanced, so that they lacked perspective and would be prone to misjudgments and to act carelessly or in haste.

Through examining the tools and weapons of the Ninja, with an awareness of how they conceived of things, it will become clear, that studying Ninjutsu even as a curious reader can open the mind to new possibilities in other pursuits. The actual weapons themselves are in some ways less important to understand than the process through which Ninja came to use them. It will further show that silly myths about the Ninja being "superhuman" are a misleading idea that only reveals the gap between what we are and what we could be. Ninja were people with a special martial culture that was related to many others, but was also in many ways different. Unlocking their unique way of understanding the world and living can reveal new potential within ourselves and dispel delusions that we may not have known we had.

We will be looking at a number of examples where tools have interchangeably become weapons, some of which are not well known, while others have been cited elsewhere, but are still worth reviewing because they contribute to a more complete understanding of Ninjutsu. Areas of interest, where innovation is particularly evident include activities like the penetration of structures—something at which the Ninja excelled. The nature of the problems encountered in this art and hence the tools and weapons used, varied with the structure and objective. Sometimes a simple solution to a typical problem could involve the use of things like stilts. These could be easily constructed from natural materials and adjusted to the correct height. They provided a direct way to scale structures (conditions permitting), with only limited exertion.

We will see how Ninja creatively used techniques employing ropes, combined with sticks and/or various forms of grappling hooks. Ninja were able to improvise methods on the spot. Ninja training required that they learn to be well versed in using the many forms of ropes and knots needed.

Another example of an unexpected innovation was how Ninja had their own early versions of the trampoline, which they used to leap onto or over walls. Yumio Nawa (1912-2006) a well-known author and researcher into Ninjutsu, proposed that Ninja even used versions of hang-glides and parachutes made from animal hides and textiles that served for silent aerial infiltration. These strange but possible proposals may have contributed to myths about the Ninja's ability to fly. Ninja conceived and created other odd tools for moving across bogs and swamps, which are clear inventions and improvisations that seem to bear no obvious relationship to an original known trade, tool or skill. These things, though some may be partially fictitious, are consistent with the kinds of things Ninja did and how they thought. The myths about flying Ninja and Ninja walking on water are very interesting and entertaining as well. Things like strange boots with cone shaped soles were meant to touch a muddy bottom of a swamp but also to keep the user from sinking too far, permitted them to move around in places likely felt to be impossible and impenetrable, like only an *invisible person* could.

Other clever and advanced ways to stay concealed were for Ninja to move across bodies of water while staying submerged. To extend their time beneath the surface, the Ninja were not only trained in apnea or breath control, but they also used bamboo tubes, strong reeds, and even a modified sword scabbard (*saya*) through which to breathe. Ninja were able to deal with their own buoyancy by the careful use of weights attached to the body. This permitted them to swim upside down under water while using a tube as a "snorkel" provided the nostrils were pinched closed or obstructed. In a concept similar to a primitive scuba tank, the Ninja are said to have brought an air filled sack with a sort of attached straw through which to breathe underwater. In reality, this sack was more like a simple re-breather, where the individual would recycle air from within their lungs. Such a system would only last a short time, but sometimes that was all that was necessary. The same sack without attached weights to counter buoyancy could also serve as a floatation device.

Examples such as these highlight the ingenuity for which the Ninja had a reputation. With the concepts of this chapter in mind, we can now look at how these invisible people remained true to their reputation and did their fascinating work. Remembering the underlying principle held sacred by the Ninja, of using knowledge before force, the reader must appreciate the extreme psychological pressure under which Ninja were expected to be able to exercise this creativity. Their enemies faced similar stress; failure to capture a spy known to have moved undetected in the midst of the Samurai themselves could have been grounds to commit *seppuku* (ritual suicide), and was certainly a part of the reason that Ninja were regarded with such fear and contempt.

Tradespeople and the Art of Ninjutsu: Carpentry and Construction

To simply produce a laundry list of Ninja weaponry and associated methods would not respect the high level of insight found within the art. Those who developed these concepts had an understanding based both in simplicity and the potential for multiple and generalized use. The tools were used without reference to handedness, since Ninja trained to be ambidextrous. Ninja were also taught to see opportunity in adversity and conflict. Conflict is in many ways the undoing of some previous system, which existed in a state of balance by the coming together of sometimes complex forces. Such systems can be psychological and within the mind, others are between discreet groups of people, based on values or financial things like resources and trade.

The process can be likened to an earthquake that occurs when continental tectonic plates that have been silently under increasing tension suddenly release and there is a tremendous discharge of energy, along with a reorganization of the landscape. That new landscape presents opportunities. Ninja did not dwell nostalgically on what was lost in a societal upheaval, but instead looked at what was new around them, adapted to it, then went a step beyond that and tried to understand where it was leading. If this could be understood, they would try to take advantage of it in some way. Adversity is associated with conflict and imposes harsh conditions on people and their systems. Under such conditions it can force decisions that might not be made in times of excess or opulence. Ninja were culturally accustomed to living with very little and were less affected by adversity and austerity. They understood how stressed societies behaved and were able to use these conditions to secure power that might not be available when it was thriving. Conflict and adversity then frequently occur as a consequence of one another.

Grandmaster Law expressed this type of observation and opportunism as looking with "funnel vision" and not "tunnel vision." In other words, Ninja were taught to see the expanding possibilities and potential within any situation rather than accepting it at face value. As a principle, it was applied even to the most mundane everyday circumstances. This concept is important in understanding Ninja tools and methods. In and of itself, this principle sounds simple and easy to understand, it is however complex depending on how and where it is applied. To illustrate, a similar or analogous concept is mentioned in the Shoninki, in the middle scroll, third part "*Shinobi ni iro o kaeru to iu narai,*" translated as "enlarging your view angle during espionage." Though it is not always used in espionage, the idea encourages looking at what other opportunities exist inherent in a particular task, situation or repertoire. It endorses indirect ways to achieve goals within limited resources. In espionage it involves getting others to divulge information that is hidden. This is done by making inferences based on data received and extrapolated through an understanding of how the people being analyzed think and behave. By corollary it also teaches the spy to detect when they are being manipulated and how to prevent being tricked into giving away guarded information in the apparent reciprocity that takes place during data acquisition. (22, p. 96).

It is also important to point out that this way of thinking was not so uncommon, especially in those areas where people were poor and living off the natural resources around them or the scraps left over from the spoils of war. It was applied from the simplest to the most complex of problems, and was most likely so ingrained that people using this principle may not have been aware they were using it, unless perhaps they were teaching this form of problem solving. It is to be contrasted with the credo of the Bushi, to live with an attitude of simplicity and to think practically although not necessarily with an eye towards expanding possibility. Many classical bushi were conservative in their thinking and were averse to moving forward with new paradigms in combat or otherwise, if they felt that their established method was enlightened and therefore sacred.

Bushi considered a life of ostentation to be a disgrace and it was clearly antithetical to the Ninja as well although in the latter case it was because such a lifestyle would have meant drawing unwanted attention. This would have made it difficult to maintain a true and effective culture of secrecy. Accomplishment and reward are known to have taken place for the services of Ninja to their Samurai overlords, as was seen in the events of Ninja aiding the escape of *Tokugawa Ieyasu* in the year 1579 from the *Warriors of Akechi Mitsuhide* (16, p. 78-79). Aside from certain well-publicized and recorded events such as these, most of their accomplishments were known only to the agents involved and their proxies.

The need to maintain a very low and invisible public profile seems to have been a primary motivator for Ninja to utilize weapons improvised from the tools of trades people. One fairly rich source of devices with this potential came from the trades of builders, carpenters and woodworkers. Not only that, but one of the things for which Ninja services were sought was the ability to penetrate structures, the so-called art of *shinobi-iri*. Because of their knowledge of construction, structures and building, Ninja had an intimate understanding and training in the use of the tools from these trades. In fact, the secrecy of Ninja society meant that they sometimes had to live in self-sustaining, independent communities, which had the necessary tradespeople to function autonomously, making them indistinguishable in many respects from other small villages in the area. Given that Ninja society was averse to allowing outsiders to live among them, all local trades people had to be from within Ninja families and held to its standards of secrecy. Thus construction was but one of the trades familiar to Ninja and just one source of tools and weapons applied to the practice of Ninjutsu.

Builders in the Far East are known in part for their art of complex joinery. Chinese woodworkers and carpenters were famous for making wooden puzzles and puzzle boxes that expressed the principles of this art on a small scale. These traditions were adopted and perpetuated in Japan as masterful works known as the *Himitsu-Bako* or "personal secret boxes" and *Sikake-Bako* "trick/smart boxes" (Ir-1). These objects, while lacking the glitter of modern games and toys, were marvels of trickery based on scaled down methods of joinery and lock mechanisms. Even today little three-dimensional puzzles and puzzle boxes are sold in contemporary Chinese and Japanese trinket stores and on the Internet. They come in a variety of shapes and sizes and can be anything from a simple sphere to a dragon or Pagoda. In the days before electronics like radio, television, and the strangely similar fad of the "Rubik's Cube" of the 1980's, these puzzles were the delight of children (and no doubt some adults) who could pass time and find an intellectual challenge in solving them.

Just as with the old board games of strategy such as *Go* and Chess, these puzzles were a form of mental exercise, developing a person's ability to think logically, to concentrate and remember. Ninja used such games to train children in these skills and to learn how to understand and open locks, from their earliest years. By the time they became adults the knowledge and concentration needed to break into buildings, decipher codes, and create devices needed for a task came more naturally to them. In a parallel manor, martial techniques applied to the human body are also subject to a number of similar physical principles found in intricate mechanical apparatuses and joinery. The workings of the human skeleton and its many adaptations for function can be considered analogously. Thus the concepts and thinking applied to these intricate puzzles was felt to be helpful in understanding some aspects of the interplay of human joints to the application of combative techniques.

Ninja are known to have made complex traps, passages and doors that are in many respects like these puzzles in and around their homes. They were expert at concealing things within other things. The weapons and tools of Shinobi would neither be kept in some obvious place nor buried in a box like in movies. They were incorporated into walls, doors, dolls, stoves or anything else that seemed to fit the task. Ninja also were adept at making the special puzzle boxes mentioned above and incorporating the same special interlocking mechanisms to larger structures so as to conceal things within objects that were in plain sight. Outside their homes they used these concepts to hide things in nature, using trees, grass, water and stone, although in these cases mechanisms were rarely needed.

Grandmaster Law would sometimes give me riddles of this kind, stressing that something hidden was in fact in plain sight, but could not be distinguished. One such riddle actually took me several years to answer. The problem I had in figuring it out was due to a limitation in my thinking of which I was not aware. The answer was in fact very simple. This kind of thinking permitted Ninja to do things like tie a man to a tree using only his own body, even when he was naked. No ropes or other gadgets are used to do this.

Making objects with secret compartments might be compared to the modern practices of lock picking and safe cracking. The Ninja firmly established an *architecture of invisibility* into their everyday thinking. Their homes, their furniture, their tools, and even their clothes were like Chinese puzzles.

The now famous Koka Ninja house at the museum of Ninja tradition in Japan's Shiga Province illustrates some of these features. Ninja folklore has well-known tales of the tricks Ninja had in store for the unwitting and unwelcome within their homes which have been published elsewhere. While the rotating walls, hidden trap doors, booby traps and singing floorboards have already been covered in other publications, there are yet things that carpentry has inspired in the Ninja arts that are less understood and known.

We were taught that Ninja entertained themselves by working wood and carving works of art like many of their contemporaries. They were known to have made frightening masks that could be used to intimidate drunk, sleepy and superstitious people into thinking they were seeing devils and demons.

The Axe

As with the warrior who sees his martial system in terms of the biological substrates of the human body and mind, the carpenter, woodworker, and builder start with a seemingly simple tree. To them it was something to be deeply understood. They have to know the various types of trees and their respective wood qualities. They also have to know how to climb them, fell them, peel them and junk them. They must then understand how to make the various poles, beams, shims and boards they will use, and know how to put them together to make a strong and lasting structure that was habitable and pleasant. The opportunities made available through "funnel vision," or broadening the scope of perspective, come to light when we examine how many tools eventually came to be used for Ninja activities and as weapons.

It was through the entire process of felling and preparing lumber to construct buildings that we see these applications come to life. Tools included saws, axes of different sizes, ropes, adzes and a few other specialized tools that are not commonly discussed as it pertains to this culture. The staff was, and remains, the most basic weapon to come from this process. It takes little knowledge to make a decently effective staff. Nevertheless the fighting art of the staff is extremely subtle and complex. The staff is sufficiently ubiquitous as to render any speculations of how it came to be a weapon essentially *sine proposito vaga est*. Given that chimps are known to pick up sticks and use them as tools and primitively as weapons for hunting and in confrontations with each other, indicates that this weapon likely goes back to the earliest humans and beyond. The fact that staffs continue to be a staple of martial arts culture is not at all surprising, due to their utter simplicity and incredible potential.

Axes and the related variants found around the world are still recognized as the tools and weapons of the commoner. Specialized axes came to be used by warriors for exclusive use in combat repeatedly throughout history. The earliest axes were made from a stone head and a handle. The axes found across the Pacific Rim are fairly similar. The Ninja had no special affinity for the axe, and neither did Asian fighting men in general. Primitive axes continue to be used by cultures that maintain stone tool use such as those seen in remote areas and islands in the pacific, and Papua New Guinea.

Early axes in the Paleolithic era and the *Jomon* period, or "Japanese Neolithic age," (10000 to 300 BC) were smaller, made with a wooden handle and a stone head that was double-beveled.

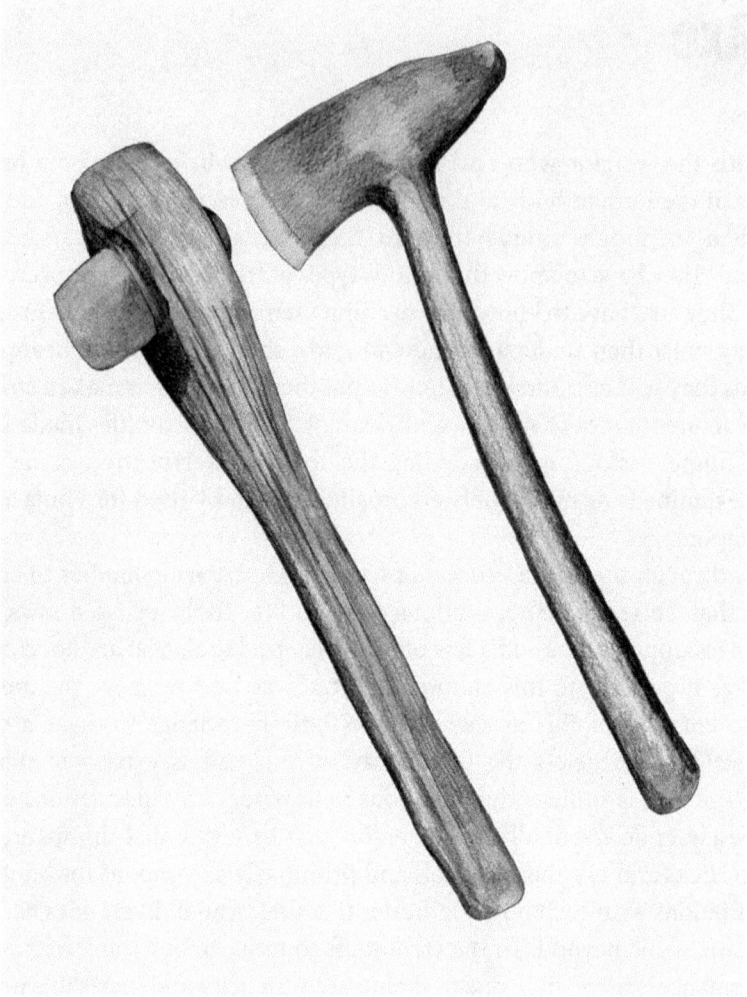

Fig. 3: Early Axes of the Neolithic period, on the left made of stone and on the right an early age bronze axe.

They were supplanted with iron axes around 300 BC during the Yayoi period (300 BC to 300 AD) (Fig. 3) with the arrival of people from Manchuria, by way of Korea, who brought axes with them.

The "Jomon people" were probably a culturally diverse population of Asian aboriginals in the Japanese archipelago (as well as other areas of Asia such as the Chinese and Korean coastal lands), while the "Yayoi people" were a wave of Sino-Asians from the Manchurian regions which later came to be dominated by China, who eventually eliminated, bred into and replaced the Jomon.

Axes were primarily for felling trees and preparing building materials, but they were also natural weapons. Larger hewing axes or *masakari* (Fig. 4 and 5) were developed later—probably by the medieval period—and were used in China prior to their appearance in Japan.

Fig. 4: A large hewing axe or "masakari" similar to those used in battle

Fig. 5: The hewing axe used to hew a log into a beam.

At some point adzes and chisels (Fig. 6) were added to the tools used by those who felled and trimmed trees. Both axes and adzes were used to hew and trim beams from trees. The hewing axe was to rough out the beam and the finer work was done with adzes and various chisels. This may explain why the findings of trace marks on the beams of ancient buildings from archeological sites reflect the marks of these smaller tools and not those of the hewing axe.

Despite the large size of hewing axes, the Ninja and Samurai did develop martial techniques for using these ostensibly impractical tools. The word in Japanese for axe is *Ono*. This name is used for the intermediate size variety of axe. The masakari used for hewing were broad and heavy, and to use them without draining all of one's strength required a method that took advantage of the particular aspects of its weight, shape, length and balance. While this is true for many other weapons as well, it must be emphasized for weapons of large mass, such as this and other Samurai weapons like the *Tetsubo* (iron staff).

The masakari was held close to the body in positions of leverage such that the burden was taken by the central musculature of the shoulders, torso and legs.

Fig. 6: Adzes and chisels of iron and wood of the Yayoi period. (R)

To swing a large axe in battle, the warrior would shift his weight and guide its fall into movements that were deadly accurate and devastating to the enemy. If the axe were swung laterally, the body swung also and acted as a counter weight, taking advantage of rotational acceleration to deliver a huge impact though instantaneous deceleration. To change and shift position, the hands were slid along the handle in such a way as to change the reach with the head of the axe without compromising grip. This permitted the wielder to swing the weapon without bringing himself any closer to his adversaries. In general, heavy weapons will feel lighter while they are in motion. The weapon, due to its movement, actually can feel lighter as it engages different muscles in its constant motion. It is kept moving with a minimum of effort by taking advantage of the center of gravity. The weapon is heaviest and offset in its balance during the starting and stopping movements, and it is at those times that it requires more strength to handle.

Such weapons could be highly effective against a mounted armor-clad warrior. These axes were capable of cleaving armor and causing crushing injuries through it as well. A disadvantage of such a weapon is that it was relatively slow compared with other weapons in the battle arsenal. In spite of this, its other characteristics, made it useful against an armor-clad warrior and the battlefield was an excellent place for an axe to be used because even though the Samurai armor is light by most standards, it still slowed them down enough that the axe retained some practicality. What it lacked in speed to some degree was compensated by its power.

It should be noted that the hewing axe was a big showy weapon and when taken out of the context in which it was used as a tool. It was not practical for the usual clandestine work of the Shinobi. Ninja rarely fought in open battlefields, thus this weapon was never a mainstay of the Ninja arsenal. Ninja did sometimes fight using the axe, and more extensively with smaller varieties like hatchets.

Throwing these in a manner similar to a tomahawk was another way in which they were used. Ninja carried them as a tool if the situation required it, but they could not really be used in infiltration because of the distinctive repeated percussive sound made when striking wood, that was easily heard at a distance.

There are variants to nearly every weapon the Ninja used. Ninja weapons were and are handmade; learning how to make them was integral to learning and understanding the art. Thus, no two weapons were exactly the same; they were as varied as the individuals who made them. In keeping with their spirit of creativity and ingenuity, Ninja made composite weapons using blades, weights, chains and staffs and occasionally other tools such as hooks and rakes.

In one such variant, a simple axe blade was attached to a chain and swung in broad sweeping circles. The blade could also be gripped and used directly like a cleaver. In some cases, the blade was wrapped and bound in cloth and soaked in flammable resin then set on fire. This was sometimes done with other weapons like the shoge, as we shall see below. Such flaming objects could, on impact, causes the resin to stick to the target and continue to burn. Blades swung at high velocity such as these were capable of inflicting serious injury and although a burn would initially be sterile, within hours it became a guaranteed source of severe, painful, and often lethal infection. Swinging something that is on fire will cause it to burn brightly because of convection, which enhances its psychological effect on the enemy. This weapon made a lot of smoke and whirling light that was used to confuse and intimidate. Against multiple enemies this was a good strategy, as they would have had difficulty organizing and mounting an attack, thereby permitting the Ninja to pick off up to several enemies at a time. It should be noted that a visible standoff as described here would only be used if the Ninja was cornered or was engaged in distracting the enemy from goings on elsewhere.

The advent of bronze, and later, iron and steel technology improved tools and weapons significantly for people previously making them from stone. Metal tools could be made lighter due to being materially stronger. They were more durable and could be made sharper without the same risk of breakage. Also, due to metals' ductile properties, they could be reheated, sharpened and repaired.

Ninja, however, maintained ancient knowledge of how to make and use stone tools, water and fire. Primitive stone axes and adzes were used for purposes other than felling trees and making buildings. Similar tools were used, just as in other cultures to make dugout canoes, bowls, various containers and vessels, dining utensils and hunting weapons such as bows and harpoons. Wedge shaped heated rocks were used to peel trees into boards. Fire was used to hollow out wood, coals and heated sharp stones were used to bore holes for the purpose of inserting pegs, and as a primitive means of accomplishing basic joinery work. Early craftsmen knew how to bend wood and bamboo using heat and water. According to Grandmaster Law, Ninja retained this ancient technology as part of their repertoire of survival skills, in the event they found themselves living in conditions without the modern steel tools of their day.

With ancient knowledge and technology Ninja were able to live comfortably in remote wilderness areas. Ninja training typically occurred in such places, far away from the prying eyes of society or other Ninja. As previously noted Ninja were not inclined to socialize closely with outsiders. Grandmaster Law explained that historically and even into the early 20th century, some Ninja families kept no birth records and those who did not survive training were cremated anonymously in the forests where they lived. Ninja were burned in their grave in such a way that absolutely no remains but ash were left. Anyone with some knowledge of forensic science would understand that this requires a specific process.

In more conventional settings we can see how axes and poles were straightforward adaptations to weapons. There were yet other tools that gave rise to weapons in ways that may not have been so immediate and clear. Making quality structures in early history, just as it does today, required a broad set of fairly refined skills. In Japan, larger homes, temples, bridges and fortifications necessitated the use of large beams. Workers used ladders to scale edifices and also used climbing skills when necessary. Just as we have seen construction workers in places like New York City walking on beams and moving about complex structures fearlessly and without supports, early craftsmen and builders likely took similar risks albeit on a more humble scale. There were no cranes or elevators available to hoist workers and materials to higher or lower levels. There were only the ladders, ropes and baskets available to move things and maneuver around on a structure. Ninja are said to have practiced climbing edifices in such contexts and to have used these skills in the field (Fig. 7).

Ninja, always watching for simple and elegant solutions to problems, and always striving to develop strategies for multiple usages with simplicity, applied these principles as they acquired and devised many applications for objects originating in the arts of building and carpentry.

Fig. 7: Ninja using one of many forms of climbing skills

Shuriken and Shaken

The *Shuriken* and the *Shaken* were amongst the tools modified and adapted by warrior culture and within it; Ninjutsu. Their use was cultivated along with a variety of other skills needed for constructing buildings, involving walking and climbing on beams and ropes and the ability to maneuver through tight spaces, each of which was essential to Ninja skills of penetrating structures.

More refined tools of carpentry developed around the 4th to 6th century AD that would eventually come to be used by Ninja to penetrate buildings such as storehouses and strongholds. These tools were originally simple carpenter's tools and included anything from small saws, gimlets, clamps and planes to various spikes and plumbs.

Naturally, any Ninja caught in the midst of entering a building using these tools would be obligated to use them as weapons; in this sense any and all of these tools were also "weapons." A distinction needs to be made, however, between tools that are used as weapons in an emergency because the urgency of the situation called for it, and tools that provide some particular advantage in combat such that they made good general weapons. Such tools may have continued to be used as weapons long after their use as a tool fell out of favor. Then there were tools that, with a little modification, were made into effective weapons. These also would be retained primarily because of their function as weapons, after the originating tool had disappeared. Matters get complicated when weapons are merely inspired by certain implements, or when they could have originated from different sources, and it can be quite challenging to understand their varying origins and transformation into martial arts forms.

The Ninja, tool in hand, in order not be awkward when it was necessary to use it in combat, had to develop fighting methods such that any object could be used comfortably and at will. Some of the original tools used by carpenters form the ancient periods do remain with us to this day, but there are very few. What has been found on archeological digs can be seen in museums in Japan and these can be viewed on the Internet as well (Ir-2). Iron was a precious commodity in ancient Japan. When tools were worn down or broken, they were likely melted down and used to make new ones. In spite of their value, such objects were not venerated as art, weapons, and jewelry and thus rarely occurred in tombs and burials. Some were mentioned in written, and shown in illustrated, records. Where this information was lacking, inferences have been made as to how and what tools were used by looking at trace evidence such as impressions and tooling marks on ancient timbers in archeological sites.

The shuriken is an elongated piece of metal that resembles a spike, nail (*kugi*) or chisel (*nomi*). It could be flattened or cylindrical in cross-section and came in a wide variety of shapes and lengths. The nail, needle and spike-like variety were generally referred to as *bo-shuriken* (stick like shuriken); the *kugigata* shuriken (nail like shuriken) is one common variety with a square or rectangular cross-section and a heavy construction. Some had a weighted tip to enhance their impact and improve stability in flight. The shuriken is to be differentiated from the *shaken* or *shashuriken*, so named because of its spin in flight. For our purposes here, *shashuriken* will be called simply *shaken*. The shaken, as we shall see later, is a flat piece of metal fashioned into a star, cross, or disc shape.

The flat and straight forms of shuriken resemble small chisels, gimlets, pry bars and sometimes small knife blades. In fact the word shuriken literally translates as "blade in hand" or "palm blade." The different types of shuriken and the many different martial arts that used them indicate that they likely originated from different sources and that any projectile weapon used in combat converged under the paradigm of shuriken. Blade-like shuriken clearly originated as knives, tanto and *yoroi-doshi* (armor piercing dagger). The tanto was typically a short slightly curved and single edged blade that could be worn by Samurai indoors when not wearing a wakizashi (short sword) or with the complete daisho (long and short sword combined) in public. They were often made from the parts of ancestral heirloom swords that had broken in battle and were cherished when this was so. The so-called *tantogata* (dagger-shaped shuriken), and their relationship to other shuriken is that they were incorporated into shurikenjutsu and modified into a more sturdy design similar in a number of ways to the kugigata shuriken.

Another variation is simply that of a modified arrow. The *uchine* and its variations clearly derive from the warrior arts of *kyujutsu*, and the fact that an arrow can be thrown as a last resort when the bow is broken. Eventually a modified, heavier and sturdier arrow was made, specifically to be thrown by hand in a manner similar to a small spear and became part of the wider arts of shurikenjutsu. Arrows can be thought of as small spears, except that they were projected by the bow.

The *matsubagata shuriken* (pine needle shaped shuriken Fig. 8), a three-pointed, v-shaped shuriken, could have more than one potential origin. The v-shaped blade is of special interest because it resembles the iron pry-bars used by Ninja to work open wallboards, pull nails in a manner similar to a modern crowbar and separate bars in windows. They also strongly resemble special spear tips used for fishing. In our school this shuriken is a preferred variety, and it is our understanding that

Ninja carried this in part because the long point could be incorporated into a dowel to add torque to prying, or the dovetailed end could be inserted into a staff and used as a spear. We have other uses for this shuriken in setting traps and as part of *hojojutsu*, which will be touched in other areas.

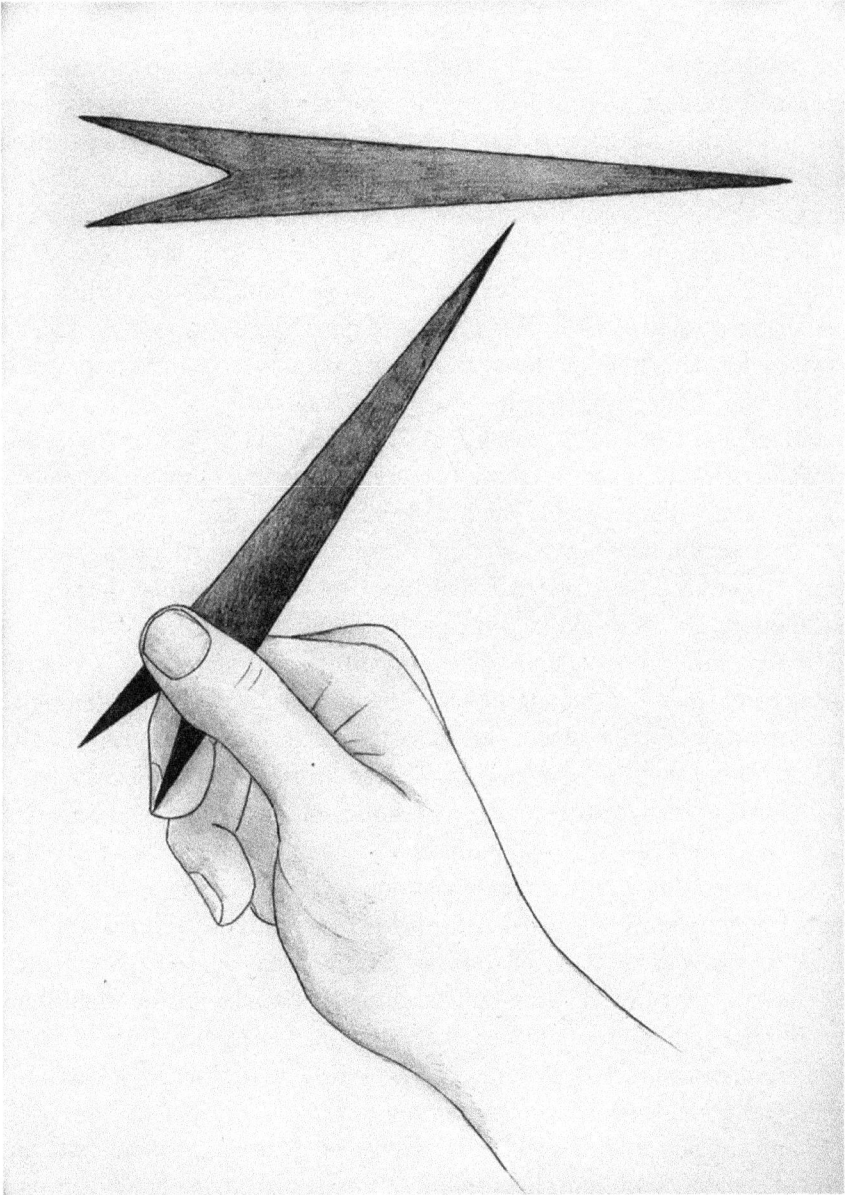

Fig. 8: Matsubagata shuriken, one variation.

We consider the most likely origin of the kugigata shuriken to, in fact, be the humble nail—a tool of building and carpentry. This, the matsubagata shuriken and the shaken are all of origin in construction and building, and are the basis for most subsequent varieties of shuriken known, which justifies their analysis in the context of ancient carpentry, joinery and building. Author and exponent of classical fighting arts in Japan, Serge Mol, is his book *Classical Weaponry of Japan*, provides a fairly comprehensive look at shuriken as they were used and understood in the Samurai Bugei. I have used this source to assure the correct Japanese terminology for the shaken and shuriken discussed here. The reason for doing so is because when we learned to use these objects, Grandmaster Law did not bother to name them. The majority of throwing objects we used would typically fall into a category known as *teppan*. These are briefly illustrated and discussed in a text called *Japanese Throwing Weapons: Mastering Shuriken Throwing Techniques* by Daniel Fletcher and featuring *Yasuyuki Otsuka* Headmaster of the *Meifu Shinkage Ryu*. Teppan are improvised throwing weapons made from sheet metal, although the term translates as "sheet metal." They came in many shapes and varieties.

Grandmaster Law's point of view was that we needed to develop the sensitivity to throw any kind of sharp or pointed object that could be thrown. Teppan allow for this. We trained in throwing anything from steak knives to screwdrivers. There is also a connection between teppan and various tools from which the metal used to make them may be salvaged. Mr. Fletchers properly draws this connection in a brief discussion about the shuko, which will be explored further.

Grandmaster Law stated that, like the many techniques in the art, giving names to these objects merely categorizes them. This can be helpful when writing about martial arts, and to some extent in teaching as well. It can become a hindrance to understanding the connectedness in form and function however, as it becomes expressed in the creative process needed to understand how tools and weapons can be used. He continually stressed, perhaps idiosyncratically, that we were to learn by observing and doing rather than by naming and categorizing, which he believes impedes understanding intuitive functionality. In addition to important insights into the origins of some types of shuriken Mr. Mol appropriately points out that shuriken were not weapons used only by Ninja as popular media might have us believe. It does remain true however, that Ninja made significant use of shuriken, begging the question of why this was so? What was it about the Ninja's art and way of thinking that made shuriken so important to them?

No one appears to know when shuriken really came into being as a serious weapon of combat, but it must have followed closely on the heels of the production of their precursors as tools. The potential of such objects as projectile weapons was obvious. The development of shuriken into highly useful weaponry, however, would likely have taken place over a longer period of time. A variety of throwing blades existed in China, and though the art of using them as weapons does appear to have come from there, as with other martial arts it went through some modification once incorporated into the Japanese bugei. These changes suited the needs of specific warrior groups and should not be taken as inferences about improvement or superiority. Certainly the tools and craftsmanship involved in building and carpentry present in Japan came from China. Most Chinese classical martial arts, however, generally did not place significant emphasis on this form of weapons training.

The shuriken, whether used in hand-to-hand combat or as a projectile, would have had little use in open battlefield conditions. It was used to advantage in one-on-one combat or in small skirmishes between groups of warriors. Its appearance in Samurai classical teaching appears at the end of the warring states period, which is long after its original use as a tool. According to Mr. Mol in the text referenced above, they were cited as early as the 11th century.

We know that construction in Japan was already very refined by this time. While early references indicate the use of shuriken by conventional warriors, it is not clear that it was in any way systematically taught as part of the common martial arts. Based on what is known about warfare from that period, with its strong emphasis on mounted fighting with spear, bow and sword, shuriken were likely a minor, off-battlefield and close quarter weapon. We can draw this conclusion from the simple fact that professional Bushi rarely engaged in menial labor or specialized crafts such as construction, and therefore shuriken were probably used against them to some effect before becoming incorporated into the classical bugei. It is likely this type of weapon came gradually into acceptance by Bushi from non-Bushi sources. These weapons were much better suited to Ninja activities than to professional warriors in open combat for many reasons, and this is the basis of our belief that these weapons, like several others, were first used by Ninja and their non-professional warrior brethren.

Many of the precursors to the shuriken remain in use today in a wider array of forms than was the case when these tools first became weapons. It is interesting that now, in many places, shuriken are illegal, while there are so many analogues available at regular hardware stores. Of course this only seems strange to a person who is trained in the use of shuriken and knows how easy they are to manufacture and conceal as tools. This is the so-called secret of the shuriken, though it isn't really a secret at all.

For centuries, some schools of martial arts kept their shurikenjutsu concealed.

Many martial arts books and media articles tell their readers that shuriken were generally a non-lethal nuisance weapon. If that is the case, one has to wonder why they would be kept secret and at other times banned. It is true that nuisance weapons functioning as a distraction can provide a decisive edge in otherwise mortal combat. Shuriken in expert hands, however, are more lethal than might be assumed. Secondarily, their easy manufacture and concealment give them a surprising edge. It has to do with the many purposes and strategies employed in their use. Of course we will hear contemporary lawmakers say these weapons are too easy for children and teens to make, and in unskilled and irresponsible hands there is the potential for a lot of injuries, hence they should be outlawed. Hopefully it will be clear, if we understand where shuriken came from and how the Ninja used them, why these weapons have such a fearsome reputation and how such interventions cannot fully address the process that produced them.

The simplest precursor to the kugigata shuriken is the nail after which it was named. Nails of certain varieties can be thrown and made to stick in a target with some practice. This becomes easier after some modifications are made to the original article. Nails and their larger cousins, spikes, were not simply for nailing boards and beams together; they were used also to extract wooden pegs and position and align beams at a specified distance from each other, preparing them for placement. Ninja probably did not have to spend much effort to manufacture kugigata shuriken; they could be purchased from a smith, manufactured, or simply stolen from a construction site, then modified to the correct shape and length. Kugigata shuriken were sure not to arouse suspicion in the hands of a person appearing to be a construction worker. According to what we were taught, Ninja infiltrated crews doing construction on the homes of important people and military fortifications in order to document carefully the construction plans for future use. Of course we can't be certain whether military officers had the workers on castles vetted for security and reliability, but even if they did it was not likely a serious obstacle to a small crew of trained Ninja. We know that Samurai had developed tests to see if a suspected individual was in fact a Ninja. We can only assume that Ninja were aware to some extent of these countermeasures and accepted it as a professional risk.

Shuriken of all types had two main purposes—to be thrown and to be used in close quarter fighting by those knowledgeable of the method. Like a knife, shuriken were easily and rapidly deployed. Multiple shurikens could be thrown simultaneously or in rapid series. This skill permitted practical non-combative applications as well. For example, they could be used for the instantaneous placement of multiple footholds into a beam, pillar, column or a tree for climbing. Kugigata and other elongated shuriken penetrated deeply into wood and were sturdy enough to support the weight of a man.

Unlike throwing knives, shuriken were sharpened only at the tip. They did not have a handle or a cutting edge, which would have made it difficult to avoid cuts when grasping, throwing or using them in any other way.

Ninja rarely used poisons on sharpened weapons because of the potential for self-inflicted injury. If poison was used, it was applied just prior to throwing, so as to minimize personal risk and to ensure that the poison was both fresh and in the proper amount. If applied too early, the poison could easily rub off onto other objects such as the clothes and hands.

The shaken is a flat piece of metal with four or more points. It has been called by the common name *hirashuriken* or "flat shuriken" (Fig. 9). We prefer to call them shaken because it is a convenient way to distinguish them from the boshuriken. In American English they are commonly called "throwing stars." As with the shuriken, they came in many sizes and shapes. There exist types with curved points and even in the form of a Swastika called *manjigata shuriken*. Shaken were named either by the number of points they had or according to their shape. It has been pointed out elsewhere that specific types of shuriken could identify the martial school of the one using it. Ninja did prefer certain types of shuriken and shaken, typically for reasons of functionality. They generally did not want to be identified by their weaponry, for obvious reasons. They occasionally used nine-pointed shaken, the so-called *kujigata shuriken, kuji* referring to the nine syllables of *kujikiri*.

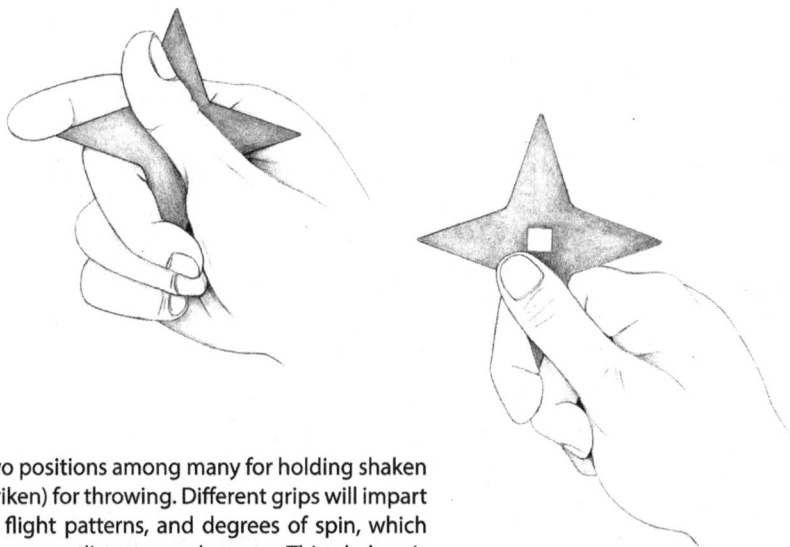

Fig. 9: Two positions among many for holding shaken (hirashuriken) for throwing. Different grips will impart different flight patterns, and degrees of spin, which affect accuracy, distance and power. This shaken is the shihogata shuriken, one of a large variety.

There is a theory that the shaken originated as weapons first from throwing rocks, then flat rocks to throwing flat metal plates (3, vol. 3) It can be inferred that throwing objects for the purpose of hunting and self-defense was potentially a critical practice in our early history in a way similar to the use of spears and slings by Stone Age people. This theory, however, does not necessarily contradict the history of metal shuriken and shaken as originating from early construction tools. I have seen no source that indicates that flat stones originally used for hunting were being copied in bronze, copper or iron as soon as these materials became available, although that could be accepted as a potential theory. Also, we have already noted that early construction tools were also made of stone. It seems reasonable to question whether throwing modified stones should be considered a form of early shurikenjutsu?

Mr. Mol writes an interesting account related to this issue in his book Classical Weaponry of Japan, calling these stones *totekibuki* and the stone throwing art being called *totekibukibujutsu,* also *ishinage* (stone throwing) and later *injiuchi.* There were even soldiers whose specialty was to fight by throwing stones. Some called the small stones *tsubute* starting around the 8th century. Mr. Mol states that in the Edo period these were replaced by iron stones called *tetsutsubute.* The interesting point about these tetsutsubute is that they bear no resemblance to shaken. They are smaller in overall dimension and thicker, and it is clear that they are intended to harm by percussion and not stick into their target. The ones shown in the manual put out by Seiko Fujita also describe this art including the proper way to grasp the stones, positioning the arms etc. In this case also, the stones bear no resemblance to shaken and the only real similarity is that they are objects to be thrown using similar postures. It should be noted that in Ninjutsu we were also taught to throw stones and various types of sticks as well.

It is also thought that some shaken were inspired by coins, though I have never seen such shaken personally. It is possible that some early shaken were simply made from coins with the edges filed down and straight but I have not so far been able to find any clear evidence for this occurring. Coins from China and Japan often had a hole in the center, as do many shaken. This similarity may have inspired either the actual making of shaken from coins or the postulated association between them. It would seem reasonable to infer that people made shaken and shuriken from whatever suitable metals were available. There is probably no one historical account that will accurately represent all that really occurred in the history of the shaken, and it probably does not matter except for what it tells us about the thinking involved in their evolution, and how that helps us with similar practical problems as they present themselves today.

It appears that the natural progression, as with the early axe, started with the humble stone precursor being used before the more advanced bronze and then iron versions were eventually made. These were crude construction tools and they were used for felling trees and then finishing and mounting wooden structures. What seems more probable still is that early Paleolithic and Neolithic stone tools were multipurpose implements used for anything from preparing hides for tanning to scraping, carving, or cutting wood and ivory and that these inspired later metal versions, at least in terms of function. It is possible that the stone axe blade for cutting wood doubled as a tool for cutting bones, scraping hides and even for things like digging. Some shuriken resemble primitive spear points as well like the matsubagata shuriken. Could this process have repeated itself whenever the need arose for a new way to throw something sharp, heavy and potentially lethal? It is not difficult to understand how such early multiple use tools were placed on the end of a stick to serve as a weapon for hunting, fishing, combat, or as a tool. Also, like the shuriken, the spear could be used both in hand-to-hand fighting and as a projectile.

Though direct evidence to support these theories may be limited and lacking,

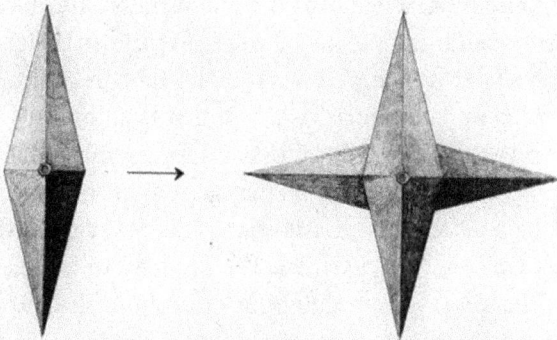

Fig. 10: A collapsible shaken

that should not prevent us from looking at the "evidence" written into the form of the object and its uses, because the goal is not necessarily to be historically accurate (though that should be attempted whenever possible), but to understand approximately what potential was seen in these tools that they should become forever memorialized as a symbol of the Ninja.

Shaken were made usually of one piece, but occasionally two pieces of metal were linked together in the middle such that they were collapsible (Fig. 10). The intent behind this was to make them easier to conceal and carry. One could well wonder if these collapsible shaken derive from scissors or gardening shears considering their similarly hinged mechanism. The analogy being that once the handle was removed, a collapsible implement emerges that has the potential to be thrown. Like with some of the other convergent findings provided, I have not come across direct evidence of this relationship in my research. It is however, well known that Ninja used garden shears as weapons and in our own training we use them and scissors, as well.

Some shaken were three-dimensional and rather like a hollow ball with protruding spikes known as *tetsumari* or "iron ball." This modified type of shaken, like several others, was particularly well suited as an incendiary device. The hollow center could contain explosives (like a prickly hand-grenade that sticks to buildings) or flammables, while the wick would be wrapped around the points. Ninja were said to use these as a means of distraction in order to facilitate escape or for lighting multiple fires since they could stick in place and continue to burn. As with other shaken they could be attached to a cord and used as a flexible weapon as well. Some shaken were made larger but had the same shape as their smaller counter parts. Larger shaken and shuriken were heavier and had greater range and accuracy.

The *kuginuki* or "nail puller" is a tool that is commonly believed to have been a precursor to the shaken and it most closely resembles the *senban shuriken*. The kuginuki in fact involves two tools that were used together to extract nails. One piece is a flat metal square, that is shaped like a shaken, the other a spike with a pointed flat tip (Fig. 11). Each has the capacity to be thrown as they were and without modification. We are taught in our school that other shaken also served as tools, in particular the four-point shihogata shuriken or shaken (Fig. 9,12). For this reason I have chosen them to be used in the illustrations involving four-point shaken that accompany the text. The illustrations also demonstrate that these shaken have specific properties and uses that the kuginuki does not, due in large part to the "v" shape where the base of the points come together, and had other uses than the kuginuki. We are taught that these shaken were also used to pull spikes, nails and extract wooden pegs or dowels. All of the shaken we used (but not all shuriken) have a hole in them to accommodate a cord. We were also taught that they were used for many other purposes and were in fact a multifaceted tool. In like fashion we learned unconventional ways to use shaken as weapons, taking advantage of this plural capability.

Grandmaster Law taught us that shaken were used for placing and holding beams in position before dropping them into place, for joinery work. A cord was passed through the hole, and the shaken, if stabbed into the supporting post or beam, could hold the cross beam in place and stop it from dropping into place prematurely before the other end of the beam was aligned correctly. When the other end was in the correct position, it too was held in place with a shaken (or kuginuki. The cords were then pulled simultaneously, removing the shaken and allowing the beam to fall into place. Naturally, the shaken or kuginuki were placed on both sides of a beam or at the ends, so that coordinated pulling of the cords made it fall evenly. Grandmaster Law reports having seen shaken used in this way while constructing homes in rural settings. He also taught that due to the fact that

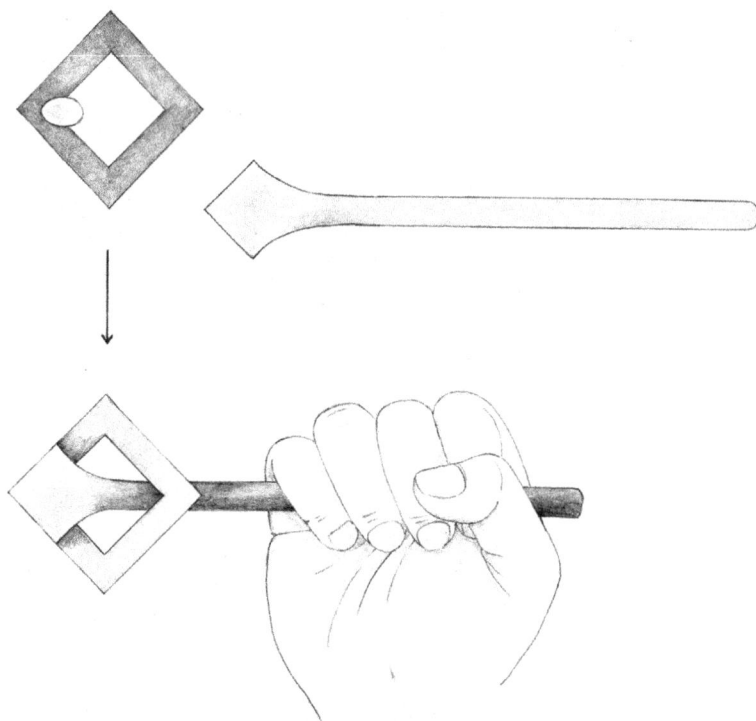

Fig. 11: Kuginuki used to pull nail, note resemblance between both components of the kuginuki and both shaken and shuriken. If necessary a kind of pliers was used to pull the nail out further.

shaken were made to specified dimensions and sported specific angles, they were a reliable tool for measurement and could serve as a square, by taking advantage of the hole in the middle as we do today with a protractor.

Like contemporary math compasses used by school children today for geometry, and by adults to measure distances on a map, running a Shaken along a surface like a wheel could be used to measure units of distance, and the distance recorded by a cord (Fig. 13).

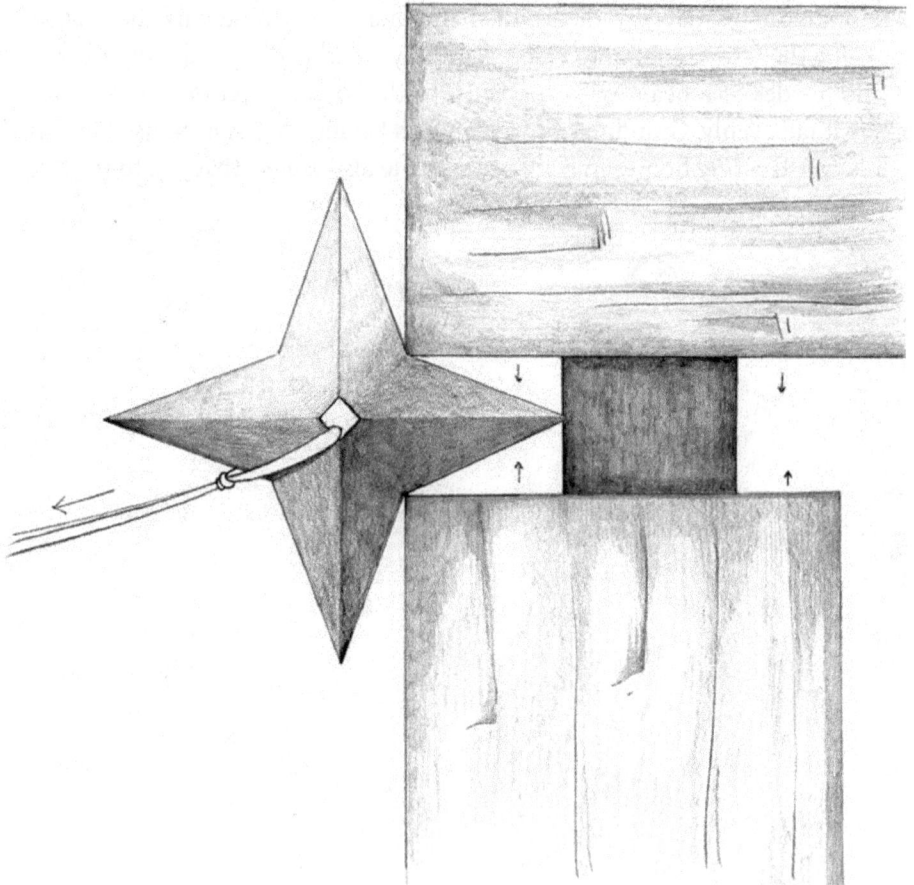

Fig. 12: Shaken used to align a beam

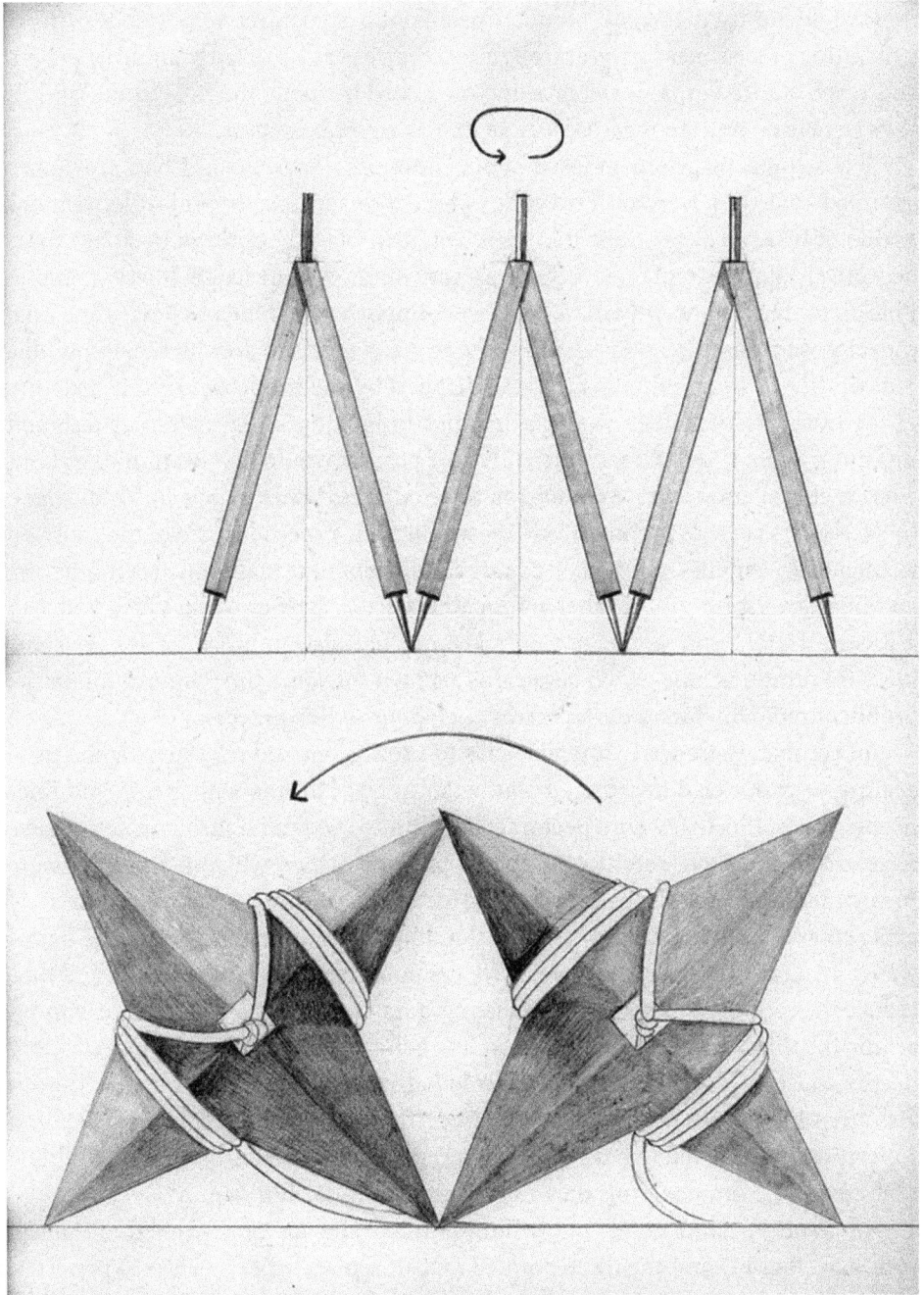

Fig. 13: Shaken used to measure distance.

Because the precursors to shaken and shuriken were of standard size or length, they could be used to hold wooden beams and structures in a stable pattern, permitting precise measuring and aligning. They were also of fairly uniform weight, and when stacked on a dowel or slung on a cord by using the hole in the middle they were used both to measure weight and as counter weights.

I was quite surprised to learn about these uses for shaken; I had previously assumed that they were only weapons and more specifically projectile weapons at that. It became clear to me that there was a whole way of thinking about these deceptively simple implements that was not common knowledge. It was then that I began to understand why these tools were important to Ninja as having the dual capacity of tool and weapon. The underlying concept has to do with seeingmultiple possibilities in simple designs that are dictated by the properties of the structure of the tool itself. The idea would be similar to looking at a problem or task and inventing a tool to get it done efficiently. The process would involve thinking about what material properties it should have to address wear, repair and reuse and other aspects such as ergonomics. You would then proceed to make the tool you needed from supplies you had or could readily obtain. It might involve modifying an already existing tool to alter its capabilities for the new task. Once you had a good solution, you would not only keep it, but also improve on it over time; ideas for modifications would come after using it for some time. Innovation in the production of Ninja weapon-tools was analogous to this process.

In combat, there were different ways to use shaken and shuriken. When used against a warrior clad in armor, it was better to have shaken with longer and finer needle-like points that would penetrate deeply into the skull if thrown into the face. Shaken and shuriken were not capable of piercing armor, which is why they were thrown at the face and the hands when the foe was clad. The face was usually the only exposed area in Samurai armor when standing naturally. Even though the hands were protected, larger shaken were heavy enough to seriously injure them, and thus reduce the capacity to fight. If the Ninja was going to use shaken on people without armor, the thinner and lighter varieties were better. Thinner shaken penetrate more deeply and can cause serious and even lethal injury. Thinner and lighter shaken also permitted more of them to be carried. The Ninja out of religious belief and superstition is believed to have typically carried nine shuriken, or another multiple of three for the same reasons they might carry kujigata shuriken.

In hand-to-hand combat the four pointed shaken or so-called shihogata shuriken (Fig. 14) and the three pointed matsubagata shuriken (Fig. 15) preferred in the Iga and Geijin Ryu were especially well suited for this because they took advantage of the leverage provided by the "v" shape created by two points

71

intersecting at their bases. They were very well adapted to catching clothing, fingers and even blades. The shaken had the added advantage of being easier to hold firmly in the palm. There was some risk of injury for the user from the reverse point with both types, and techniques were developed in order to minimize this. In fact this reverse point concealed within the palm and wrist was essential to this type of fighting. The reverse point was good for hooking either the enemy's skin or clothes and to immobilize them. Shaken used in this manner also caused severe lacerating injuries with significant bleeding. The art of using shaken in fighting by necessity utilized vital areas, especially in the neck, and several other locations where major organs, vessels and nerves are found just below the skins surface. Hand-to-hand combat involving these targets could easily kill.

Fig. 14: A classic shihogata (hira)shuriken (see below) or shaken as it would be held in hand-to-hand combat applications, note that some schools will keep the fingers extended and spread out for this, as would be the case when performing primarily a slashing movement.

Fig. 15: Illustration of matsubagata shuriken and shuko in action.

Ninja had to be able to throw shaken and shuriken in many ways and from different and even awkward positions. They were thrown in vertical and horizontal planes. The vertical throw is generally more powerful. This is because the downward swing of the throwing arm takes advantage of gravity and is also a more natural movement, resulting in the transference of more bodyweight and thrust into the projectile. Most available video and books on shurikenjutsu show practitioners throwing at stationary targets from a standing or kneeling position. In reality Ninja practiced throwing from all kinds of postures and movements. They threw shaken while lying down on their backs, stomach, across the front of the body, while spinning around, backwards, from their sides, backward through the legs and so on. They also practiced throwing while running and rolling. They threw shaken at moving and swinging targets. Taking the skill to this level required considerably more practice than simply throwing at a tatami mat. Ninja threw shaken and shuriken into wooden targets, which required more power. Note that the grain of the wood influences the ability of the shaken to stick.   If they hit in a plane perpendicular to the grain they often bounce back.

One relative disadvantage of shaken compared to shuriken is that they do not penetrate as deeply. This is important to remember when considering the purpose for which the tool would be used. In order to improve durability, shuriken tips were tempered. In the cases where Ninja needed to retrieve shaken, they would attach a cord to them (Fig. 16). Done properly, the cord did not interfere with the shaken's flight. Some types of shaken were more highly valued as both tools and weapons and took greater effort to make, in addition to leaving clues to a Ninja's presence if left behind. Therefore whenever possible Ninja tried not to lose or waste them.

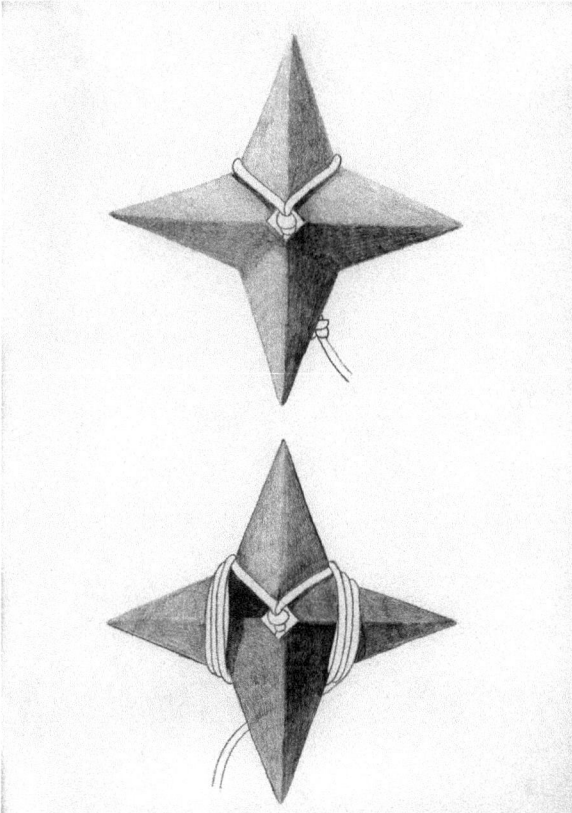

Fig. 16: Cord winding on shihogata shuriken

An additional creative way in which shaken were used was to string them in series along a knotted cord (Fig. 17). This weapon was easily assembled and disassembled with slipknots. This device could be used as a form of ladder, with the shaken acting as toeholds. As a weapon, it would be swung and wound around any limb or the neck. Like other flexible chain and rope weapons, this method was useful for disarming any enemy by winding it around the weapon hand, followed by a quick yank.

Fig. 17: Multiple shaken strung along a cord as both ladder and weapon, on the right, one method for making a stable horizontal toehold.

Grandmaster Law taught that shuriken were sometimes worn on the body in strategic places where they acted as a form of armor from beneath the outer layer of clothes and within its folds (Fig. 18,19). One of the first things he taught me was how to conceal weapons on the body so that they provided strategic protection against attempts to cut vulnerable areas. This applied to any weapon a Ninja might carry and not just shaken or shuriken.

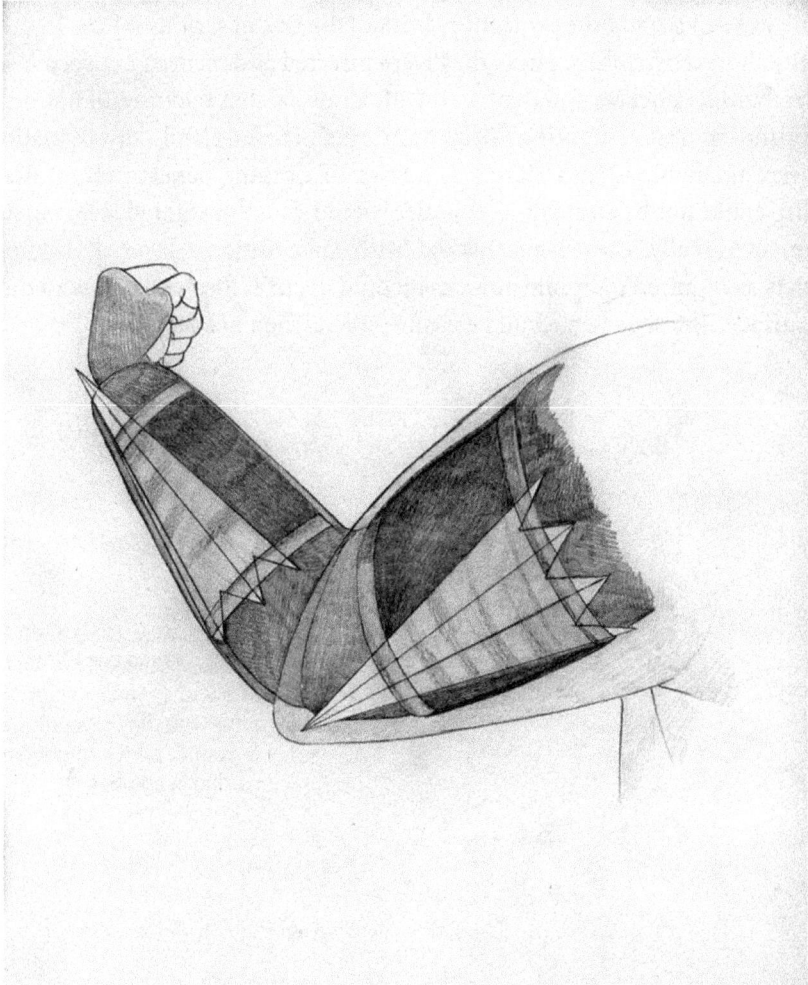

Fig. 18: One way to carry shuriken, in this case intentionally providing a protruding point which was not usually desired when activities involved penetrating structures.

When wearing shuriken, sometimes the points were intentionally positioned in such a manner as to protrude a short distance when the limbs were bent and acted as hooks or for stabbing depending on the position. To work in the capacity of concealed armor and enhance combative techniques, they were placed on areas like the shins, thighs, forearms and upper arms. They enhanced the weight and severity of strikes while protecting against blades and other weapons. It should be stated that being struck on one of these areas even when protected by metal is still painful, but less so, and the protection reduces the risk of serious injury. In order to keep the shuriken firmly in place, they were inserted and secured between layers of cloth rather like pockets and tightened with straps so that they would not dislodge while running and/or fighting. Straps can cause chaffing and cut circulation, so they were made broad and there was a layer of clothing beneath them. Also the clothing could not be stretchy, as this also would cause unwanted swaying during movement. Finally, they were covered with an additional layer of leggings or gauntlets as required to muffle noise that could occur if they collided with another hard surface. The shuriken could be easily pulled when needed.

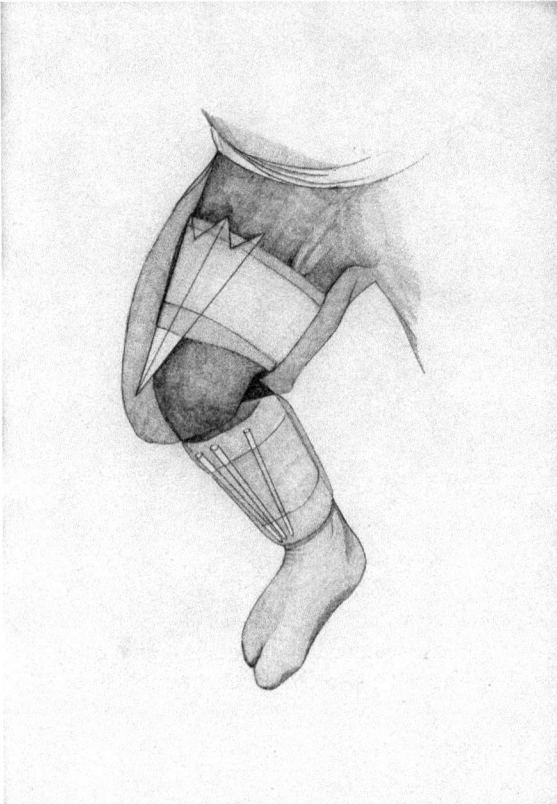

Fig. 19: A method for carrying shuriken on the legs. Note that often the inner thigh would otherwise be covered because it was a prime target area for cutting in combat.

Similar in concept, but unrelated to the use of shuriken and shaken, Ninja attached other weapons to their bodies. One consisted of an iron or wooden horn-like spike or short blade with a flat base imbedded into a leather band and worn on the forehead to be used for head butting (Fig. 20). Grandmaster Law explained that such devices were used to enhance striking capability, especially for less experienced Shinobi. Masters in the art were said to be able to go into battle sporting less or no armor, as it was felt to be cumbersome. They did however use weapons liberally and without reservation.

As previously mentioned, shaken and shuriken were incorporated into the methods of hojojutsu. Texts produced by Seiko Fujita (3, vol. 1) show the *kaginawa* (see below) used in this way. Like the kaginawa and *kakushi*, shuriken and shaken combined with hojojutsu were used to immobilize, inflict pain and paralysis. Just as the striking attacks using shaken and shuriken involved atemi, hojojutsu techniques utilized both knots and shuriken or shaken at anatomic points of vulnerability. Kagi (hooks), which by necessity were attached at the end of the rope, caused severe pain and injury to peripheral nerves while also providing an anchoring point for the rope where it was pierced through clothing and flesh. Shuriken and shaken could be strung anywhere along the rope, permitting the decision about where to place it for a desired effect. It was not necessary to have them at the end of the rope for anchoring. The hooks, shaken and shuriken sometimes were inserted so as to dig into and lacerate nerves and blood vessels. If the captive struggled, they also caused severe pain, bleeding and even death. The result of using these methods would depend on various factors that were known to the Ninja and is not knowledge suitable for public consumption. Other target areas included tendons, sensory organs, and weak points and angles in the skeletal structure. Here again the concept arises that a broader understanding of how to utilize these areas in any form of combative activity maximized the efficiency techniques by causing greater physical injury with fewer movements. Implied in this strategy is the underlying concept maintained in Ninjutsu, that due to the unpredictable nature of combat and typically unfavorable odds, the opportunity to strike might only occur once, so each strike, cut, or slash must count maximally.

Having reviewed some aspects of the incredible versatility and effectiveness of shuriken and shaken as both tools and weapons, it is clear how they came to be valued in the Ninja arsenal. Although versatility is essential for any Ninja weapon, other aspects were equally important. These elements include portability, ease of concealment, and to a certain extent, disposability. It should be noted that concealment in this sense also infers that weapons appeared to be simple tools, and were "concealed" in that their true purpose was not obvious even in the

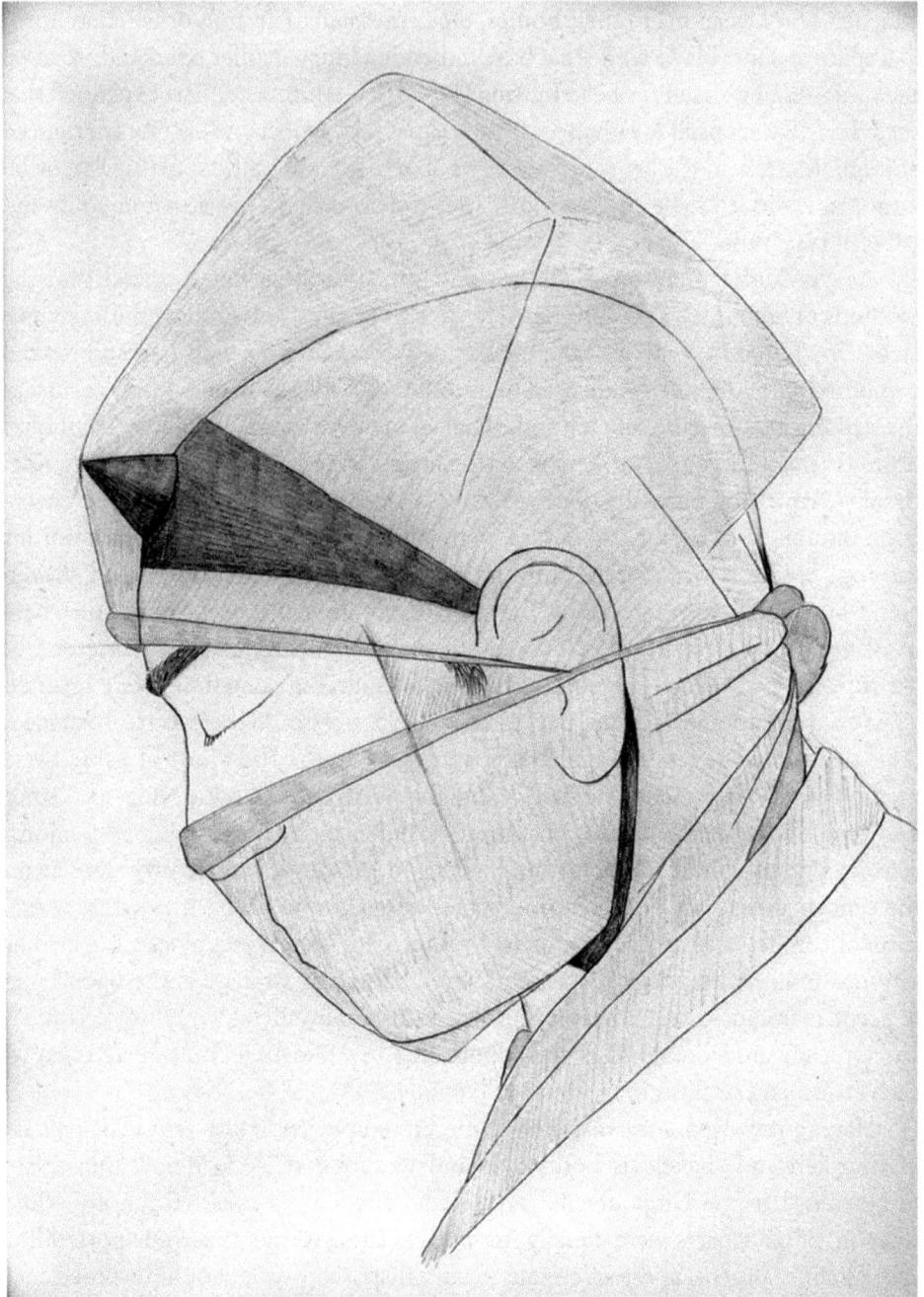

Fig. 20: Devils horn

plain sight of others. Since Ninja viewed their own everyday objects as potential weapons, it is probably impossible to know when and under what circumstances Ninja incorporated specific ones into their martial culture. In all sources reviewed for this book, shaken and shuriken in their "weaponized" form do not appear as conventional tools of construction and carpentry like their analogue originator tools the kuginuki and the kagi. Neither text nor photographed collections of tools from various ages show kugi and kuginuki in these weaponized forms like the shihogata and matsubagata shuriken, thus the versions we are seeing as weapons were modified and derived. It has been repeated by various authors that tools like the kuginuki and kugi are believed to have been one of the main sources of inspiration and even the raw material for producing shaken and shuriken. In some cases the weapons were nearly identical to the tools from which they originated. Though I am not privy to any densho of Samurai bugei, it would seem that research into the koryu arts and Ninjutsu do converge on this account and support it. Some of the added details and uses outlined in the text above are explanations given by Grandmaster Law to help further contextualize this account and provide insight into the subject of how and why these weapons were significant in Ninjutsu

Weapons bearing a methodological relationship to the shuriken in hand-to-hand combat and similar in form are the *suntetsu* and the art of *suntetsujutsu*. The suntetsu is a relatively small hand-held iron rod bearing an attached ring in the middle through which a finger or a cord can be passed. These have also been made of wood or bone. The ring of the suntetsu was sometimes a simple cord or was made of the same material as the shaft itself. Suntetsu and the related *tenouchi* were often crude and blunt but some were tapered according to the user's style and preference. Some schools of jujutsu call this weapon and the tenouchi by the name *yawara*, which, in Japanese kanji is the same character "ju" as in jujutsu and for which the terms are synonymous. So as not to confuse things, we feel it is best to speak of suntetsu and tenouchi as distinct from yawara, which is terminology best reserved for the actual martial art of yawara or jujutsu.

The Kasugai

Other important building tools in the repertoire of the Ninja were the kasugai (Fig. 21), of which there were several forms. Kasugai were used by Ninja as tools more than as actual weapons. This is equally true of such other building and carpentry tools as *shikoro* or "leaf saws" (Fig. 22) and the *tsubo-giri*—a boring tool with a half-moon shaped double point, which differs from the gimlet, (also a boring tool), which has a corkscrew or triple point. Kasugai were shaped rather like large staples and were used in building to join beams together. These were used by Ninja for other purposes, such as for climbing, hanging and when necessary as weapons with a dynamic similar to that of the suntetsu except with a claw-like hook on either end. Ninja used kasugai to jam doors preventing access and pursuit. Some versions of kasugai had the points diverging at right angles to each other according to how they were to be used in joinery. Tools similar to kasugai are still being used in places like China today and there are analogues of this tool in the West being used to hold rove frameworks together.

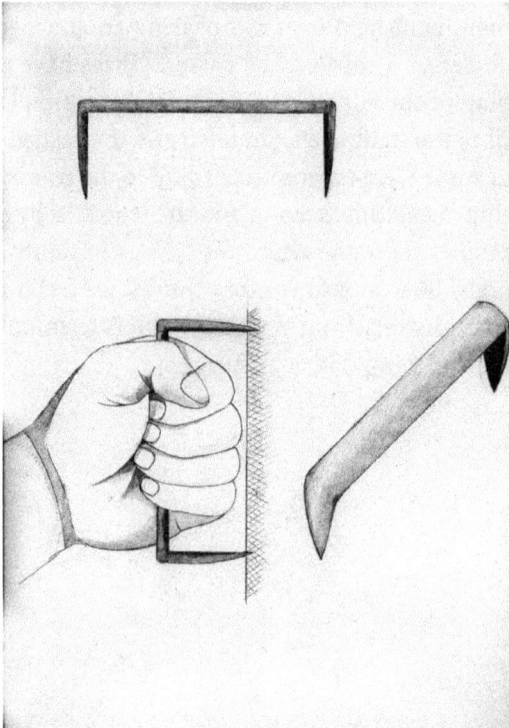

Fig. 21: The Kasugai

Fig. 22: A form of Shikoro, or leaf saw

The Kunai

The *kunai* is yet another formidable weapon with probable origins as a tool. It is similar in appearance to a knife without a cutting edge, and also in some ways resembles Bo-Shuriken. It has a simple rod-shaped handle which is often bound in a cord. As a weapon, the kunai is a very sturdy piece of iron that can be used as a projectile and like a suntetsu or tenouchi. It has a sharp point for stabbing but because it lacks a sharp edge it is not suited to cutting. Like other tools with similar shapes it was easily adapted for setting traps by being used to hold a delicately balanced structure. For penetrating buildings it served generally as a pry-bar or lever to pry through boards, roof tiles and also to dig through thatch (Fig. 23).

It isn't entirely clear where it came from, but we were taught that it originated as a plumb. It was used to ensure vertical alignment and to mark locations on wooden surfaces by sticking it in place. Another purpose was to mark lines along beams as a guide for a saw cutting. The cord was unwound but kept taught and threaded through an inkwell attached to a spool in a device called a *sumi-tsubo* (sumi; "ink," tsubo, "jar" Fig. 24). The thread was drawn, pulled upward and released, in manner similar to a guitar string being plucked. In so doing it would make brief and momentary contact with the surface and mark a straight line (Fig. 25). The same concept is used today with chalk-covered thread that is used to make straight lines on floors as a guide for laying tile.

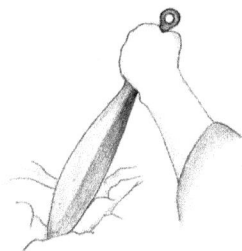

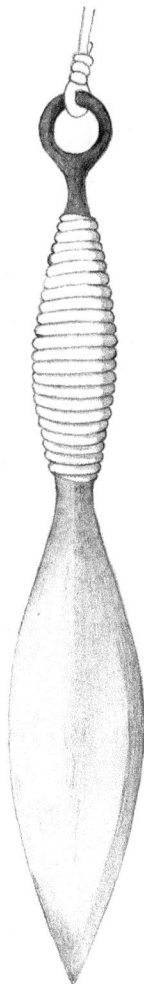

Fig. 23: The Kunai, used for digging and as a pry bar.

Fig. 24: Sumi-tsubo or "ink marking jar." Note that there are handles projecting on either side and that the base is notched to allow it to be hooked in place.

Fig. 25: Sumi-tsubo and kunai in use.

Tools of Fishermen, Hunters, and Farmers

A number of other trades appear to have contributed tools and skills to Ninjutsu. As discussed in the previous chapter, Ninja living as commoners were intimately familiar with their trades and ways of living. It has already been noted that when not active in the field, Ninja supplemented their livelihood through various professions. In this way Ninja as commoners when not completely isolated were subject to the same oppression imposed by the Samurai class on the peasants, along with conscription into major undertakings requiring mass labor such as land works, fortifications and into the army to fight battles. Ninja are also believed to have voluntarily joined battles so as to test their fighting skills, and probably to acquire weapons as well. Not all segments of Ninja society lived in rural areas, although it was preferred because they were further from the reach of Samurai officers working for strong local families and landowners. We have noted that living in hard to reach areas also meant less interdependence with other communities, which meant less interaction and intrusion, and thus it was easier to conceal their training activities (Fig. 26). Added benefits were that rural families of this kind were less economically important to the central powers and as such there was less pressure to pursue them to pay taxes and respond to governmental demands. In this way, Ninja families and communities were able to maintain the privacy required by their way of life.

Because some Ninja families had stronger social bonds with common people who made their living off the land and seas, commoners were a source of knowledge and inspiration to Ninja society. A significant proportion of Japan's livelihood was derived from the ocean and the thousands of miles of coastline surrounding it. Hunting and gathering ocean resources predates the arrival of agriculture in Japan. Most agricultural practices in Japan were imported from China. Agriculture and the domestication of animals took place in China at least as early as 7500 BC during the Neolithic Era (11).

The Japanese have for millennia hunted, fished, and gathered food and other necessities from the sea. They hunted whales, harvested kelp, sponges, corals, crustaceans, sea cucumbers, mollusks (shellfish and pearls), echinoderms like sea urchins, and minerals (salt containing iodine needed to ward off iodine deficiency which causes goiter, found among inland people often living in mountainous areas). They fished a wide variety of ocean catch, including such mainstays as octopus and

Fig. 26: Ninja training in remote areas.

squid. Some areas were known for their pearl divers who were adept at spending fairly long periods of time submerged and were able to tolerate cold temperatures. Divers and fishermen developed a repertoire of tools to assist them in their work. Several of these may have inspired Ninja weapons and devises.

Certainly the incentive for the development and use of weapons by common folk and warriors existed throughout the region and its history. From the earliest years of Imperial Japan, 500 AD to the 12th century, there were numerous campaigns versus Korea where battles were fought against Chinese and Korean armies. The Japanese also fought battles at sea during these campaigns, the *Gempei* wars, during the attempted invasion of Japan by the Mongols and various other battles with Korean forces when Hideyoshi's armies later invaded there.

The Japanese were famous in Asia for the pursuit of piracy. The *"Wo-k'uo"* (Chinese term for Japanese pirate armadas) rose up in the 14th century, becoming very powerful by the 16th century. Based on the islands of Honshu and Kyushu, they were a renowned and powerful pirate force on the South seas of China. They numbered in the thousands and were actually a blend of Japanese and Chinese fighters. Interestingly, two-thirds of their forces were Chinese, indicating a unique condition of martial culture cross-pollination. They arose in response to the edicts from both China and Japan restricting trade. They began to use islands off their respective coasts to conduct illegal trade. In order to protect their interests they created armies. Chinese fishermen who were prohibited from exercising their livelihood by even more stringent Imperial restrictions in their homelands also joined the pirate's rebellion. These restrictions irrationally forbade the use of all boats by what appears to have been a paranoid and xenophobic Chinese Imperial Ming Dynasty increasingly concerned with keeping foreign influences out of China.

The pirates fought pitch battles on land in China, defeating several Ming armies. They were poised to seize major coastal Chinese cities. Among the pirates, the Japanese fighters used their sword fighting skills, which were said to be formidable in open battle. They also successfully used Japanese battle tactics. Chinese pirates were taught these sword and battlefield skills by their Japanese counterparts. Japanese warrior pirates wore Samurai armor to make themselves look fierce, and it was said to have intimidated and discouraged Chinese conscripts. By necessity, the defending Chinese peasant soldiers were deployed into small units of three or more that were specially trained to kill these fighters. One man wielding a bamboo stick with intact branches used it to interfere with the enemy's sight and sword; the other two were equipped with spears to thrust at and kill him. (23).

This long history of sometimes dynamic warfare between the islands of Japan and its neighbors maintained intense pressure to produce the same level of high quality warrior culture and influence in the coastal areas and at sea that was present in the central provinces. Restrictions on trade and the patrolling of the seas and coastlines ensured the permanent presence of fighting men there. People living in that environment were subject to the same degree of oppression and taxation as their agrarian counterparts inland. With essentially the same social forces at work, the need for spies and other groups like Ninja was no less important. It therefore follows that some aspects of Ninjutsu probably reflect the influence of life in coastal communities. It is also by way of the sea that all cultural exchange with China took place. Such arrangements would have necessitated a well-established relationship between central areas and the coastal fiefs. There must have been many important political activities going on involving these various groups of people.

The Chinese influenced Japanese martial culture repeatedly over the centuries as they did the many other facets of Japanese civilization. The well-known, and probably overemphasized, case of "Chin Genpin," a Chinese national and interpreter living in Japan during the 17th century who studied 13 months of *Shaolin* (*Shorin* in Japanese) and jujutsu in Japan, is probably but one case within a long continuum of steady cross-cultural influences (5). Both Chinese and Japanese commoners used similar tools for their livelihood and both cultures incorporated some of these into their respective martial arts. In some cases it appears that the Chinese led this process and the "tool" was adopted into Japanese martial arts after it had already made the transition to weapon status in China.

Some of the tools used by commoners living in coastal areas are recognized today as weapons in Samurai bugei and in Ninjutsu. These weapons share certain general properties such as the capability to hook, snare, and tear. In some cases this is combined with the features necessary for apprehending and binding a live enemy. These tools are not core or essential curricula to the samurai arts; they are instead specializations that round out the capabilities of warriors, with skills that are not generally intended for the battlefield. Some were intended for police work, others for use at court or in holy places where it was forbidden to draw swords and spill blood. In some instances a Samurai did not wish to stain his prestige by using his sword on someone he considered beneath him and not worthy of being cut down, and would then resort to these kinds of weapons to deal with such an enemy. The Samurai generally did not associate closely with common people, and regarded their labors as unbefitting a Bushi.

A brief and perhaps obvious distinction should be made as we move forward into a fuller discussion of the tools of hunting, gathering, and weaponry. It should be noted that hunting tools, as opposed to gathering tools, are already weapons, and it is only the quarry that changes. Gathering tools and the tools of a trade are much more of a conceptual transition during incorporation into a fighting process and for subsequent modification to meet the challenges of training and combat. It is important to retain this this ideas because the concepts of weapon and tool become blurred and sometimes difficult to keep separate.

The Kagi and Kaginawa

The banal fishing hook was assimilated into Ninjutsu. The hooks used in the martial arts are usually large and fearsome. Like all of the other tools used by Ninja, hooks had multiple applications. Larger hooks were used as grappling hooks, others used to set traps or even as implements of torture. This later variety and those intended for fighting were sometimes barbed. When used in combat, they essentially required close engagement of the enemy. These hooks were nearly always attached to a rope; they were occasionally fitted to a staff similar to certain special fishing spears made for hooking salmon by the Japanese aboriginal people. Examples of such can be viewed on museum and archeological websites where the smaller varieties used by divers are displayed (Ir-3, 4). Although hooks could be swung, the smaller varieties were too light to effectively stop an armed and determined enemy. They were most effectively used with the application of taijutsu techniques, especially those involving throws and immobilization, where the hook was first inserted through clothing or flesh and all subsequent struggles served to bind the enemy with the rope. As such, all martial curricula teaching the use of the hook also teach variations of hojojutsu. Together the hook and rope combined are called kaginawa (kagi meaning *hook* and nawa meaning *rope*).

In the absence of a hook, hojojutsu methods require the use of a loop or snare, which accomplishes essentially the same anchoring but without as much immediate pain and injury and hence less dependence on submission through pain. Using the kaginawa in fighting a warrior armed with a sword or spear demanded the utmost of competence and fighting skill. The fighter using the hook had to move in close and would sometimes use a sword or staff to engage the enemy's weapon before deploying it. Ninja are said to prefer to move in with the staff when fighting an enemy armed with a sword because, according to Grandmaster Law, Ninja were taught to use the staff in such a way that the sword would cut into and get jammed in the wood. Locking the sword in this way provided the staff special leverage and it could be used to either break the blade or force the enemy to let it go. This was an effective means to disarm the swordsman. This strategy for infiltration to close quarters permitted the opportunity to pass the hook through clothing, hair or flesh. Sometimes clothing was better to hook because the absence of pain did not telegraph its presence, and the enemy could be bound before they realized the hook was in place.

Ultimately, either method was quite effective. When hooking flesh, typical targets were the webbing of the neck, the ears, mouth, nostrils scrotum, armpits, and thighs and sometimes the large tendons of the popliteal fossa (area behind the knee) and the Achilles tendon.

Hooks came in many configurations. Some were bound or welded together at the shaft in doubles, triples and groups of four, but never more than that. The hooks used in Ninjutsu have not changed in form since the Neolithic period, and were originally fashioned from bone and sometimes tusk especially in Northern areas (Fig. 27). Some hooks bore a strong similarity to the threading needles from that period used to sew hides that were often straight or slightly curved. Hooks combined with the rope as used by Ninja were mainly an all-purpose general tool, that were extensively utilized to facilitate breaking into places, remaining suspended, moving objects at a distance, tripping people in their own homes, setting traps and many other applications. The kaginawa was a routine implement of the Ninja's retinue.

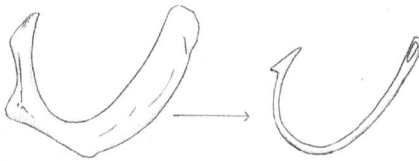

Fig. 27: Kagi and kakushi from bone here

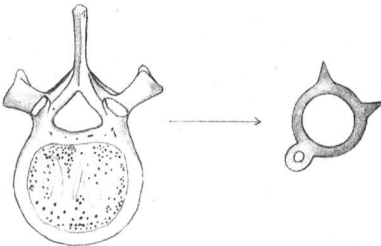

Nets

Nets have a truly universal and indispensable design. They are very ancient and are already widely understood as tools for catching fish, but also for carrying loads and less conventional things like setting traps. Being so utilitarian, it would have been surprising had they not been found in Ninjutsu. Used as a weapon, nets were not unique to the Ninja or to Japan. In the West, the net is often best remembered as a weapon used by Roman gladiators. In Japan, however, few other groups than Ninja used nets for the purpose of actual fighting. Samurai may have used nets sometimes for capturing a person that was to be kept alive, or who lacked the social status to be cut down with a sword. The net does not appear, however, to have been a formalized weapon in the traditional bugei. This is in spite of the fact that it was highly effective because of its property of limiting even highly trained fighters from using their weapons. Ninja used nets in combat and for many other purposes.

The taking of specific people prisoner for interrogation was one of the many things Ninja were hired to do. The net was used for this purpose and was sometimes combined with hooks of the type used with the Kaginawa, so that it would not require hojojutsu binding as part of the method. Using a net to immobilize an armed enemy was easier than moving in and applying the kaginawa. Theoretically, the net could be categorized with hojojutsu by virtue of the fact that it can bind an enemy, but cannot involve the use of complex knots unless the net itself was equipped with added lengths of cord.

The net was another ideal all-purpose Ninja tool because it was light, easy to carry and use, and did not arouse much suspicion provided the disguise was appropriate. Ninja, like many commoners, knew how to make nets. Outside of combat and field operations the net was used to capture game or fish, and even served as a comfortable bed when hooked up as a hammock. It could be used to keep the Ninja's food supply high in the branches of a tree and away from animals, or as a sack, slung over the back to carry an injured party, goods, and various other things. Sometimes the net was worn like a sort of apparel or used as a cover through which branches and grasses could be passed, transforming it into a highly effective form of camouflage rather like a crude Ghile suit. We have used this method in the bush and students have walked to within inches of disguised parties without detecting them.

Using the net in actual fighting involved throwing it in an arc from over the back, shoulder or arm and having it spread out in the air and drape onto the enemy.

It could then be used to good effect by twisting and tightening it like a wet rag, then unraveling and providing slack as necessary for combative taijutsu movements. When held up as a flexible barrier it was effective at stopping weapons, especially projectiles such as shuriken and shaken. Ninja used nets for setting traps in a manner similar to that seen throughout the rest of the world.

Few people carry nets today, but an elastic variety is common in the trunks of cars to hold down groceries and just about everyone uses blankets, sheets, coats and tarps. Any of these items can be used in a manner similar to a net. A knife-wielding intruder in a home can be neutralized with the proper use of bed sheets, a comforter, or, even better, a heavy coat. To add effectiveness, weights can be incorporated into it permitting the sheet to be swung like a ball and chain weapon. Coats and jackets have sleeves that are very useful for binding and immobilizing an enemy, especially if the intent is to control them without harm.

Training with the net is a case that clearly demonstrates how using very ancient methods can translate into effective self-defense strategies for today, without the need to purchase special weapons. It also directly illustrates that with the proper understanding of everyday objects in our surroundings, Ninjutsu offers special tactical insight in the realm of combat and survival.

The Shoge

The Shoge (Fig. 28) is a weapon strongly associated with Ninjutsu that may also trace its origins to several possible sources. It has three basic parts. It has a knife-like weapon that consists of a handle with a split blade made typically from a single piece of metal. One of the blades is reversed; curving back and opposite in direction to the other with a shape similar to a gaffing hook. The straight blade is usually double-edged. The curved blade can be single or double-edged as preferred. The handle is made of wood and bound with bamboo strips, leather or cord, or simply left plain; it is connected to a rope that can vary in length according to need. The other end is equipped with a ring attached to the cord by a knot.

The shoge is commonly called by its full name *kyoketsu shoge*. The term "kyoketsu" is a composite of "kyo," commonly meaning distance, especially when used as a suffix in the second half of the word. When used as a prefix, as is the case here, it has the more archaic meaning of "ankle." It is difficult to be certain, but the word may be a clever moniker since this weapon utilizes distance as a major part of its strategy and the ankle is one of the most commonly targeted areas on the. The reason for attacking the ankle is that it is a highly vulnerable target especially against a mounted warrior (warriors' and horses' ankles) or un-mounted and armed with a sword or spear. I have also been told that ankle in this case may refer to the ring or annulus being made from the anklebone of a water buffalo or cow. These bones are strong, fairly large and hollow. A cross sectional cut of such a bone could make a useful ring.

The second character "ketsu" translates as "spring to one's feet" phonetically. The kanji I have read for this weapon however in *Classical Weaponry of Japan* by Mr. S. Mol translates as "implement" and "practical effect." Both are interpretations that intuitively make sense. This is a puzzle I have not yet been able to resolve, but would defer in this case to a person with a deeper knowledge of the language.

The word "shoge" is also a composite term. "Sho" used here as a prefix, means to "wade" through water, shallows, and the like. The suffix "ge" which can also be pronounced "ke" means "hair." This, of course, is what the cord was made of in ancient times.

The translation I have provided of the meaning for the name of this weapon is a literal one that uses the combined translated meanings of the actual individual kanji. When incorporated into a name, however, the meanings can be different and culturally idiosyncratic.

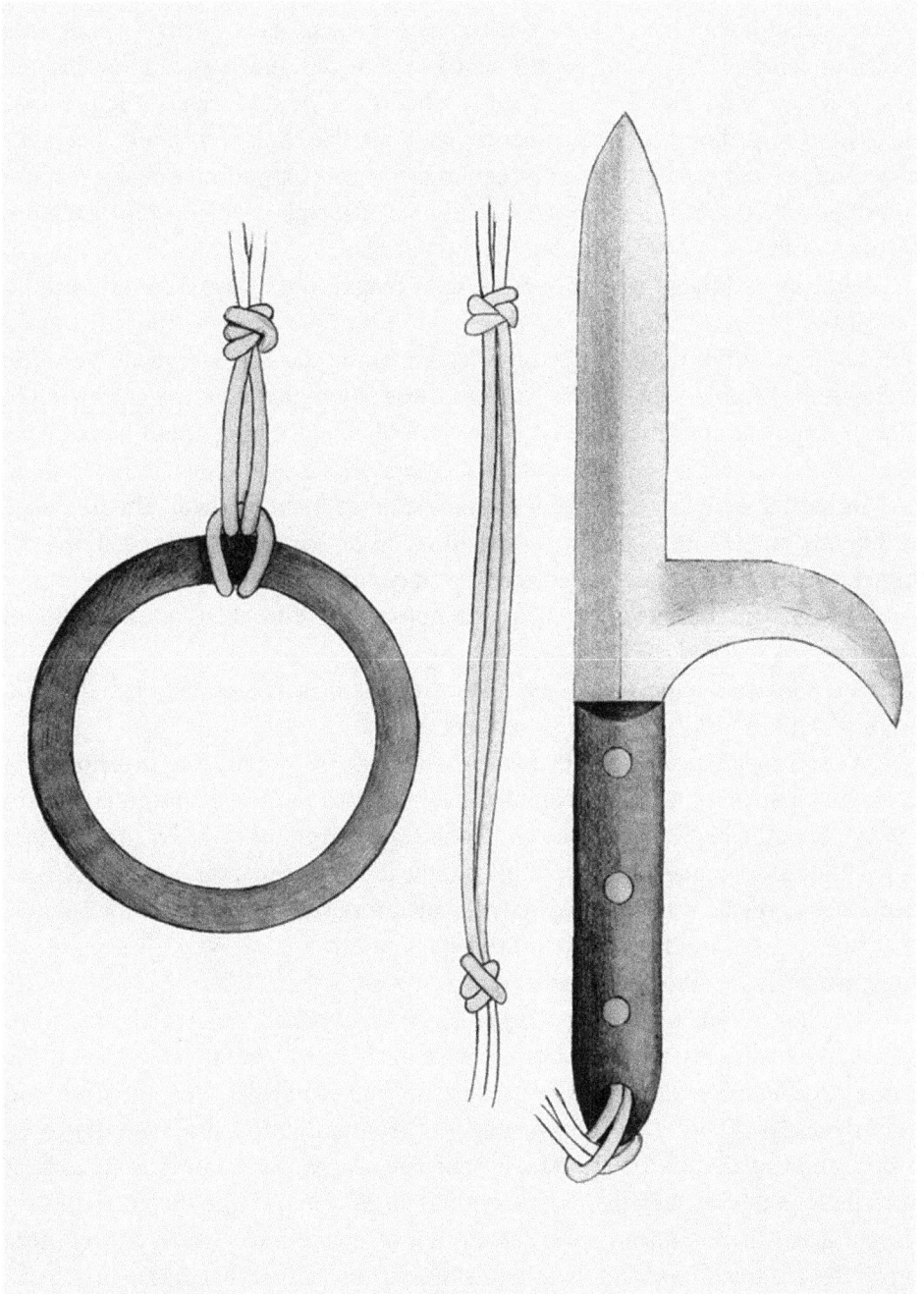

Fig. 28: The Shoge, showing the three elements of the ring or annulus, the unique blade and the cord, in this case with knots, as used in our Ninjutsu tradition. The knots shown here are of the variety that can easily be disassembled.

Indeed, this name can mean many things, but seems mostly to imply a versatile tool and weapon that incorporates specific strategies and applications that are practical to a Ninja and a traveler in the wilderness. As was seen in the previous discussion regarding the various names used for the Ninja, tools, and weapons, also changed and acquired different names over time. I have found that it is more informative to examine the properties and uses of such implements rather than to trying to infer too much from what they were called.

Like many of the other weapons we were taught to use in our school; early or primitive versions of the Shoge are believed to have been made of bone. The blade was fashioned from tusk, long bone or antler, while the ring was made from the hollowed body of large vertebrae, such as those from whales, or the anklebone of a large ungulate. If these materials were unavailable, the ring could be made of hardwood or carefully selected round flat river stones ground down in the middle.

Only later were the rings made from a flattened band of metal. The ring edge was gently tapered, but not sharp. Thus it could be handled without risk of self-injury, yet in striking at high velocity and with circular acceleration it could actually cut. A larger and heavier metal ring was not only able to break bone, but could actually even sever a limb.

The cord was often fashioned from the hair of a horse's tail, sometimes a woman's hair as well as rope, but rarely a chain.

When I met Master Junichi Kawakami in 2009, he told me that the shoge was especially associated with Iga Ninjutsu. He also said that their understanding of the origin of the blade is that it comes from a spear point, cut off and attached to a rope. Though intuitively attractive and simple as an explanation, our school does not exactly concur with the simplicity of this proposition. It is no doubt possible that the shoge comes from a cut-off spear point; but if it did, was it from a spear used primarily for combat, or some other purpose?

Looking at analogous rope weapons with attached blades coming from China, the blades resemble the tips of spears or halberds. In fact, the shoge blade bears a strong resemblance to the Bronze Age halberd blades form the Chin and Han dynasties. These Chin weapons appear around 220 BC and are likely to be a derivation of the "ko," (Fig. 29) a bronze-age "dagger-axe" dating to its earliest incarnations during the Shang dynasty of 1500 BC (23). While the ko is called a dagger-axe, which is a near literal description of what it looks like, it carries some attributes of early bronze and stone age axes and those of the what the Japanese refer to as a kama (sickle) used for harvesting rice and other grains. I have repeatedly heard attention being drawn to the resemblance of the shoge to the common kama in a variety of settings, where people were proposing the relationship as a theory for where the unusual shoge knife comes from. Indeed, if you were to take the kama and add an extra blade to the tip of the shaft, you have what looks like a shoge knife and you have a modified ko with a straight blade at the end, like the Chin dynasty halberds. This is precisely what appears to have been done during the Chin dynasty, making what was possibly a harvesting blade into what is essentially a shoge knife. We could then well ask where the original *ko* came from? Did it arise from the kama combined with a spear tip, as seems to be the case? This explanation is possible, though I did not find any sources that clearly demonstrate it.

At the end of the Paleolithic era began the Neolithic approximately 10,000 years ago. Among Neolithic defining characteristics was the domestication of animals, pottery making, and the beginnings of agriculture. We know that Jomon Neolithic people in Japan practiced a blend of hunter-gatherer living and agriculture. Archeological studies indicate that they were already cultivating barley, millet, buckwheat and rice on a relatively small scale (Ir-3). I have not found any information that pinpoints the general era during which the kama would have come

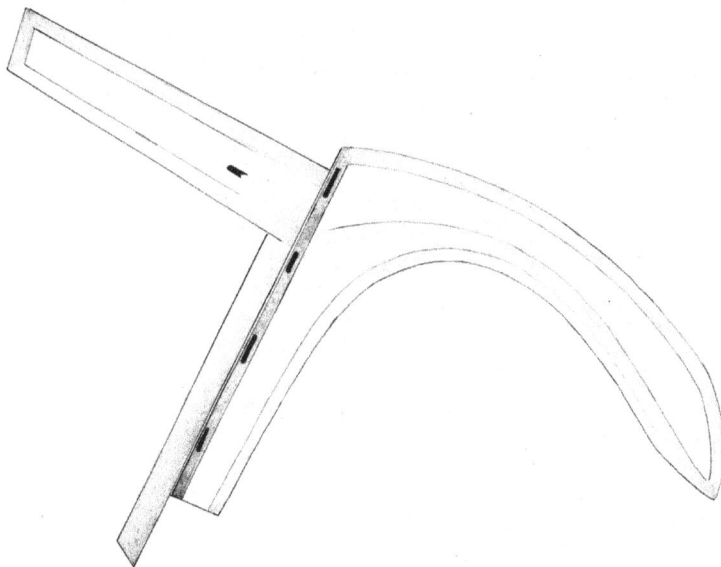

Fig. 29: The ko blade, it should be noted that some ko blades had a third straight point emanating from the shaft.

into existence. I would posit that it is ancient in form and predates the bronze-age with analogues made of other materials developed specifically for the cutting of plant stems and later rice and other grains. I would further suggest that the shoge blade predates the kama and may be its source tool, with the extra straight blade portion being abandoned for ease of use and reduction of risk of injury during rice harvesting in rice paddies where workers operate very close to and behind one another. Derivative theories of the kama having a clear connection to the shoge knife will probably not be able to be confirmed. In our school we hold that the shoge blade is the predecessor to the kama, which was modified from a tool for hunting and skinning to one better suited to harvesting grains, when this practice began. In fact the kama blade is different in shape than the curved shoge blade in such a manner as to suit its harvesting functionality.

Non-agrarian Northern people of the Pacific Rim and arctic regions maintained an almost exclusively hunter-gatherer way of living, and their remaining cultural practices can to an extent be considered a living window into a way of life that existed prior to the advent of agriculture, or possibly after having lost it and preserving only the former. My research, as limited as it was, revealed a dearth of information indicating if the Jomon people of Japan engaged in any kind of serious warfare. If they did, it does not appear to have been systematized. It is commonly assumed that the Kama as a tool and then weapon arose in China, since they advanced earlier in technology. In the Neolithic period, Northern China, Korea, and Japan were populated with the various tribes of aboriginal peoples that predate the rise of Chinese civilization, as we know it from recorded history. Therefore, I make no effort to determine whether such tools arose in any one of these regions and the distinction seems irrelevant to the proposed underlying evolutionary technological processes.

What becomes very interesting in this study of ancient tools is how and why the concept and development of reverse pointing blades and hooks took place. It may not seem like much today, but in fact this was an important innovation, presenting new capabilities and economy of movement over the simple knife or pointed rod. They also indicate an advance over conventional stone tools, in that reliable reverse blades would have been hard to make from stone. The original reverse blades were probably made from materials like wood, antler and bone and designed to combine the ability to hook and cut.

The kama is a reverse cutting tool. If some form of straight cutting tool preceded it, the use of a straight blade would have entailed a different and less efficient type of movement for cutting bunched plant stems. If the kama existed prior to agriculture, then the direct source tools came from the non-agrarian tools of hunter-gatherers from the late Paleolithic era. In fact, we see reverse cutting tools preserved in the strictly hunter-gatherer societies of the Pacific Rim. Some continue to be used today. The concept of hooking using a reverse point appears in very early civilization primarily for catching fish. It is very well represented in cultures living off the ocean and in areas where salmon run. We know from archeological work that salmon was an important food source for the Jomon people of Japan and the rest of the Pacific Rim. We also know that they hunted whales and likely other large animals from the oceans.

Looking back at the idea of the cut-off spear point bearing a reversed blade portion, we can see it deliberately and beautifully represented in the common toggle harpoon (Fig. 30). Though the harpoon is a form of spear, it was not originally designed as a weapon of combat. Take the wooden spear shaft away from a toggle harpoon and you effectively have a shoge, ring and all.

Note that I have illustrated below several toggle harpoon heads from Northern cultures (Fig. 31,32), which effectively illustrate the reverse points and display a fairly clear resemblance to the shoge blade. A mere changing of the location where the rope is attached and thinning of the blades makes the shoge knife. This resemblance is further reinforced by the presence of the rope and ring in a manner exactly analogous to a toggle harpoon.

I would add that there is an interesting and logical parallel between the shape

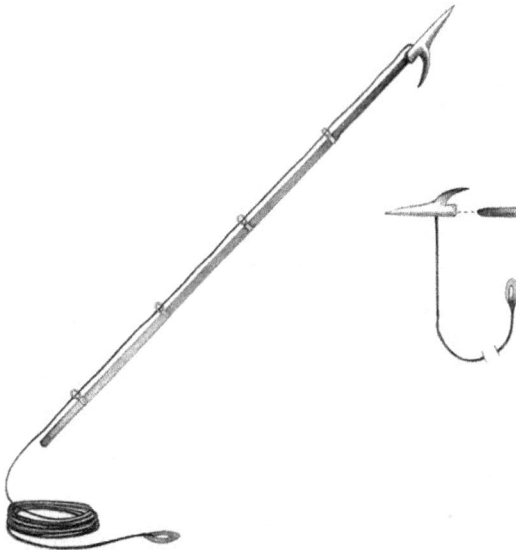

Fig. 30: A toggle harpoon showing all three components of the shoge together, in addition to the presence of the staff.

of the shoge knife and skinning knives used for removing the hides from large animals and gutting fish. The shoge knife, whether pulled downward or lifted and pushed forward, will cut a hide neatly. When researching the translation of the name of this weapon the character "ge" (or "ke") in shoge can mean "animal fur" as well. Although I drew a connection between this character and the cord of the weapon being made of hair, my inclination is to believe it is a reference to skinning hides. This connection fits very well with the shoge knife being the business end of a toggle harpoon and once the animal is captured doubling as a skinning knife. Since the ring and rope in combination with a skinning knife seem to make a possible argument for the shoge being a derivative of the toggle harpoon, we can then ask about the purpose of these components. Why the ring? The answer lies in how the toggle harpoon was used. When the spear was thrown into a whale (think also large fish, seal, and other animals), the spear shaft drove the blade deep into the animal. The shaft then separated from the point and stayed attached to the rope outside the animals body, while the harpoon head stayed lodged in the animal and

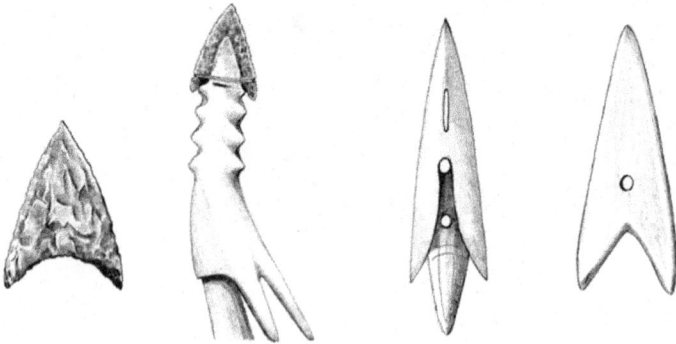

Fig. 31: Neolithic harpoon points, made initially of flint then incorporating bone and related materials like tusk. Note the presence of the reverse points, which are designed to keep the blade in the struggling quarry. Note also the interesting resemblance to certain forms of shuriken.

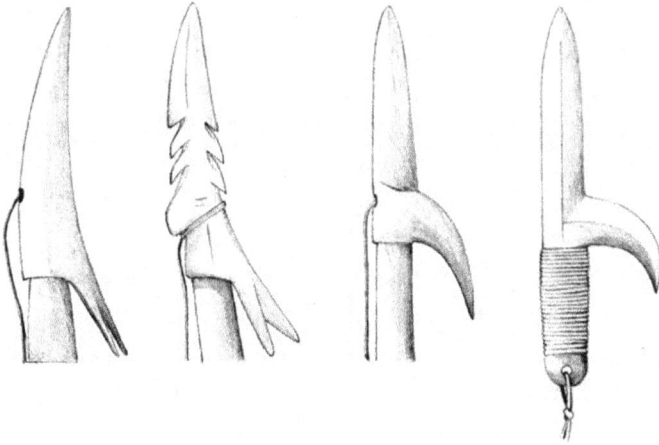

Fig. 32: Various toggle harpoon heads, showing a progressive resemblance to the shoge knife, the connection of which is proposed by this author.

securely connected to the rope (typically well below the skin). The long rope was then attached to a solid immobile and grounded object, effectively mooring the quarry to land (or ice, as the case may be) causing the injured animal to struggle, bleed, and die in place. In this way, hunters did not have to work against an animal much larger and stronger than themselves. They would simply wait for it to die, then haul it in. Of course, if necessary, the animal could be further controlled by the use of two or more toggle harpoons together.

This was the main use of the toggle harpoon, but as we have already seen, ancient hunting tools were rarely used for one purpose alone. Most modern hunters will tell you it is best to travel light and efficiently. They know that the less equipment they carry into the field, the more meat they would be able to carry back, with less meat going to waste. Hunters want tools that are light, strong, durable, and have multiple practical uses. The fact that porous bone typically floats is, of course, important especially when working in rivers or at sea. The added precaution of adding a rope to the spear means the carcass could be dragged using that rope from where it was killed. If it was wounded but managed to get free, the tool might still be retrieved.

Broadly speaking, the toggle harpoon shares characteristics and methods of handling conceptually similar those used with a fishing rod. The main difference is that a fishing rod isn't thrown at the prey to get the hook lodged into it. Also, the fishing hook is typically much smaller. It therefore isn't surprising to see the same people using toggle harpoons also using fishing lines and fishing poles as well.

We have been taught in our tradition that the shoge originated with coastal hunter-gatherer cultures. While it cannot at this point be proven definitively with the information provided here. It nonetheless supports the notion brought to light by other convergent evidence that Ninjutsu may have origins and influences that are disparate, very ancient and not merely an offshoot of conventional Japanese warrior culture or simply an importation of Chinese espionage expertise. An interesting internet site adds convincing congruence by showing an example of a "fishing spear" that is essentially a shoge blade (Ir-5).

To further support this perspective, it seems that far northern pacific people were very much in contact and in fact traded with their Southern counterparts, and specifically those with a developed warrior culture. It is not well-known in martial culture, but Northern peoples like the Koryak of the Northern Pacific Rim actually wore lamellar armor and used shields when engaged in combat (Fig. 33). Though they are not generally reported to have engaged in any major conflicts, the presence of this armor clearly indicates a connection with peoples of the Northern Japanese/Sakhalin archipelago, the Kamchatka Peninsula where they lived or via a Siberian/Northern Chinese connection. This would provide the necessary link for a tool like the toggle harpoon and the derivative shoge to make its way to China and Japan from these regions where it may have originated. Or it may indicate, as we propose here, that the shoge derives from Neolithic populations that used toggle harpoons antedating the rise of Sino-Asian populations in the lower pacific regions that are now China, Korea and Japan. These harpoons and derivatives were used contiguously by Northern populations as well, who preserved their practices long after they had disappeared in Southern regions, except as a weapon: the obscure shoge. The shoge would not have returned to lower Japan, but for the integration of Emishi warriors into the Japanese shinobi warrior caste after the colonization of Emishi lands.

In the first chapter of this book I proposed that Japan's first aboriginal inhabitants contributed to the art of Ninjutsu. They also contributed aspects of their general culture to the new Yayoi people similar to the way Native Americans contributed to the developing culture of early settlers in North America. In so doing, they very likely contributed their hunting tools to the art as well. This theory by no means negates the possibility that a shoge was a cut-off combat spear point from a later era. We might also consider that the conventional spear, with its reversed point like the shoge knife, itself derives from an ancient tool that came before and inspired the later production of the toggle harpoon, which in turn gave rise to the shoge. This

Fig. 33: "Koryak Warriors wearing lamellar armor, which may have originated in China (or possibly Central Asia to the Middle East) as early as 500BC. These men are modeling armor purchased for the American Museum of Natural History." (public domain)(Photograph is from American Museum of Natural History, negative #1543)

theory could account for the inclusion and presence of the ring, which isn't quite so easy to explain if we assumed the shoge simply originated with a cut-off spear point from a much later era and culture. If that were the case, we might expect to see a weight used instead of a ring as is the case of the *kusarigama*. This explanation of course implies that the ko, as used in China was a modified hunting spear that turned out to be very well suited to combat, especially for mounted warriors. It would seem that the shoge really did originate with a cut-off spear point, we will never know whether that spear was a toggle harpoon or its rigid intact cousin consisting of a staff with a shoge-knife at one end similar to the ko.

Though it is always possible that this weapon was reinvented several times in history, there is an important rationale for looking at these events as a progressive evolution. Early people, whether hunting or in the early phases of developing agricultural practices, were often resource poor and existed at or near a subsistence level. They were vulnerable to the variations of the seasons, natural disasters and their own ability to influence the environment. Not securing adequate foodstuffs simply meant starvation, potential cannibalism and death. So the creation of tools was not a trivial matter. Starvation and pressures of the Darwinian kind drove the process.

It is an appealing fantasy to think of someone sitting down one day and having an epiphany; saying "wouldn't it be great if I invented a weapon/tool that did this!" Casual experimentation must have helped in some instances, but to rely on it alone was a bet weighted in favor of extinction. The ideas for these tools and weapons appear to have come from people who used them every day and were keenly aware of their limitations. When innovations occurred, not only did they often rise to address critical situations, but also there was confidence that they would work. This is because the inventors were practical people. The effect of coming up with new, efficient ways to perform tasks did much to alleviate the stress of hunger and suffering. These innovations provided humanity more free time to develop their cultures and civilizations. To serious martial artists, the shoge is an active connection with their past, represented by a tool that can still be used today for many things.

In Ninjutsu, the shoge maintained its composite nature as tool and weapon. Shoge were used to set traps for animals and men alike. Usually the trap involved the release of a snare intended to capture the individual or to swing/release an object designed to strike, injure, and possibly kill the target.

The blade was sometimes put on the end of a staff, thereby regaining its usage as a specialized spear point. The shoge hook-knife was used for gaffing and hooking anything that needed retrieval, be that a large fish, animal, underwater baited trap, or a basket gone overboard. It could even be used to hoist goods up into a tree. It could be used to moor and tie boats into a cluster when not in use or when fishermen needed to bring them together to accomplish a specialized task.

Ninja knew that the shoge was well suited for climbing trees and walls. By doubling the cord, loops were made (see Fig. 28) that in addition to strengthening the cord itself also served as footholds. Another ladder-like climbing device was made by incorporating the shoge into a bamboo staff with holes bored into its shaft, through which bamboo slats or loops of rope were passed. This was faster to climb because it was more rigid and stable than a loose rope with loops in it. The ring at the end of the cord itself acted as a toehold that could support a man either upright or even hanging upside-down.

The ring was used for rappelling down smaller walls or precipices still too high to be scaled easily or rapidly by other means, and which might take too long to climb. We were taught that Ninja might use more than one shoge to move from one high place to another, by hanging from one while swinging the other into place, retrieving the first and so on.

The shoge was especially useful for crossing difficult obstacles such as moats and deep gorges. As with the kaginawa, the shoge was sometimes combined with *mizugumo* (Fig. 34) (a sort of floatation device), adapted either as a seat in its larger form or for the feet if smaller, such that Ninja could cross a muddy bog or small and very shallow bodies of water without sinking in. The mizugumo is believed to have been developed by rice farmers for crossing their muddy paddies. One internet resource (Ir-6) incredibly shows a very similar device illustrated by Leonardo da Vinci (1475-1480 AD) as so-called "water shoes" made from hides! This method was sometimes needed to avoid traps hidden below the surface. It is this process that seems to be referred to by the root term "sho" in shoge.

In combat, the ring worked effectively to strike and ensnare. By winding around the head, hand, any weapon and so forth, it served to immobilize and restrict the enemy's movement (Fig. 35). When a weapon was seized it could be torn from their opponent's grasp. The ring was not always held in the hand or dangled via the cord; occasionally it was slid up the arm with or without grasping the cord and in this way was anchored for movement. Bringing down the ring while grasping the cord would create an instant snare.

The shoge knife was also used to lock and immobilize limbs and tear away any weapons the enemy held. The straight blade portion permitted cutting, slashing and stabbing while effectively maneuvering the hook to trap the enemy's movement. This prevented the Ninja's opponent from wrestling away the shoge knife.

The hook tore clothes and flesh, causing severe lacerating injuries while

Fig. 34, The Mizugumo (water spider), here shown as a large version in which a person can sit. As noted there were smaller devices that had the same construction and fit on the feet. Here the Ninja is depicted using a short bow. Note also the modified geta.

hindering the enemy's ability fight. Unlike the to and fro slashing movements typical of knife attacks that quickly release and resume again, the hook-blade dug into the enemy while the rope ensnared him. This created a strong and desperate impulse for the enemy to try to escape, and divided his attention between fighting and getting away. The enemy thus often injured himself further during their attempts to escape. The shoge blade was used to hook warriors even in full armor, thereby ensnaring them for capture or a final *coup de gras*.

Ensnarement and striking could be executed with great versatility and freedom by swinging the shoge in many different directions. Either the ring or blade could catch the enemy. Ensnarement techniques were similar to those previously described for the kaginawa and shaken, although the shoge was more effective. All rope weapons used in Ninjutsu involved some degree of hojojutsu. In this regard, the shoge was no exception.

The ring was well suited to holding flammable materials, used either to send a nighttime signal, or as an intimidating and confusing weapon.

What is perhaps unique about the shoge is how deceptive it was for an enemy

Fig. 35: This is a fanciful illustration of the shoge being used to ensnare a ronin. It does show the process of entangling the enemy and his weapon while readying the shoge knife for a cutting slash or capture by the Ninja to be subsequently used for direct handling.

to face. The distance of the swing was constantly and easily changed along with its trajectory. On swinging impact the knife was capable of cutting, tearing, stabbing, or binding the enemy. Ninja combined rolling and taijutsu in its use as well, amounting to a formidable capability enhancement. Its versatility in combat when combined with what would otherwise be empty-handed fighting skills was such that it fit naturally with Ninjutsu fighting methodology.

The Shoge is not a simple device to master and its manipulation can be tricky. The methods used to handle it to a certain extent resemble those seen with both the Chinese "meteor hammer-ball" or *sheng-bao* practiced in WuShu and in other ways a kusarigama (Fig. 36). The sheng-bao and kusarigama however, are equipped with a percussive and ensnaring iron ball attached to the chain or rope instead of a ring. The shoge ring, though percussive and ensnaring, allows cord to be looped through it creating additional possibilities. Common demonstrations of the sheng-bao show it used primarily in its percussive capacity, although it is hard to imagine that in reality it was used only in this way when it was still a relevant weapon of combat.

The shoge's resemblance to the kusarigama in form and strategy may justify conjectures that one is possibly a derivative of the other. They were both commonly used as weapons for ensnaring and immobilizing a well-armed enemy. The kama blade and handle of the kusarigama are different sizes, weights and shape than the shoge and operate differently in hand-to-hand fighting. Anyone having tried the two in combative training will be struck with the difference. No one seems really sure when the rice harvesting tool, the kama (Fig. 36), became incorporated into routinely practiced fighting skills of peasant conscripts let alone professional warriors. We now see kama used ubiquitously in martial systems, possibly as a consequence of its use in Karate, which has enjoyed enormous popularity around the world. Properly reinforced, it was used to stop a sword and take control of an enemy. Versions of this weapon used in combat had the handle reinforced with steel so that it was hard to cut through. Ninja used kama liberally, as did some of their warrior counterparts as seen in illustrations showing the kama placed on the end of a staff (*kamayari*) (19) and being used by both the bushi and non-professional warriors. Perhaps because of its use as a peasant tool and various technical limitations the kama never developed the status of the *katana* (long-sword), *yari* (spear) and naginata (polearm similar to a Halberd). Nevertheless the kama and its analogue the kusarigama are distinct in certain fundamental ways from the shoge. Though it can be placed in the same general category of flexible weapons, it carries its own unique functional niche. This niche will always be strongly, though not exclusively, associated with the Ninja.

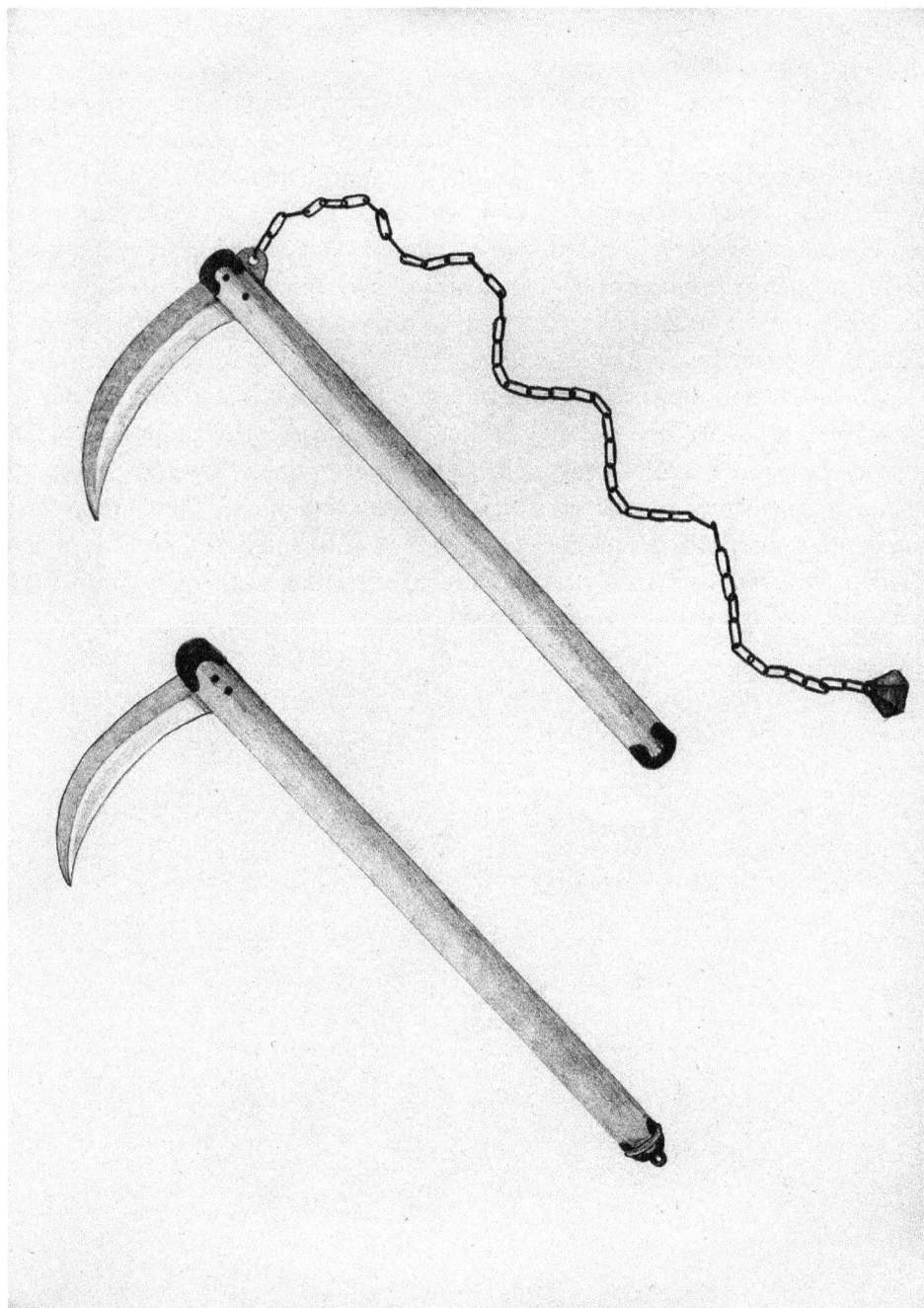

Fig. 36: Kama and kusarigama

It requires a great deal of practice to take advantage of shoges multiple dimensions. The respective individual parts are not as challenging to use as the ensemble. The complete shoge is more than the sum of its parts. A synergistic application of its three components permits the user to find its true potential. To the Ninja it was this potential that justified the extensive training required for mastering it and they learned to be familiar with it in all aspects.

To make the use of complex weapons and tools like the shoge easier and more intuitive, Grandmaster Law stated, that as children, Ninja played games with them. By playing games similar to ring toss or horseshoes, they learned to develop their accuracy with the ring. They would play with them by swinging from trees and using them to climb.

Finally, in response to a comment made by Master Kawakami that Koka Ninja used the kusarigama and not the shoge, Grandmaster Law proposes that the distinction is loose, as Koka (like other Ninja organizations) are known to have many subgroups that maintained contacts with Iga and others. These groups had some interconnection, though they were often at odds and kept secrets from one another. The various martial arts and strategies relating to these weapons were neither completely in one camp or another.

Spears and other Polearms

No discussion of martial arts weapons would be complete without some exploration of the spear and related polearms. These weapons, be they originally for hunting or warfare, were ubiquitous and are very ancient. To assert that they have any one specific origin in any culture or any part of the world would be folly. Although it may exist, I have not so far seen any clear evidence proving when polearms first made their way into warfare or where it occurred. As hunting tools they are likely far more remote in origin. Even chimps and orangutans have been seen making crude spears or clubs for hunting. It is possible their actions were learned from observing humans, or perhaps our common ancestors used them. Many martial arts include systems using polearms, or teach methods to defend against them. There have been adaptations to polearms that are specific to groups of warriors, martial art traditions, and regions. Some of these have endured and are well recognized. Reasons for including polearms in this chapter have more to do with specific types of this weapon and their relationship with tools than a need to explore them as a category in their own right.

Human use of spears as hunting tools is known to have existed from at least the later part of the Paleolithic period. They were used to hunt game on land, in rivers, streams, and large bodies of water. Spears are but one variety of polearm, which encompass many forms, some of which clearly are more related to tools used for other purposes, especially farming, and occasionally for unusual applications like firefighting.

As with all other tools, their properties have evolved with their uses. Some of these required little modification to suit martial purposes. Spears themselves came in many varieties, depending upon their cultural origin and/or the type of game for which they were intended. The Inuit and Native Americans are excellent examples of people who have developed the use of specialized spears for hunting anything from ungulates to walrus and whales. They are also well known for their ability to deftly harvest spawning salmon. Unlike the Neolithic stone spear tips that were usually crafted to a simple elliptical or triangular shape, the tips used by people hunting game in and on the seas, rivers and streams eventually came to employ hooked and barbed tips like those described in the discussion of the kaginawa and kyoketsu shoge.

Polearms with a barbed hook have been used throughout the world, and their primary function was for the hook to remain lodged in the flesh of the quarry no matter how much it struggled. Their size and shape depended on the technique and purpose for which they were designed. Such hunting and game harvesting tools were not practical for the battlefield and were intended only for seizing, immobilizing and capturing animals.

Hooked polearms without barbs do have a place on the open battlefield, but they were not the primary type used by bushi. They were typically associated with the work of foot soldiers using them to pull down mounted warriors. Mounted warriors had tactical advantages over foot soldiers. They were also more expensive to train, equip and maintain. Being a mounted warrior was also a matter of significant status, and as such they were often well-trained fighters.

Foot soldiers with hooked and ensnaring polearms (Fig. 37) frequently worked in teams, and while one soldier pulled the mounted warrior down, his peers would use regular spears or swords to kill him. A second purpose of hooked polearms, as we had noted previously with the shoge, was to take away weapons from enemies. The distance afforded by polearms could in part compensate for lesser fighting ability by keeping, an experienced swordsman out of striking range. Finally, hooked blades were used for snagging the leggings and armor of bushi and they gave the fighter the ability to pin down enemies more easily at a safe range. These are all significant advantages, but hooked weapons could also slow the fighter down as he used it for the more complex maneuvers needed to accomplish pinning and killing armor clad warriors. On a battlefield where enemies were moving quickly and efficiently, it was generally undesirable to be slowed in any way. The other members of the team would therefore be charged with the task of protecting the soldier charged with this vital first task.

In the discussion about the advantages of the shoge, it was mentioned that the reverse cut provided a certain economy of movement as it applied to the work of harvesting plants and for skinning and gutting game. It was also mentioned how this contributed to its natural inclusion into the Ninja arsenal. Above and beyond these matters, there is a whole strategic understanding associated with the concept of hooking as it applies to combat in Ninjutsu.

The concept of the reverse point, be it a blade or hook, is central to the way in which martial arts are conceptualized in Ninjutsu. Many Ninja fighting techniques are designed more for hooking and trapping an enemy, than either dispatching or immobilizing them. Interfering with the enemy's movement creates a significant combative advantage provided that it sacrifices nothing. Reversed and especially bidirectional blades are ideal for these purposes. As was described with the kaginawa, we see the utilization of the hook as a weapon for capture and control. Associating a pole with a hook added another dimension that is different yet shares

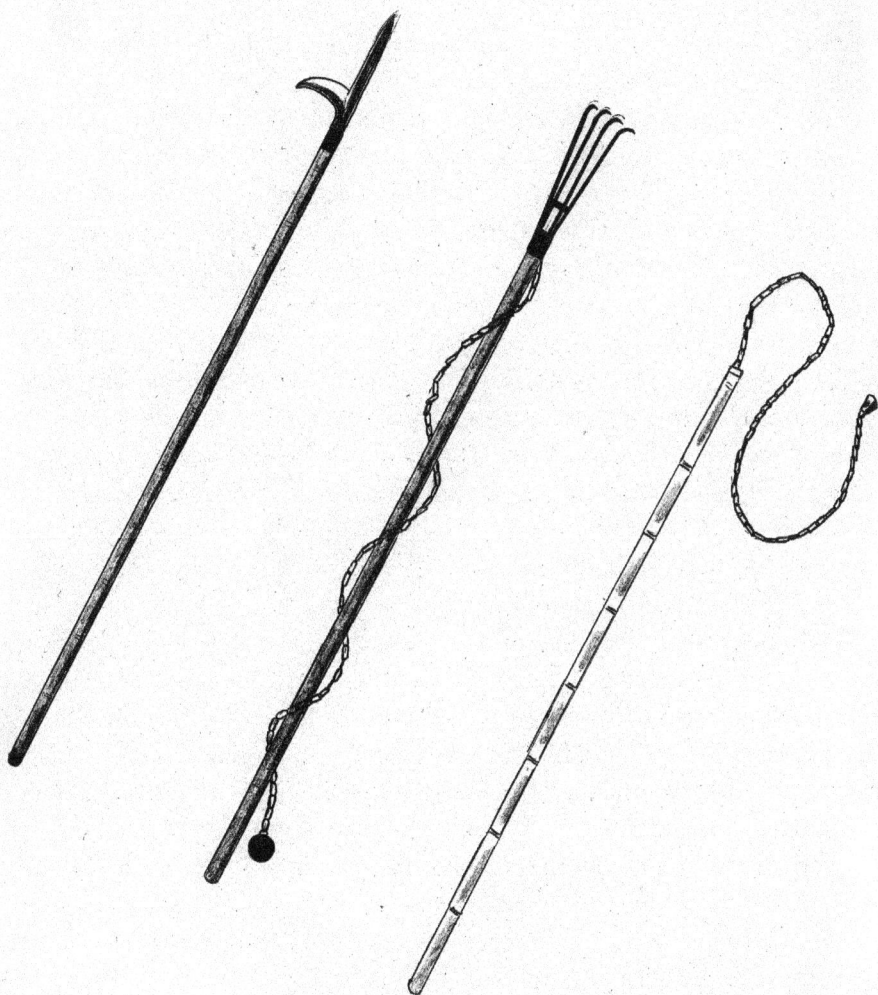

Fig. 37: Examples of various polearms that had different combative applications.

some common properties with the rope-hook combination.

Master Law took pains to teach us the utility and importance of being able to use not only left and right equally, but also to be able to understand and perform techniques in a forward and reverse manner. Initially it was disorienting for most of us, especially for those of us previously trained in linear striking arts. When movement is reversed; the techniques change, as does the fighter's way of seeing them. This perspective on movement and thinking is by no means unique to fighting methods; it can be used to understand art and structures (for example by viewing them using mirrors), a sequence of acts or steps, and so on. Reverse pointing blades are more easily used by a person trained in this manner and permit a more thorough understanding of the techniques. These weapons are not unique to Ninjutsu, they are, however, essential to understanding the commonality between combat weapons, hunting weapons and tools from the Ninja's perspective.

In the empty-hand fighting form of Ninjutsu called taijutsu, using natural "hooks" of the body is critical to a successful outcome. Some other martial also take advantage of this, in particular the grappling arts. This aspect of training was heavily emphasized in taijutsu and all the weapons fighting systems based on taijutsu as well. These techniques differ from the linear stabbing and slashing style movements favored on the open battlefield, once again highlighting some of the fundamentally different purposes of different martial arts.

Reversing strategies used by conventional warriors created fear based on the impression that Ninja were unpredictable. It was in part this ability to move in and through, forward and backward freely that created the illusion that the Ninjas was untouchable and even invisible. Imagine the terror of encountering an apparition that can at first be seen, but then vanishes. For those who understand the subtle and inconspicuous reverse stroke of the katana in many standard cuts in bujutsu, what is being discussed here is similar in concept, but extrapolated to a greater degree and applied to nearly all movements.

Often during practice, newcomers to the art of Ninjutsu will sense strong familiarity to techniques seen in jujutsu, but will have difficulty doing them the new way because the similarity, though apparent, is only superficial. Applying hooking and reverse movement deliberately interferes with the adversary's chances of escape and their freedom to fight back; Ninjutsu psychologically destabilized the enemy from being able to use their ingrained martial fighting patterns. The key idea here was that fighters, whose techniques had become second nature through constant repetition, would not be able to improvise and adapt at the moment or instant when it was most needed. This being so because learning was through repetition and not improvisation itself with a large technical vocabulary. In combat, this prevented the adversary from organizing serial or further attacks. They were effectively neutralized.

The spear was distinctive from other polearms due to its straight edged blade. Although we understand that spears have primitive origins as hunting tools, we now typically think of spears as battlefield weapons. They were equally well suited for mounted fighters and foot soldiers alike. Classic battlefield spears were simple and were used to kill by stabbing followed by quick extraction so that the warrior was free to move against the next enemy without hindrance.

Hooked polearms like some of those associated with Far East Asian martial arts also appeared very early in Chinese warfare (see discussion regarding the "ko" above). In general, Ninja trained to fight with, and especially against, the spear. It was one of the classical weapons of Samurai warriors and their antecedents. Spears were not a favored weapon of Ninja, who frequently found themselves fighting in close quarters or forested or enclosed settings with uneven terrain and obstacles. Ninja did, however, have significant uses for modified and especially hooked polearms. Even so, they preferred to use flexible or collapsible hooked weapons and tools over these due to their needs for ease of transport and also the ability to conceal such weapons.

Modified polearms were primarily used as tools for moving into a compound or building. They were used to snag branches, ropes, rafters and doors. Thus they could be used for climbing, wedging a door shut or open, tripping an enemy, remaining suspended, tipping things over and so on. If a Ninja were discovered, or encountered an enemy who was not yet aware of his presence, the weapon was useful for killing that person at a distance and potentially from a hidden vantage point.

Interestingly, when the roles and needs of the warrior class changed during the relatively peaceful Edo period, there was increased use of modified polearms and greater emphasis on methods of trapping, pinning and capturing individuals alive in the bugei. This is best shown by the new and modified arts developed by Samurai for police work, putting down public brawls and small-scale rebellions.

Another earlier context in which arts of this kind existed was in the courts of Daimyo, and aristocratic persons, where decorum required that blood not be shed at court as a matter of etiquette, respect and spiritual purity. Thus warriors were expected to quell any disturbance in these quarters without resorting to the sword. Techniques applied with these restrictions were not as easily learned and executed as the more direct assault methods of attacking and killing with a sword or other weapon. Techniques involving kicking and punching, which are executed at full force, also did not require the same degree of sensitivity and control as grappling used to take down a warrior clad in armor or other seizing and control methods. The late Edo period was a time of innovation in unarmed combat and in the practice of using small and concealed weapons by warriors as well as commoners. Members of the merchant class and other occupations made inroads into learning martial arts, but rarely did so openly.

It is rumored that non-professional fighters and some of the police style martial arts utilized by generally low ranking members of the warrior class had techniques either derived from or influenced by Ninjutsu. This belief seems to stem from claiming that Ninja who were no longer employable with Daimyo found other ways to keep their skills alive and such opportunities existed in professions like police work, bounty hunting, and within organized crime networks. Some of the methodological similarities between taihojutsu and taijutsu certainly make this seem plausible but I have found no explicit and clear links in the translated literature to support this. In fact nearly all the taihojutsu methods I have seen appear derived primarily from Samurai bugei. They are of the variety common to traditional Samurai jujutsu, bujutsu and taijutsu. It is, however, no secret that authorities will at times hire enemies and covert specialists to develop methods to apprehend others of their own kind; thus, it is conceivable that Ninja may have contributed to Edo and Meiji period policing methods in some relatively minor way.

A modern equivalent of this approach would be when the FBI or a corporation such a bank hires a computer hacker to test the security of a computer network or to track down another hacker. We were taught that historically Ninja were hired as security consultants to *metsuke* (see below) and Daimyo for the purpose of enhancing their own personal and military security against not only Samurai rivals but against breaches by enemy Ninja groups. This function was typically performed by Ninja loyal only to a single domain or warrior family. These same groups were sent when necessary to infiltrate enemy camps, fortifications and other important elements of security. It should be noted that the link between Ninjutsu and some highly ranked Samurai families (shoninki and others) is well established , but does not negate the lower-class roots associated with Ninja martial society. In spite of such links, the association was one of necessity only. It was not uncommon for people to view others of so-called lower classes in disdain. Even peacekeeping warriors from respectable families such as higher-ranking *hatamoto* (standard bearers) and *gokenin* (house retainers) looked down upon their Samurai brethren given the duties of apprehending criminals. To them it was impure even to interact with common people. This probably contributed to the necessity for covert exchanges to take place between the lowly Ninja and the loftier Samurai who employed them to go through multiple intermediaries. Not only that, and the need for secrecy, there was also the issue of trust. Higher ranking Samurai would not generally feel secure having direct contact with Ninja operatives, unless their loyalty had been completely assured.

Bakufu authorities during the Edo period, adopted weapons like the *jutte* and the *torimono sandogu* (sleeve entanglers) into the taiho arts. These weapons were used within the narrower repertoire of techniques characteristic of the taiho schools of martial arts. The torimono sandogu was an interesting example of highly specialized adaptations to polearms. We were taught that Ninja were familiar with arresting implements and the tactics associated with their use because such weapons had the potential to be used against them. Ninja were more desirably captured alive because it was believed that as spies that they could provide critical information or be turned into double agents. Ninja had methods of their own to deal with the authorities; they also had their own torture methods.

Another polearm associated with both Samurai and Ninja that merits some attention is the *naginata* (Fig. 38). In English, the naginata is considered a kind of halberd or more properly a glaive. There are several other weapons resembling the naginata, such as the *nagamaki*. These weapons can be traced back through the Samurai arts, including their early use by both high-ranking warriors and foot soldiers alike. The naginata appears to have had its start in Japanese warfare around the 12th century when these weapons were first mentioned in accounts of conflict in Japan (24). This weapon was widely used by warriors in the employ of military strongmen, aristocracy and monastic communities, which, along with the monk's cowl and wooden high sandals, later became among the stereotypic defining characteristics associated with the *Sohei*.

The so-called Ninja version of the naginata is said to have had some differences with those traditionally used by Samurai, being both shorter and lighter. We believe this to be something of a fabrication of a later age like the image of the monastic warrior as a Sohei. It is possible that Ninja, in the interest of practicing with this weapon, made modified versions for battle against groups of other warriors or mounted Samurai. It was not a very important weapon in Ninjutsu, but, again, studied to develop the skills necessary to fight against it in field operations.

Naginata are either associated with traditional bugei or now with naginata-do, an art still dominated, as it was in the past, by female practitioners. It is not coincidental that the naginata came to be favored by Samurai women. It afforded definite advantages for the smaller and out-numbered person fighting against a group of sword wielding attackers. The naginata was an imposing weapon and could be quite heavy. There were, however, effective ways of using it while conserving strength even for persons of smaller stature and weaker physique. Such a weapon

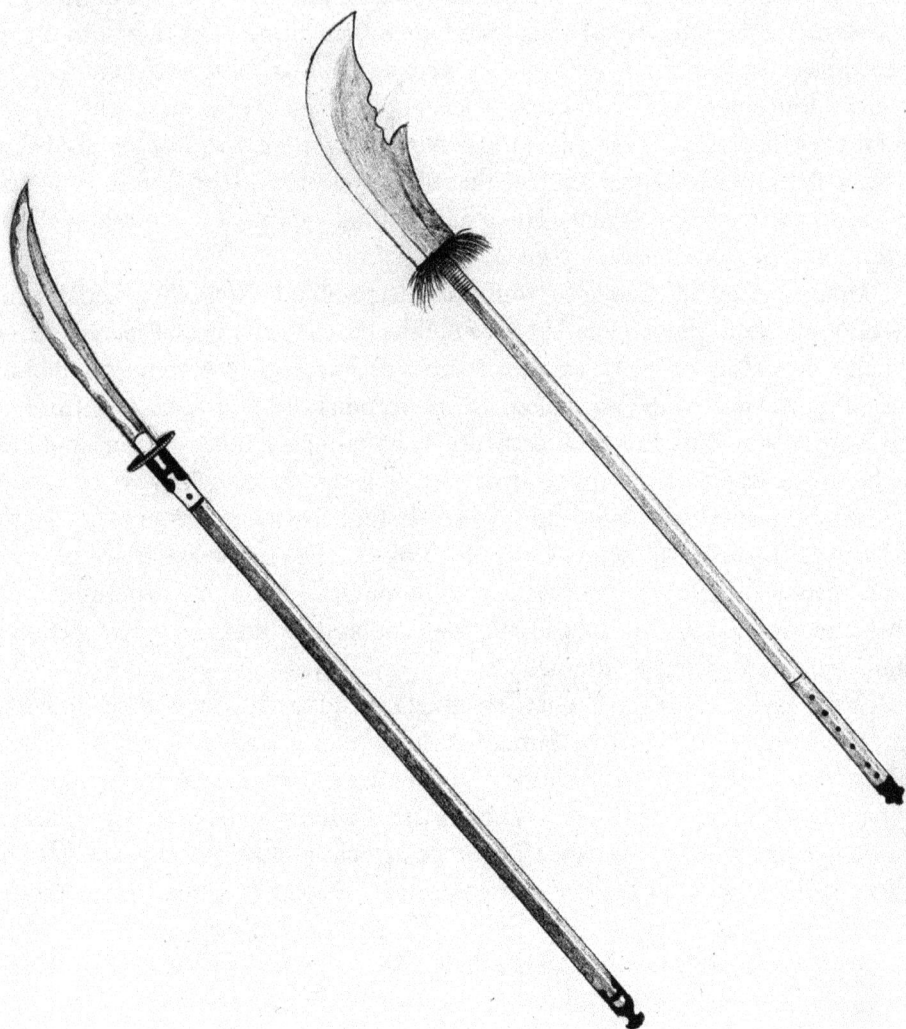

Fig. 38: Comparison of the naginata (left) and the kwan-dao

could be encountered by Ninja entering a home, where the naginata was at the disposal of women, and especially the wives of Samurai, to protect their families.

As to its actual origins, there is little easily accessible information available to the layman. Although it is said to bear resemblance to stone axe-headed pole tools from the 3rd century BC in China, this seems less likely than it having originated from the later *kwan-dao*, as still used today in Chinese WuShu. The Japanese appear to have modified this weapon to suit their needs. A nearly identical weapon to the naginata was seen in China much later during the 19th century (23). It is not clear if this weapon was originally of Chinese origin as a modified derivative of the kwan-dao, or the naginata making its way back to China from Japan.

If the early naginata has an origin as a tool rather than as a weapon, that origin is unclear. There are tools that bear a strong resemblance to the naginata, and there are early polearms that do as well. In this case a broader sword-like blade was placed on the end of a staff. The curved blade of the naginata actually resembles tools bearing both broad and curved blades used in the cutting meat or flesh known as "fleshing knives." Such tools have a long history and are found around the world. A fleshing tool that bears an uncanny resemblance to the naginata is the blubber knife used in whaling.

Coincidentally, the Okhotsk culture in Northern Japan and on the Siberian peninsula, dating from the 5th to the 13th century, had a whaling tradition that coincides with the early development and eventual use of the naginata in Japan. I was not able to find any direct information linking these facts historically, but it seems worth consideration to anyone interested in the subject of weapons innovation to look at this possibility as a source of both the kwan-dao and its Japanese cousin the naginata.

Having the intellectual freedom to think unconventionally about martial arts and many other activities is a core value in Ninjutsu. Like scientists, we never assume there is only one explanation or that all that is known is all there will ever be to know on any subject. We believe that humble attitudes such as these keep us open to new discoveries and the possibility that the orthodox view on something may change. This kind of thinking led to the willingness of Ninja martial society to abandon ceremony and superstition along with irrelevant elements of cumbersome Confucian ideology regarding combat as they entered the modern age. This spirit endures and means that Ninjutsu will continue to evolve as it reinvents itself.

The Kumade and Shuko

The word *kumade* is simply the Japanese term for a rake. The kumade as a polearm with little substantial alteration appears in an ancient illustration, called the "*Kasuga Gongen Kenki e*" circa 1300 (2, 24). In this document, it is shown being used by a mounted warrior to pull another off his horse.

The kumade, as used by the Ninja, was a sturdy rake made of heavier and more durable material. Ninja living as common farmers and gardeners handled rakes as a daily work tool. Kumade, like so many other tools with good capacity for use as weapons, eventually became a variety of polearm. Innovations were of course made and so we see kumade with cords or chains affixed to one end adding special capabilities (Fig. 37, middle specimen).

Other similar modified tool-weapons included the so-called *kamayari* (sickle-spear) and the *chigi-rikki*. The aforementioned torimono sandogu (sleeve entanglers)

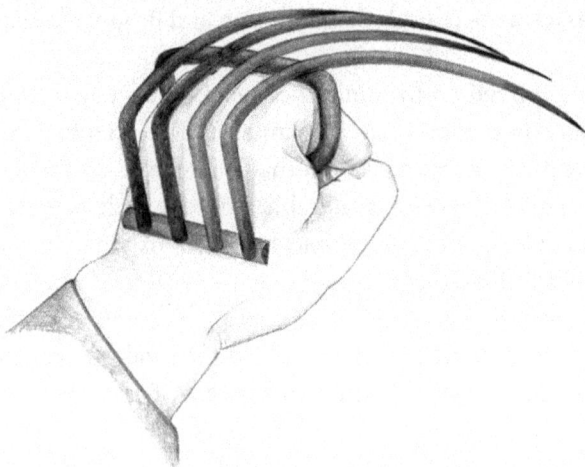

Fig. 39: One version of the shuko

used for capturing fugitives and criminals had one polearm with similar properties to the kumade called the tsukubo.

The kumade was well suited for capturing and locking swords and flexible chain weapons. It could devastatingly grasp and tear both clothing and skin. Like some of the previously described Ninja weapons, it too has reverse-pointing blades or hooks. Modern rakes, if solidly built, retain nearly all these properties, and work very well for disarming anyone armed with a knife or machete. They are perfectly legal and can be used without special modification. They are inexpensive and there is no real hardship in destroying a rake to save a life. Discussion about the kumade as a polearm could have been elaborated upon in the previous section but for an innovation that is very popularly and strongly associated with Ninjutsu,please consider the *shuko* or hand-claw (Fig. 39, 40).

Functionally and conceptually there is some overlap between rakes and pitchforks. The two are distinct and used differently but closely related in design. Although we speak of the shuko as being related to the rake, it actually bears properties of both the rake and pitchfork and these influenced the techniques and applications of the shuko. Some shuko were very simply the business end of a rake/pitchfork fitted to the hand (Fig. 39). Others were made with a band of steel, leather or wood, through which the hand was passed, and which bore the claws (Fig. 40). Claws, in some cases were made from the teeth of a rake-like grain-thrashing tool called a *senbakoki*, which also appears to have been used to make teppan, shuriken and other small improvised weapons (13).

The claws were either emanating from the dorsal (back) side of the hand or across the palmar surface. Palmar claws were, by necessity, shorter and had a strong resemblance to the claws of a bear. Shuko were often lightly tethered to the forearms by an additional band or ring over or within the sleeves. This was linked by a strap to the hand device. When not in use they were usually concealed in a cloth around the waist or within the outer layer of oversized pants (modified hakama) if possible. Shuko eventually took on a favored role like the shoge as a composite weapon-tool that fit perfectly the purposes and needs of Ninja. We should note that they were used for climbing—but unlike in the movies, not smooth stone or, in later times, concrete! They were used for scaling trees and wooden structures. Shuko were also ideal for handling anything that Ninja would not touch or handle directly in their hands such as digging through hot coals or touching uncertain items that might be toxic or imbibed with poison.

As a weapon, the Shuko was unequalled for its capacity to disable the adversary and defend against a well-armed attacker in hand-to-hand combat. Variations of the shuko may be seen in different schools of martial arts and techniques were modified according to the type used. The heavy steel with which shuko were made and into which the claws were set delivered bone-crushing power to any strike. This eliminated the need for years of painful hardening exercises, pounding the knuckles and other parts of the hands to develop calluses for hitting; a practice that continues to be seen in many martial arts today. The formidable claws can ensnare an attacker's blade, rip through chain mail, and eviscerate any exposed area of the body. However, Ninja would never block a direct strike from a sword by placing themselves in the line of the attack despite the fact that the shuko could stop a blade. This kind of technique is far too dangerous when facing a skilled swordsman. The preferred method would involve avoiding the blade altogether through evasive movement and directly counterattacking the limbs holding the sword or the neck or body of the adversary. Striking the enemy's hands or limbs would immediately disable him and end the attack.

In keeping with Ninja strategy and methods of stealth, the shuko was ideal for the silent attack. Unlike larger or more cumbersome weapons such as swords, staffs, and even some of the flexible weapons, the shuko was perfectly adapted for hand-to-hand techniques and freely permitted the use of rolls. Wearing shuko on the hands permitted all the freedom of movement seen in empty hand combat without the risk of being disarmed. It also required relatively little training to use if the Ninja was already competent with the empty-handed techniques of taijutsu. Shuko were easily disengaged from the hands without risk of being dropped because of straps that kept them attached to the forearms. Strategies using smaller weapons like the shuko, shaken, and weapons suited to the rope tying arts were ideal for the type of close quarter combat preferred by Ninjutsu practitioners. These weapons permitted the best control over the adversary and rapidly finished any encounter.

Ninja also used a form of shuko worn on their feet. These were called *ashiko* (foot claw). Ashiko were not just shuko adapted to the feet, and it is unclear if they evolved separately. We were taught that people working in climates where icy weather and slippery conditions were likely to be encountered used variations of ashiko. The concept was not far removed from the snowshoe, except that snowshoes were intended not just to maintain grip but also to prevent feet from sinking into the snowpack. We believe that this tool was widely adapted by people in various circumstances, who used them to climb and keep their footing on any kind of slippery surface and in this way they are analogous to modern crampons.

As with the shuko, ashiko enhanced the effect of certain techniques, including kicking and foot-sweeps, and added a devastating effect to stomping and tearing into the adversary put to the ground. The spikes were either saw-like or curved like claws and could vary in length though typically shorter than those worn on

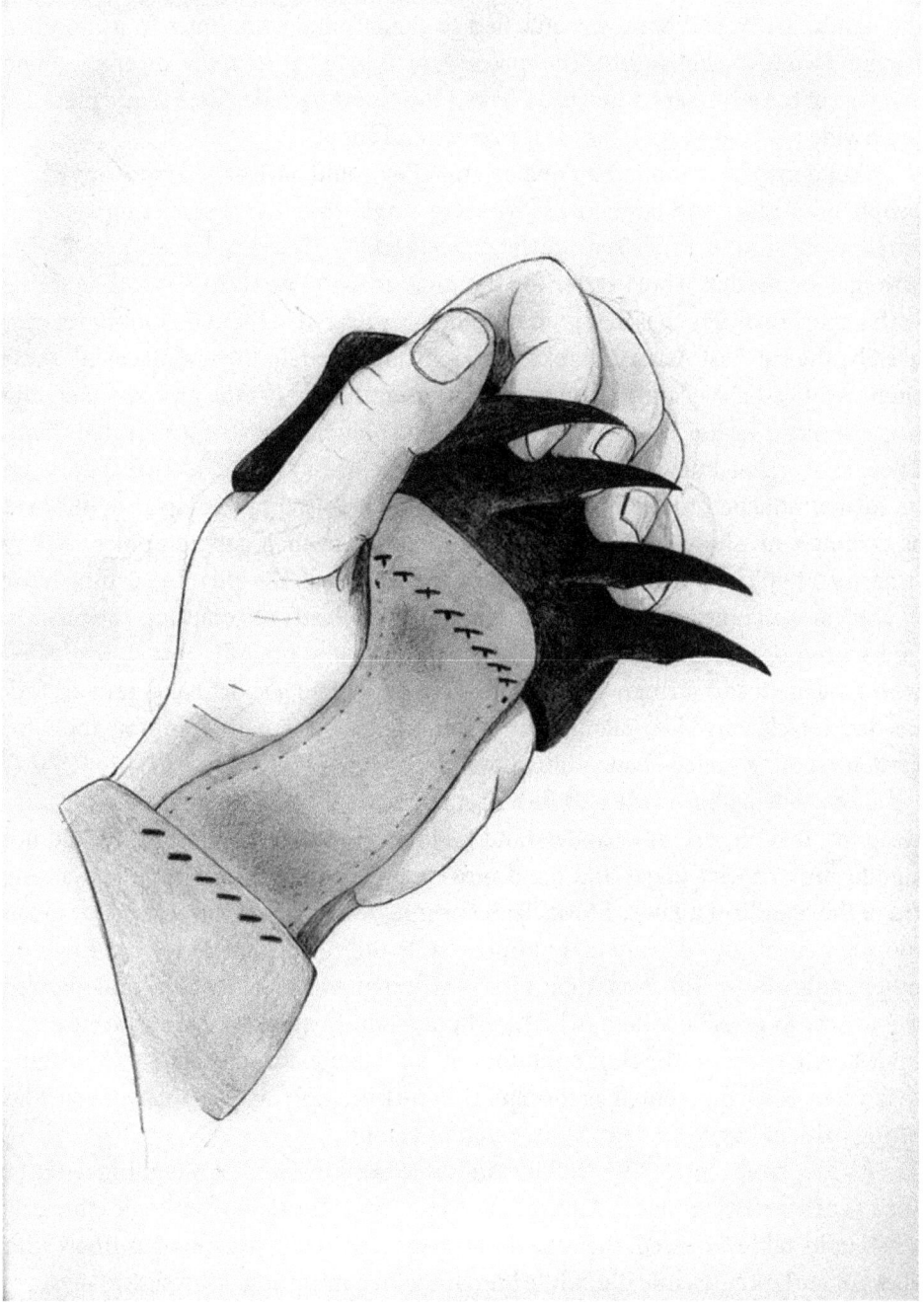

Fig. 40: Shuko with the claws emanating from the palm, with a leather strap keeping it attached near the wrists. These do not resemble the rake as much and functionally are closer to the claws of an animal such as a bear.

the hands. The metal base was attached to sandals and sometimes to a modified Japanese wooden clog or *geta*. The spikes were used to rip open the lower abdomen and legs of the adversary when used in kicking. Some varieties were made precisely to provide traction needed for escape on ice and snow.

Shuko may have more than one origin. They could have arisen from anywhere people used rakes and large forks. We were taught that divers collecting sponges, coral, shellfish and other sea life from reefs might have used such a tool. The rationale being that it was easier for the diver to swim wearing claws than doing with a short rake, which is likely what would have preceded them. In looking at gear used by the Far East Asian divers of the pacific, we can find the use of a small short single pronged claw called an *uni tori* (uni meaning *sea urchin*, and tori meaning *harvester*) and various utility knives, depending on what was being collected (Ir-4). These short rakes-like claws were sometimes attached to a cord, so that they could be further attached to the boat or floatation bucket used by the diver or the arm as is done with shuko. This tool is really no different than gaffing hooks used by fishermen to pick up large fish by hooking them through the gills. The gaffing hook is used in a manner resembling the shuko, which leads to tempting speculation of a shared origin. Another more likely source for the shuko is that it originated with gardeners and farmers who would have developed a short hand-rake or fork needed for clawing dirt, planting and seeding. These remain common tools for gardening today called "hand cultivators."

Those having both rake and fork properties are the most versatile as tools and weapons. It is important to understand that the band type shuko (Fig. 40) did not significantly restrict finger and hand movement; an important reason for getting rid of the handle of a rake or fork. Transforming the tool in this way made it much more practical, and considerably improved its utility and power for fighting and other applications. This was important for combat and working alike and allowed the wearer to grasp any item, whether slippery, thorny, hot, or having some other undesirable effect on the skin or clothes. It is probably not satisfactory to imagine that a tool of such potential as the shuko came from only one singular use such as lifting bales of hay in analogy to the pitchfork alone.

It's easy to speculate that shuko could have been inspired by watching wildlife, such as bears clawing logs or fishing in a stream, or by the sight of an eagle clutching a fish in its talons. Indeed, the rake itself seems inspired by watching animals with claws or antlers efficiently dig, while humans with contrastingly soft sensitive hands were really limited in this way. In fact, early Jomon people made rakes out of wood and antlers for tilling soil, which seems to corroborate these intuitive connections rather well. Animal claws are also fighting tools and it was likely such an observation that made evident their dual nature as survival/work tool and weapon. No doubt people of ancient times were very familiar with the devastating effect claws could have on an opponent after witnessing encounters with predators such as bears and tigers.

All martial arts traditions have their stories and myths regarding the history and origin of the implements they use. These stories vary by place and from the relationship of one tradition to another. So whether shuko came about from gardening tools and/or other tools inspired by animal claws, it is important to appreciate not only the potential truth behind these stories, but also the creativity and innovation they reflect. A convenient way to understand this point is to realize that a tool becomes a preferred Ninja weapon *because* of its diverse capability in both domains.

The Bow

Interestingly enough, the bow, though very ancient and primitive, has never lost a place in the contemporary Ninja arsenal even if it may have lost its prominence. Ninja understood that the more primitive a tool or weapon was, the more easily it could be made from common everyday materials. Ninja counted among their skills the ability to make tools and weapons. Today, the ability to make weapons from scratch using materials all around us amounts to a valuable survival skill. Such weapons lack monetary value and are easily destroyed or discarded after use. This practice is in keeping with Ninjutsu principles.

Today most would only consider the bow as a weapon for sport and hunting, all the while recognizing that it was once an essential weapon of the battlefield and could not have had such an enduring history without being very effective. There have been many forms of bow developed over the centuries. They vary in size, weight, and tension; they also vary according to the materials used to make them.

The bow favored throughout the Far East was the composite bow. Typically the Japanese made them from a hardwood core and multiple layers of bamboo laminated together. The materials were further tightly bound at certain points often with animal sinew or leather. The glue used to laminate bows varied with the culture. The best materials were those that resisted moisture and permitted elasticity of the bow. Good quality bows were also lacquered as a further measure to retard moisture and prolong life. The bow used by Ninja was much like the rest of their weapons in that they were concealable, simple and utilitarian. Although Ninja did not usually fight from horseback, the bow they used was of a smaller variety like that favored by mounted warriors from the Asian continent like the Mongols and the Northern Chinese tribes. The advantage of this kind of bow was that it was lighter and easier to transport and conceal, especially when the collapsible version was used.

Making high quality bows is a labor-intensive craft, and though the Ninja preferred strong durable weapons, sometimes out of necessity they used bows that were crude and intended for one single encounter at fairly close range. These simpler bows could be fashioned in a short period of time from common materials and were disposable. In general, however, Ninja used their hunting bows in combative operations, much like early American militiamen who used personal hunting rifles or muskets. These smaller bows were well suited for hunting game in woodland and meadow environments. Using such bows meant Ninja had continual practice and needed no special training to transition them for use as combat weapons. It was particularly important to gain experience hitting moving targets in highly varied and nocturnal conditions, as would be the case in actual fighting. Ninja also found ways to conceal arrows in natural places and on their person. This sometimes required that the arrows be shorter than the variety used by Samurai on the battlefield and it limited their range and accuracy.

Samurai used highly developed bows and excelled in archery, both on foot and on horseback. The technology used in making the Japanese bow is quite ancient and dates back to beginnings in the Jomon era. The traditions of *Kyujutsu* and *Kyudo* continue to be widely practiced in Japan. Other challenging arts, such as *Yabusame* (shooting targets from horseback in full gallop) and the art of *Yadomejutsu* (deflecting arrows) can be seen at popular festivals or *Omatsuri*. Yabusame dates from before Heian period, and was traditionally the subject of competitions. Like other martial arts practiced by bushi these are felt in contemporary society, to represent a high level of martial and spiritual refinement and exemplify certain aspects of the Japanese ethic and religious experience.

In Ninja tradition, martial arts are viewed with a high level of pragmatism and our current understanding is that Ninja did and do practice martial arts with an underlying interpretation of universal causality, but that the practice is not religious in the sense that that it is neither static nor very ritualized.

The Samurai codes endorse a life of service unfettered by petty desires and worldly concerns as the consummate expression of a life of purpose. Life must be simple and therefore dispassionate, thus liberating personal karma and permitting expression of one's being. This ethic and philosophy is memorialized beautifully in the Tea Ceremony. Worldly matters are things to be managed with an appropriate display of honor and dignity that reflect this understanding. Carried further, one of the purest experiences for the Samurai's spiritual growth was through a brush with death and in dying itself. Ethical and spiritual purity was sought through the ultimate sacrifice of one's life in service. Bringing great honor to the family name was its own reward.

In contrast, Ninjutsu tradition as we know it teaches that Ninja saw life itself as a reward, and only through living could one enjoy the spiritual benefits that life offers. Consistent with that view, Ninja have a core belief that the individual must live free from tyranny. Some Ninja had hard and strict lives and regarded martial arts as dangerous. These dangers were accepted as part of living fully. Thus, Ninja did not generally seek high refinement through the practice of any martial art; it was only a means to living free.

It is interesting how these divergent views are reflected in the differences between the weapons used by the Ninja and their Samurai contemporaries. The Ninja used weapons that were practical and utilitarian while the Samurai used refined weapons covered with symbols of superstition and their beliefs (such as the ornamented objects seen in religious and royal services).

It is widely known that Ninja used poisons with projectile weapons; the compounds used for these were originally developed for hunting larger game that could not be felled with a single arrow. The art of producing and using certain poisons was tested and practiced through hunting. Understanding that sudden death could come silently in this manner must have been a terrifying prospect for any potential victim. The psychological impact of an arrow coming from the darkness is not far removed from the modern experience of being the target of a sniper.

The bow had other applications for survival. It was used for trapping, fishing, starting fires, and even climbing, among other things. Simply detaching the cord at one end and putting bait on the line transformed the bow and string into a fishing rod. Anchoring the bow on shore permitted the user to fish while going off and attending to other tasks, which was not as labor intensive as fishing done by shooting arrows. In fact, we used this method during our training to live and survive in forests. Another variation on this theme is to use the flexible bow and string combined with a variety of knots and snares for trapping small game.

When a Ninja needed, for example, to cross an expanse of water or move from one tree to another without touching the ground, this could be accomplished by launching an arrow attached to a rope and hook such as the kaginawa, which could be secured at the shooter's end by the use of a special knot permitting retrieval of the rope after having crossed. These knots release or tighten according to which line is pulled. Another method would be to not secure the rope at the shooters end and then to swing down and across to the target area. The beauty of using arrows in this way was that the rope did not need to be swung in circles and arcs as would have been done with a grappling hook alone. To launch it across an expanse in this manner was an advantage in tight spaces and wherever there were a lot of surrounding branches or other obstacles.

An arrow fired into a tree does not typically have the strength to support the weight of a man. Therefore putting a grappling hook onto the head of the rope attached to the arrow or using a hook as the arrowhead itself was necessary. The arrow must be allowed to pass by the target then be pulled back and taught into place. Launching light grappling hooks with arrows provided greater range than swinging with arm power. Preparation and practice was important for this kind of work, because Ninja had to know in advance to use rope that was not too heavy, yet strong enough to bear weight. They knew to inspect their rope ahead of time to make sure it had not come unraveled or become frayed. When required, they created loops in the rope at intervals to facilitate climbing; most importantly, they had to know the range of the set-up. Ninja had methods for estimating range and knew how far an arrow with a rope could actually go.

Crossing water in extreme darkness, Ninja shot rope just above water level to guide their passage across to the exact spot they intended to go. As mentioned earlier when discussing the shoge, the rope assisted the use of the mizugumo and rafts. Note that grappling hooks were often bound in cloth to muffle their sound as they collided with targets and were dragged until into place.

Ninja were famous for nighttime assaults on fortresses and for helping to break sieges. For this task, they used burning arrows to rapidly set fires in a dispersed pattern. This distracted the enemy, enhancing the element of surprise and thus permitting attack while the enemy was busy responding to the fires. Fires created panic and confusion; Ninja took advantage of this and the smoke to cover their movements. They moved in close to the ground in in order to see better, avoid the heat and toxins and take advantage of cleaner and cooler air. Ninja sometimes wore specialized clothing called shozoku (Fig. 43) for this kind of work, which will be discussed in greater detail later. The shozoku had a hood and mask that protected against fire and smoke inhalation. Gauntlets worn on the forearms were in part adapted for archery and protected the skin from being injured by arrows and the bowstring. A glove was also worn for added protection. These types of assaults required that Ninja be specially trained in shooting the bow from different postures to permit use in unusual circumstances. Shooting while lying down, sitting and rolling, as is done today with guns and other projectile weapons was necessary when firing from positions of concealment.

Fukiya-Blowgun

A hunting weapon associated almost exclusively with Ninjutsu in Japan, but that is common in many other cultures, is the blowpipe or blowgun called *fukiya* (Fig. 41). The darts are called *fukibari*. Strategically it was employed in a way similar to the bow, especially in sniping unsuspecting enemies with poisoned darts. It was silent, compact, and accurate at relatively short range.

The blowgun or blowpipe was another weapon that was especially well adapted for hunting small game in the forest. Ninja blowpipes were generally small in size (though larger ones existed) and the fact that a blowpipe could be dismantled or disguised made it easier to conceal. The blowpipe could be made from common materials and incorporated into objects such as a flute, staff, sword scabbard, or smoking pipe. Modern versions are only limited by the imagination.

In comparison to the bow, fukiya were not as lethal; to enhance their effectiveness, poisoned darts were often used. Non-poisoned darts could also kill as long as the hit was accurate, but the risk associated with missing the target by even a small distance was great. The use of paralyzing poisons that stopped breathing or caused nearly instantaneous losses of consciousness was preferred. When employed in this manner, the fukiya was a weapon of capture and assassination. Darts could be fired through very small openings and were virtually silent. Ninja kept the poisons for their darts in small vials on their person. Darts and arrows were usually dipped into the poison just before use. This practice, as with shaken and shuriken, lessened the risk of accidental poisoning during handling. There were also ways to store poison in darts, such that it would only release on impact. This required different and special preparation before going into the field but actually saved time.

Materials such as bone, feather stems, certain types of wood, and the woody hollow stems of plants combined with rice paper were good for making darts. The cup in the back of the dart for catching the air was made of paper, but could also be fashioned from a leaf or thin bark. Adhesives made with resin (pine pitch) or cooked rice were used ubiquitously. Resin is very sticky when fresh, and also flammable. It is durable for a relatively short time after which it dries out completely and crumbles. Rice glue was more stable and reliable but could come apart when wet.

Fukiya were not used in open combat, they were used for operations requiring stealth, in which Ninja moved close to an unsuspecting target, or to silence dogs guarding a compound. To achieve longer range, some fukiya were increased in length. This, of course, would limit how easy they were to conceal; hence the need

Fig. 41: Ninja sniping an unsuspecting Samurai guard.

to make them so that they could be dismantled or reassembled.

In darkness, a blowpipe could be used against an attacker even when the user was in full view. At night it would be very difficult to tell if the adversary was carrying such a small weapon. In these circumstances a blowpipe could defeat a technically superior adversary armed with just about any weapon short of a firearm, provided that the soft tissue targets were hit. It is easy to understand how the fukiya have remained essential to the art of Ninjutsu.

Hunting Traps

As a special mention in this chapter, it is helpful to describe the use of hunting traps. Traps were extremely varied, and sometimes complex; the principles, however, were simple. They typically involved the use, combined or otherwise, of gravity and tension in cords and branches. The potential energy stored in a static system under tension generated the trap's movement. The release was a switch that unleashed the mechanism. In some cases, the tension was provided by the game itself, as in the case of a simple snare. Projectile weapons, such as shuriken, shaken, bow (and the related crossbow), nets, hooks, spear and Shoge all had applications in hunting traps.

Traps used against people utilized essentially the same methods as those for animals. Anyone knowledgeable about trapping understands that the location and type of set up chosen is very important and should take into consideration the behavioral profile of the game. Advanced knowledge of an enemy's tactics was very valuable to a successful outcome. The use of non-lethal traps took into account that the quarry would try to escape and/or signal for assistance. In such cases, it was necessary to find a way to lure them to a spot where aid was unlikely.

Some traps were designed to take on large groups. Multiple traps could release in series or sequentially. Traps could even be designed to produce a strong psychological effect on the enemy. They were used to give off signals of pursuit and for many other purposes. The most efficient traps were made easily, quickly, and from everyday materials. Part of the reason for this was that traps were disposable. The user generally did not intend to retrieve the materials. Despite the fact that some people thought traps to be underhanded or cowardly and that they should not be part of the conventional soldier's training, they were conceptually and philosophically in line with the doctrines of the *Art of War* by Sun Tzu, which admonished the warrior to win with the least struggle or fighting (1).

One of the main goals of Ninja strategy was to level the odds against a superior foe. The intelligent use of traps did just that. Bows and crossbows could be combined with traps to release arrows. This could confuse the enemy into thinking they were being fired upon by snipers. In this way, Ninja were sometimes able to create the illusion of greater numbers. People respond to what they perceive, not necessarily to what is actually there.

Various Specializations

By the time of its developmental apex, Ninjutsu was a seamless and coherent art. Many of its tools and techniques had migrated across region, society, and culture. This was also true of other combative systems around the world. What is perhaps unique about Ninjutsu, however, is the fact that its coherence was not just the result of the cultural influences from invasions or even trade bringing technologies together. It was the credo of the Ninja that made it what it was.

The art(s) of Ninjutsu were studied, developed, and integrated to the point that the principles contained therein made it into the formidable masterwork of fighting strategy for which it was reputed. Ninja actively sought knowledge of martial skills and found that they existed and correlated with the everyday activities of living. This fact made it ideal for covert purposes. Simple, everyday objects and activities could be made into the most natural of combative expressions by those who understood this principle. They would know the properties and potential of any "weapon" in their hand because it was a tool of their everyday work. In fact the object was only really a weapon when used as such; otherwise it was *only* a tool. It also meant that less time was spent in the formal training required to acquire weapons mastery. These themes remain manifest throughout current Ninjutsu practice.

Ninjutsu also became something of a repository for arcane arts of war. The Ninja never abandoned weapons and strategies that retained utility. As we have seen, they used methods and weapons that were indeed considered by some to be archaic. They only laid to rest those tools that had been definitively replaced by superior and accessible common technology. The gun and related weapons are a case in point. The Ninja now train only with or against modern firearms instead of muskets, even though a large part of the principles and strategies remained unchanged.

The contexts in which Ninja operated were essentially all those areas relevant to the collection of needed information or any venue or platform likely to influence events critical to them and their mission. Some Ninja dwelled and operated in urban settings, particularly during the Edo period, when populations in urban centers were exploding. Grandmaster Law pointed out many times to us that some historical Ninja operated as well-connected *Yakuza*. The Yakuza were analogous to the Western Mafia in many ways. They continue to be referred to as the Japanese Mob or Mafia in books and films. Their operations were ideal for collecting information on the street and also special insights on the habits and lifestyles of specific people. Nobles and merchants alike would pay handsomely for this kind of information when it was needed.

Organized criminal gangs ran extortion rackets, smuggling, prostitution, gambling, drugs (opium) and even murder for hire. These activities brought them into contact with powerful people of all kinds including politicians, military personnel, pirates, entertainers and sometimes subversive groups. Through such connections Ninja were able to obtain state-of-the-art weapons, tactical military manuals and intelligence, as well as rare goods, which could be used to pay off and extort others. It was in this domain that the boundaries between Ninja and unethical thieves were blurred. Some Ninja did not partake or reveal connections to these activities because they were viewed as self-serving and disloyal, thus weakening the trust a potential employer might have for them. Ninja groups dedicated to a single family or domain distanced themselves from these questionable elements of Ninja culture. Some took pains to associate themselves with religion as a way of changing the opinions of those who might seek to employ them.

Gangsters often lived double lives like their Western counterparts and with the right incentive served higher government authorities. In such cases they might report to a *han metsuke*. The word *han* referred to a clan territory or fief under a Daimyo, and metsuke can be defined as a political administrator in charge of law enforcement and management of social order within the clan's direct employ, extending to the commoners when the clan was affected (25). They were known to utilize people for gathering intelligence, some having groups of Ninja loyal only to them. This was not so different than the specialized police operations of today when officers go under-cover for law enforcement. Members of secret societies, be they criminal organizations or political ones, used layers of go betweens, secretive meeting places (often changing) and had places of refuge where they could hide from authorities.

A modern analogy to this practice would be the safe houses used by the various secret services or the hideouts operated by gangs. Ninja blended in with any trade including entertainers, or as those who arranged entertainment and ceremonies (in particular as monks). With this disguise they were able to gain access to the residences of important people and learn about their homes, the number and type of guards, and a wide variety of other personal and vital information. This happened because, monks, like priests in Western society, were spiritual guides and confidants of the people they served. The same was basically true for those posing, for example, as skilled tailors or kimono makers who would be called to the homesteads of wealthy clients.

The so-called "floating world" or *ukiyo* of pleasure seeking, where *kabuki* was found and entertainers such as geisha and various other artisans lived, was an ideal place to plant female spies known as *Kunoichi*. They were experts at collecting information using special methods of subtle interrogation, socializing, and plying people through trust by knowing a lot about their lives and getting them to talk about themselves. They used alcohol, seduction, or sometimes even cruel torture as the case required.

They used many disguises. As women living in a rigid patriarchy, they were generally not viewed as threatening to most males, who might relax their guard around them. They understood how to find the psychological weaknesses in their targets and exploited them to attain their objectives.

Some Kunoichi were known to marry into influential families and have extended relationships with the person or family on whom they were spying or even intending to kill. Ninja were known to plan well ahead. Sometimes it was required that an assassination take place at a specific time. Ninja could wait years, living patiently under an assumed identity, until the time came to strike. Otherwise they might spend years slowly poisoning their intended target who was by then believed to be suffering from an intractable illness.

Aspects of various entertainment arts were incorporated into the methodology of certain Ninja groups and were even expressed in their combat skills. We were taught that Ninja learned skills from entertainers able to act and perform magic tricks. This was especially exploited by Ninja, both in non-combative ways and, at times, in combat as well. Magic is essentially a way of deceiving the perceptions of others. Ninjutsu fighting skills and tactics exploited this strategy as much as possible.

Samurai warriors also aspired to be inscrutable in their movement and strategy, but did not rely upon trickery as heavily as Ninja. Many Ninja and Samurai warriors worshiped the Buddhist cult of *Marishiten*. This deity was popular with warriors because she was believed to enhance the fighting skills of those who followed her and provided them with the capability to be invisible in their intent and to confuse the minds of their enemies. Worshipping an actual deity with these assumed powers indicates the importance attributed to skills of this kind. Those wishing to know more about Marishiten and her importance to Japanese warrior culture will find an interesting discussion on the subject written by David A. Hall in the book *Koryu Bujutsu: Classical Warrior traditions of Japan* Edited by Dianne Skoss (14).

Disguised Ninja would have been readily ferreted out unless able to convincingly play the part their disguise and role demanded. The ability to assume an identity and elicit certain reactions in others was an essential skill Ninja learned through acting. Many entertainers' livelihood depended on this ability. Often it had to be maintained under stressful conditions and the stakes were highest for the Ninja in the field.

Entertainers, be they magicians or otherwise, were rarely held in high regard in the Far East and except for the most accomplished artisans this meant association with the lower classes among whom the Ninja often belonged and felt quite comfortable.

The *Kugutsu* represent a group with whom Ninja were believed to have been associated. The word Kugutsu means puppet in Japanese. It has been suggested that this group of people were descended from wandering nomads that lived all across Central Asia and who traveled the Silk Road, eventually finding their way to Japan. Their name became the word "puppet" by association, as it was the craft of puppetry for which they were most renowned. This included the famous *Bunraku*, puppeteers who wore distinctive black and very Ninja-like apparel, which made them nearly invisible on stage and allowed them to operate in the background.

Another suggestion was that the Kugutsu came from groups of displaced aboriginal clans that were forced to travel the land and subsist on their entertainment skills. There is even a legend that the famous younger brother of the first Shogun *Minamoto No Yoritomo, Minamoto No Yoshitsune*, during the 12th century, who was being hunted in the aftermath of the Gempei War, traveled in secret with such a group to reach Oshu from Mount Kurama. After the annihilation of their rivals the Taira clan, the Minamoto family hunted down Yoshitsune, who apparently was a key figure in the success of the Minamoto securing the power of the Shogunate and founding the Kamakura Bakufu.

There are additional stories and myths about this pursuit, and how a Sohei by the name of *Musashibo Benkei* aided Yoshitsune. The old myths and stories that the legendary Tengu and *Sojobo* trained Yoshitsune on Mount Kurama are steeped in Ninja lore. Sojobo has been characterized as the "king of the *Tengu*." He is often drawn and represented as a Yamabushi, as are most of the Tengu themselves.

The mythical Tengu are reputed to be those who developed and guarded the secret arts of the Ninja and those of other martial arts as well. The same is said of the Yamabushi. If there is any truth behind some of these myths, then this period would denote a time when there was greater contact between the early versions of Ninjutsu martial arts, those of the bushi and some ascetic groups.

Entertainment groups who practiced puppetry and magic, which could have included other arts like alchemy, tended to be involved in many types of performance, as is seen today with circuses. Comedy with clowns, fortune and storytelling, music, and tightrope walking were among their many talents. Fortune and storytelling appear especially well suited for the transmission of intelligence.

Many such groups were impoverished. Perhaps not surprisingly, their main source of livelihood was hunting and fishing. Early accounts of these people portray them as having no agricultural practices, as having no loyalty to any lords or administrations, pursuing late-night religious ceremonies to their own gods, and showing open disrespect for the authorities (15).

These descriptions imply a great deal about whom these people really were and who they came to be. Nocturnal religious practices may conjure images of witches and Satanism in the West, but would have nothing to do with the practices described here. During the repression of Christianity in Japan during the 17th century, Christians also worshipped at night so as not to attract the attention of the authorities. If these people were indeed oppressed and displaced aboriginals or secretive nomads, it becomes easier to understand their lifestyle and relegation to the lowest classes. Even the now revered Bunraku was advanced by members of among the lowest social class, the *Eta*.

The skills of a Kugutsu could earn the savvy character quick money needed to survive in urban environments. These skills were also used for swindling and theft. Such practices were highly valued in some circles and could help to get a Ninja initiated into a gang or group into which they could blend. This might be desirable if the Ninja's task involved getting information via the underworld. The underworld, then as today, was for hire to the highest bidder and was often called upon to do unpleasant things that the wealthy or well-known patrons could not risk. Vital intelligence could gain a victory for the Ninja without the slightest amount of physical violence.

Gangs also controlled the prostitution trade. Information could be collected through these resources in a similar way to that performed by the much more sophisticated Kunoichi but with less reliability. Ninja were able to persuade lackeys to do their bidding through the promise of various rewards and, if necessary, threats. Such individuals could be used to test the defenses of targeted places and people as well as to assess the vigilance of the authorities. It is during the Edo period, after the end of the great wars, that Ninja were rumored to have been employed for the pursuit of the intimate and personal political agendas of ambitious and typically wealthy clients. This era and context was where we see the highest development of the *kakushibuki* or small-concealed weapons. Ninja were expert in this kind of weaponry. These are sometimes confused with *Ningu*, which are in fact "Ninja tools" that are of course both tools and weapons.

Similar terms that touch on this theme are *hibuki*, "secret weapons" and *shikomibuki*, "trick weapons" (6, 21) and *Mijikimono*, "common items one would wear." All these terms have slightly different meanings and are technically somewhat different as well. The shikomibuki are weapons that are concealed within everyday objects and thus disguised. This is a common feature of Ninja weapons, which are intended to go unnoticed even when carried about casually. As a matter of perception, it should be pointed out that any implement that is only recognized as a tool but has potential as a weapon should be considered by definition a concealed weapon, even when it is not specifically modified. Certain tools of the Ninja arsenal became popular in the Edo period with the strict implementation of the caste system. With only Samurai and specifically honored professions such as physicians and law enforcement officers of a certain rank allowed to carry swords, commoners needed weapons that could help even the odds if caught in a fight with a swordsman.

Implicit to the arts of using kakushibuki are several other martial arts practices, these are: *mutodori, shiharadori, atemijutsu* and *kyushojutsu*. Mutodori meaning "no sword" is the art of disarming an attacker who has drawn their sword. Shiharadori is the art of "catching live blades" (6), which is not what the name would imply in most instances. Mutodori and shiharadori are different terms for essentially the same thing. Note that most techniques in these arts do not involve actually *catching* a sword, but instead employ methods for immobilizing an attacker's ability to use one.

Ninja spent a good deal of time training in *Atemi*, popularly known as "striking" in the West. The art of atemijutsu involves understanding all of the different methods of how to strike specific points of the body that are vulnerable to attack and which yield a unique advantage. The vital points are called *kyusho*. Calling them "vital" is to some extent misleading, because most of them do not lead to death when attacked. There are many in number and kind. There are vascular, neurological/sensory, skeletal, deep organ systems and even endocrinological (e.g., the thyroid gland) points. Some were used for psychological control, as through the use of pain, but inflicted little or no permanent physical harm; others were sometimes used to cause either definitive or temporary disability in opponents.

Some had instantaneous effects, while others caused a delayed effect. These arts also involved knowledge of how to cover and protect one's own vulnerable spots as well as knowing how to properly expose them and which parts of the body to use to attack them. For atemi some body parts needed to be conditioned for striking, while others were naturally tough enough for the task. The subjects of atemijutsu and kyushojutsu are highly complex and well beyond the scope of this text. For our purposes here it suffices to understand that the small-concealed implements of the Ninja as with empty hand fighting were especially well suited for enhancing atemi and kyusho attacks.

Small-concealed weapons continued to be used well after the abolition of the Samurai class. As citizens of the new Japan were not permitted to bear arms openly, they resorted to other strategies for self-defense. The salient advantage of these implements was the fact that they maintained the element of surprise. This was particularly important for any tool used in combat, whether the strategy was attack or defense. Due to their small size, and when combined properly with well-executed taijutsu and related atemi, some of these weapons were difficult to detect by witnesses, extending the concept of concealment as not only applying to the enemy but also to onlookers.

Witnesses and juries today are often reluctant to believe that the aggressor could be a person of lesser stature or strength. They might find it equally hard to believe that a slight or tiny female for example, could defeat a much larger and stronger opponent. This imbalanced perception was known to Ninja and was used to give the enemy the false expectation that they were dealing with an easy target. As a corollary to this line of thinking, the greater the perceived imbalance of power, the greater the advantage of surprise. For this reason, Ninja made extensive use of kakushibuki for small-scale confrontations.

Ninja exploited the strategy of creating a perceived power imbalance further by employing children. Ninja trained from early childhood. By young adolescence they were already formidable fighters. At this young age, they would accompany the older Ninja on missions, gradually and increasingly participating in clandestine operations. As soon as they were competent in their skills, they were employed.

Children also enhanced the disguise of traveling Ninja. As with women, children were not perceived as threatening and in fact would be dismissed by others as a burden to a warrior on some kind of mission. But by this age, Ninja were already adept at eavesdropping, spying, and other methods of gathering intelligence. According to Grandmaster Law, Ninja children and sometimes adults were taught to present themselves as intellectually impaired or of diminished capacity as another way to get others to let down their guard around them, since such persons were likely to be considered incapable of comprehending what was being said in their presence.

Due to their small size, lesser weight, and greater flexibility, children were better able to climb into buildings and move through confined spaces where they could steal information, eavesdrop, spy, set traps, and even kill just as their adult mentors did. Entering enemy strongholds would also permit them to prepare the way for other Ninja to gain access. By the time Ninja reached adulthood they were experienced agents and masters of their trade.

All Ninja, regardless of the setting in which they operated, needed to understand

140

signaling and gathering intelligence as part of survival and espionage. The type of signal used depended on the identity they were assuming and the situation in which they operated. A signal had to be ordinary enough to blend into the environment and unusual enough to stand out for the anticipating observer. This worked as long as the person receiving the signal was trained enough to know what to look for. Signals could include ribbons, clothing items sometimes indicating the presence of hidden messages, which were typically coded, and which, if discovered would seem to convey something meaningful but unrelated. A hidden nonsense message aroused more suspicion than one left for a benign secret. The Ninja had their own written characters and methods of hand signaling as well. Their hand signaling was not very different conceptually from the modern sign language we use to communicate with the deaf. Ninja were also able to read lips. Both these techniques permit silent communication and leave no evidence that such communication had taken place. The other obvious benefit was that a deaf individual or one who has lost or needs to conceal their voice is still able to communicate. Note that the Ninja could still do these things without giving away their identity. Hand signals and lip reading were performed, of course, with a direct visual on the person conveying the information, typically while disguised.

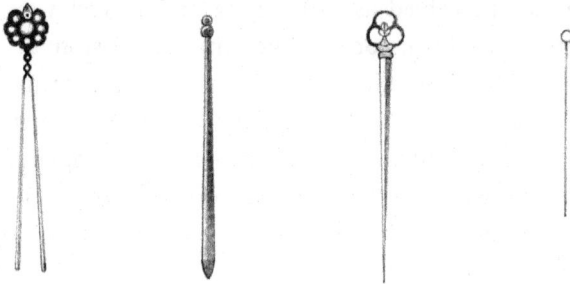

Fig. 42: Various ornamental Kanzashi.

Other Ninja weapons considered kakushibuki or as hibuki are an array of pins and hair ornaments known as *kanzashi* (Fig. 42) and short stabbing weapons called *kaiken*. Kanzashi included very fine needles used both medicinally and as weapons. Ninja also had an effective knowledge of acupuncture. This is analogous to the way that they used toxins both as a weapon and as medicine.

Traditional Japanese hairstyles involved assortments of ornaments. These included pins with or without tassels, combs and ribbons. Depending on their relative thickness and length, pins could be used to conceal written information and even substances within their ornamentation. The Kunoichi were especially adept with these kinds of weapons and the strategies associated with their use. Hair ornaments were found in very ancient societies, and like other ornaments adorning the head were usually associated with social status. Such ornamentation could indicate for example whether a woman was unwed, wed, or widowed. This meant that Ninja had to be aware of the styles of the prevailing culture in an area when deciding what tools to choose for their disguise, and what kind of disguise would serve best. In some cases these ornaments certainly appeared as though they were designed with self-defense in mind.

The kaiken were no more than very short and small often needle-like daggers that were also used as concealed weapons by women and some men where necessary. They reached usually no more than 8 inches and they bore no ornamentation. They generally resembled very short tanto, others may have resembled kugigata shuriken.

Clothing: Obi, Ribbons and the Shozoku

Examining how Ninja used clothing, we see a whole microcosm of diverse strategies under this theme. Disguises were naturally a major element here. It is widely accepted that Ninja operated primarily in disguise and only for specific needs did they wear the shozoku (Fig. 43). Outside of the standard seven disguises mentioned in a number of historical sources on Ninjutsu including children's books on the subject, Grandmaster Law taught that Ninja used any disguise necessary to get their job accomplished. By disguise, it should be clarified that we are referring to an assumed identity and this is to be distinguished from disguising one's presence entirely or as that of an object or animal. Conceptually, a disguise should be thought of as a form of social camouflage because its purpose is to hide the appearance and intent of the individual and thereby their true and actual identity.

The seven standard disguises were intended primarily for the purpose of travel, not necessarily the more refined task of getting close to an intended target. They were as follows: *Komuso* (priest of the *Fuke* sect of Zen), *Shuke* (ordinary Buddhist priest), *Yamabushi* (Mountain acetic, see chapter 1), *Shonin* (merchant), *Hokashi* (magician, entertainer or acrobat), *Sarugakukushi* (dancer), and *Tsune-no-kata* (ordinary commoner, which could include a Samurai/Ronin). Most of these disguises were chosen because they were based on common people whose lifestyle included travelling from community to community, and as such were not unusual or suspicious. Note that one of the seven is the "commoner," which, of course encompassed many potential identities (17, 20).

We were taught that Ninja had to know how to actually make their disguises. In some cases, as would be the situation today, the clothing could be purchased anonymously, but not in every case. Ninja therefore, like many commoners of that time, knew at least some basic sewing. This knowledge could allow a Ninja to disguise himself as a tailor. However, to successfully assume that role or any other, he had to be competent or even expert in any trade he chose to impersonate. Otherwise he would not gain the attention and employment to get where he needed to be.

Using tools of the common man was not necessarily helpful for a Ninja unless they were able to convincingly play and look the part of the person who actually used those tools. A more sophisticated disguise technique was the ability to wear clothes the right way and appear natural when doing so.

In some trades a Ninja could not simply show up in a town, hang a shingle and make a living in some trade. They had to have a believable story. Ninja were known to use forgery to make documents of licensure and letters of introduction that could get them into the graces of established houses with reputations. The story had to incorporate a blend of true information with falsehood that fabricated circumstances to justify their presence. Today this is called disinformation. In cases like this, the Ninja agent would be fed information from a superior who had access to intelligence needed to get them started. Once set to work however, the individual agent decided when and how to do what they were sent for. Carrying the example of a tailor further, it was then that small implements like needles, which were part of the tailor's working retinue, became the weapon of choice.

Often Ninja did not operate under such an elaborate scenario. When necessary they would weave a story on the fly that was, of course, false, but which bought them the time to do what they needed before anyone was able to check or realize that something was suspicious.

In line with this overall strategy, we were taught that Ninja therefore used clothing to cleverly conceal small weapons on their person for use when they closed in on their target. Allegedly some Ninja were able to even conceal needles in their mouths and were able to spit them at their adversary (6). It's hard to imagine how much a person would have to train to make this an effective combat strategy! In terms of spitting, we were taught instead to spit substances that were not strong enough to be corrosive in the mouth but acidic or spicy enough to burn or irritate the eyes. Coating the spitter's mouth in vegetable oil will reduce the impact of a substance there, as long as the substance is water based. However, a substance that mixes with oil will make it harder to remove and prolong the effect. Just as with the shaken and shuriken, the Ninja were aware of the potential for self-harm associated with their various tools. Pins were easily concealed in many places on their person, and could even be thrown very short distances or used hand-to-hand. Their virtue, like all other weapons in their class, was that they were difficult to detect by the enemy.

The Ninja also used articles of clothing such as the ribbon and the sash as weapons. These were used in a similar context where the Ninja was close to a target they intended to kill or capture. But ribbons were used for other purposes such as to pass on information, at times using color-coding, location and frequency. As a weapon they were used essentially like ropes, for strangulation, and hojojutsu. Ribbons could be combined with other concealed weapons in improvisational ways. Sashes, which are essentially larger ribbons, were combined with the sword or staffs and used for creative methods of probing around in the dark. This was done in such a way that the weapon could be instantly deployed the moment the target/obstacle was encountered.

The *Obi*, a long wide sash wrapped around the waist for wearing the Kimono was used as a weapon and for stealthy movement where it served to muffle footfalls when Ninja laid it over gravel or dry leaves. In such cases it was sometimes necessary to wet the obi. If water was unavailable, it could be soaked with urine. This was one of the ways that the flat broad shape of the obi gave it unique features not available with ropes. One way to use the obi as a weapon was to wrap a stone or other solid object into it, tie it, and handle it like a weighted chain. It did not, of course, have the strength, weight or resistance to cutting of a chain, but it would wrap around any adversary in a way applicable to combat. Its capacity for wrapping, tensile strength, and inherent applied traction made it strong enough to support the weight of a man and useful for applications as varied as an improvised cast for a fractured limb or a tool for climbing a tree. Only the length and the material from which obi and sashes were made limited the versatility of their use. Otherwise, they retained many of the characteristics of the universal rope.

To further illustrate the technical similarities and distinctions between ropes, ribbons, and sashes, it helps to discuss the rope tying arts a little further. The art of hojojutsu was an essential element of warrior culture throughout Japan. Hojojutsu was practiced in all complete martial traditions. From the ancient periods through the modern reforms, hojojutsu was combined with the weapons of open combat on the battlefield and also with the covert operations of Ninja. While it was commonly known as a method for the Samurai on the battlefield and for those charged with the task of law enforcement, hojojutsu was also a dreaded and deadly form of torture used for interrogation employed by the Samurai and Ninja alike.

The Ninja agent usually hid rope on their person for all manner of uses. Advantages of the rope are many, but mention of a few of the more significant applications is helpful to emphasize the reason why hojojutsu evolved to the level of complexity that it did.

When properly used, the rope afforded the ability to exert various levels of control over the enemy and applications such as rapid neutralization, immobilization, pain, and transient to sustained injury, and death.

Generally speaking, Ninja did not use the same degree of complexity found in the hojojutsu techniques of the classically trained Samurai. Samurai were bound by strict codes of conduct according to rank that were at least known among their peers and their tying methods could reveal from which tradition they had learned the art or to which clan they belonged. They tied persons of different rank, gender and age in different ways required by the captive's social standing as a matter of respect or lack thereof. Samurai and law enforcement officials also used rope of a specific thickness and color. Thinner ropes and twine were more painful and injurious. Twine was particularly crude and unacceptable for use by a warrior with social standing. It was also unacceptable to tie a respected captive with it. By the same token using a ribbon, sash or obi to tie a captive was not what a respected warrior would use unless it was an emergency.

Given the covert nature of Ninja activities, they engaged in methods that were practical and expedient. Ninja would use the same knots to bind enemies as they would to make footholds in their climbing rope. Ninja paid little or no attention to the rank of their captives, unless it was specifically required by the nature of their assignment. Using twine and painful thin rope was a matter of course for Ninja. A rope could be fashioned under even crude conditions using ubiquitous plants and animal parts (such as strips of hide, tendon, hair and sinew). Ropes required little actual practice for Ninja to use because they were employed ubiquitously and daily like a pen or a pocketknife might be for someone today and therefore were deeply understood. As such, they were not regarded as weapons unless in the hands of an experienced warrior and they did not arouse suspicion in the past any more than they would today. Ropes were used by all households and by most trades. They were combined effortlessly with nearly all Ninja combat methods and tools.

As in some of the Samurai traditions, the Ninja practiced techniques to bind multiple enemies and to carry captives. There was little overall substantial difference between the core techniques of hojojutsu as practiced by the Samurai and those used by Ninja. The arts of hojojutsu have been slowly dying out and are practiced in depth by only a few extant ryu-ha.

As many Ninja communities were in the mountains, often isolated from outsiders, Ninja families learned to weave, dye, and stitch their own specialized garments. Ninja did make clothes with hidden pockets and folds into which they could conceal anything they needed to: information, medicine, food and weapons. The clothes of commoners or members of the working or so-called peasant classes were inexpensive and easy to obtain. They required little specialized knowledge to make. These clothes were easily modified to possess hidden capabilities useful to Ninja.

Leaving as little as possible to chance, and realizing that survival in large part depended on intelligent preparation, Ninja clothing was considered a form of survival gear. They understood that bearing weight slowed and tired them and that this problem was resolved by having objects fit the body as comfortably and closely as possible.

Ninja used their understanding of rope tying and textiles to configure ways to carry objects, sometimes for long distances and through awkward conditions.

They made special features in their clothes to protect against extremes of cold, humidity and the effects of smoke and fire. It is with these features in mind that we can discuss aspects of the shozoku.

In modern dramatizations, Ninja wear black (or gray or rusty brown if the producers are trying to be realistic) clothing strapped to their body with hoods fashioned in a variety of ways, sporting secret pockets in which to hide their concealed weapons. This depiction, as already noted, was not completely divorced from historical reality as best we can tell. In those cases where Ninja did wear camouflage, of which the shozoku was a version, it was usually a reversible piece of clothing that was easily converted into conventional clothing. In this manner it served as both camouflage and disguise combined.

However, the shozoku was not limited to this popularly depicted form of dress. Ninja camouflage was rarely black. Black casts a shadow in all but the darkest conditions. We were taught by Grandmaster Law that Ninja from different groups preferred different colors for their shozoku with a fairly limited range of possibilities. Some preferred blue, others reddish-brown. The camouflage of our group was either moonlight gray or blue. A sort of mottled reddish brown was also sometimes used. The dyes used for these garments were made with extracts from a variety of earthen dyes, vegetables, seeds, and tree bark.

Layering was a very important element of the shozoku. The near full body covering and up to three layers of the shozoku protected against irritants such as thorny shrubs, spiders and stinging and biting insects. Since, Ninja used methods of stealth and infiltration at night, mosquitoes could be a real source of suffering. The shozoku protected against smoke, fire and humidity by virtue of these layers. The outermost layer being larger and baggier created a dead air space separating environmental contact from the inner layers. This was very warm while Ninja operated in cold mountain air.

The head coverings served to muffle coughing, sneezing, heavy breathing and the sweaty smell associated with physical exertion. The layers also tended to prevent blood from dripping and leaving a trail. Parts of the outside layer could be removed in order to make a carrying device, tourniquet, sling, or improvised cast. As mentioned earlier, Ninja carried their weapons and tools between clothing layers to minimize noise, friction and the need to carry them by hand or in a sack.

When concealed in the mud, the covering over the mouth provided a pocket or space for breathing, and prevented it from entering the mouth. The rest of the head covering protected against sweat getting into the eyes. The cloth above the eyes and over the nose was often folded to provide a thicker barrier when needed and a visor if necessary. Ninja moving through underbrush could get cuts and scrapes, which could give away the Ninja's nocturnal activities when the head and the rest of the coverings were removed and they had to return to their assumed identity.

There were other applications for related textiles like sheets and clothes. When a rope-like tool was needed, most textiles like sheets and clothes could be torn or twisted into ribbons. Depending on the material, the ribbon could be doubled or rapidly braided to provide the necessary strength for activities such as climbing or remaining suspended. Part of Ninja combative training also involved ways in which to use clothes and household textiles, both for defense and for attack and capture. This was explored to some extent above in the discussion on the net. There are examples where textiles were used to cause very smoky and smoldering fires, and could be soaked in volatile chemicals that release when exposed to steady heat. They were used to create visual barriers in darkness and signals that were not easily understood when observed.

Fig. 43: Ninja in shozoku using a shoge.

Tabi

A very special feature of Ninja clothing and gear was their *tabi* (Fig. 44). Tabi are a form of footwear that, in some cases, resemble a sock and in others a boot (though not in the conventional sense). They are still used today by many Japanese for usual day-to-day living, but not generally in the workplace. They are worn either as part of formal or traditional attire, or casually around the home. Their special feature is a glove-like split for the big toe, separating it from the other digits. This feature confers greater freedom of movement but also makes it easier to wear sandals without as much chaffing of the skin. As was their practice, Ninja altered tabi and sandals for very specific purposes. Ninja made tabi specially designed for stealth.

In general, Ninja spent most of their time barefoot. Their feet became rugged and tough, which of course helped enhance kicking and sweeping techniques. On many operations Ninja went barefoot, but when required to move in very close proximity to others it was necessary to take extra precautions and control anything that could make noise. This, of course, included the sounds produced by clothing, breathing and feet. Associated with the use of tabi, Ninja often wore leggings (*kyahan*), which are a sort of short cloth wrapped and tied around the lower leg and shins, combined with either short indoor tabi or a longer boot like tabi that fit the leg rather like a glove or long sock. In our school the longer boot-like tabi are preferred and leggings were used at times to add an extra layer of protection, warmth and a place in which to conceal objects. But one of the main purposes of leggings and layers wrapped around the limbs was to prevent clothes from rubbing during movement and thereby reduce unwanted noise. It is important to mention that sound reduction is not merely to avoid making noise that would be heard by others but also to not mask environmental sounds and enable the ability of the wearer to hear the surroundings.

The leggings and long tabi were also intended to cover any exposed ties from underlying clothing. Uncovered ties or knots could create problems during stealth operations requiring penetration into enemy terrain where traps or tight spaces might snag any protruding loops or excess clothing. We were taught to fold the ties over and inward to reduce any protrusion. Anyone having moved through bush and thick forest at night can appreciate this point. Broad or large movements caused by struggle with underbrush create a lot of noise that can be easily heard or seen by others. Mistakes such as these might result in capture or death for field operatives.

The specialized long tabi of the Ninja were double layered. There was an inner and outer layer. Between the two, at the sole, there was duck down, cotton or horsehair as padding to cushion footfalls. Duck down was sometimes preferred because it was water resistant. The tabi were made of fine and supple leather from the hide of a newborn or unborn calf that had been worked and softened to the point that it was like a second layer of skin. Ninja sometimes accentuated their stealth by wetting their clothes, including the tabi. After use, the inner tabi could later be everted from the outer tabi to dry. The leather could then be worked again so as not to shrink and lose its softness.

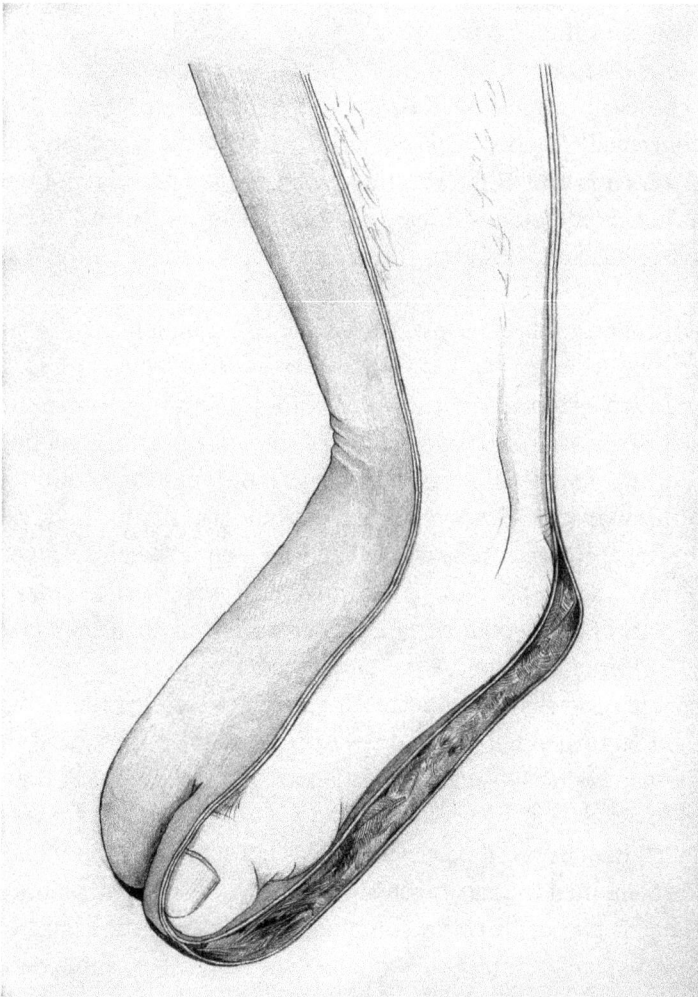

Fig. 44: Double-layered boot tabi with duck down.

Kakushi and Kakushibuki

Kakushi can have different meanings according to how you write it. It seems common in Japanese martial arts to find names for things that have multiple meanings or implications by the sound and pronunciation of the words. It is interesting that *kakushi* means "horned finger," a term used synonymously with kakute "horned hand," but kakushi also literally translates as "pocket," add the word *buki* as "weapons" or "arms" and you have the word *kakushibuki*, or "pocket weapons," also meaning "concealed weapons" as kakusu means "to hide and conceal." While these words are spelled differently in Japanese, the play on words phonetically borders on amusing. Kakushibuki is a generic term used to refer to any small and concealed weapons. There is also the use of the word *kaku* as meaning "to scratch," which is one of the meanings we were taught this tool was used for (see below). Just as there are overlapping meanings to this word there are many overlapping technical and strategic principles to consider for all these weapons as a category.

The kakushi are odd weapons fashioned from a simple ring that has small spikes protruding from it (Fig. 45). While they appear to have originated from a ring that was then deviously transformed into a painful instrument, they more likely have a history as multipurpose tools used by lay people including builders, farmers, fishermen and others for making markings, punctures and for grasping anything slippery or wet. They enhance a person's grip significantly, rather like a shuko for the finger instead of the whole hand. This could be useful when climbing a tree, handling things in the rain, or anytime a sure grip was necessary. Fighting a naked and sweaty enemy would be easier using a kakushi. Fighting in wet weather, hooking the koshirae (handle) of the enemy Samurai's katana, and/or making a really strong foe drop his weapon are all ways in which a kakushi was helpful. The ring could be turned inward or outward so that the points faced the palm or outward in a manner not unlike that of a brass knuckle, but made only to fit one finger or the thumb.

Like the kaginawa described earlier, it was used as a weapon in close quarter fighting often combined with an attached rope or twine cord. The points on the ring usually numbered two or three. In combination with taijutsu, kakushi were used to prevent escape and to inflict severe pain especially when applying atemi. The techniques of submission used with this weapon were frequently combined with rope tying methods to bind, ensnare, and immobilize an enemy. This composite

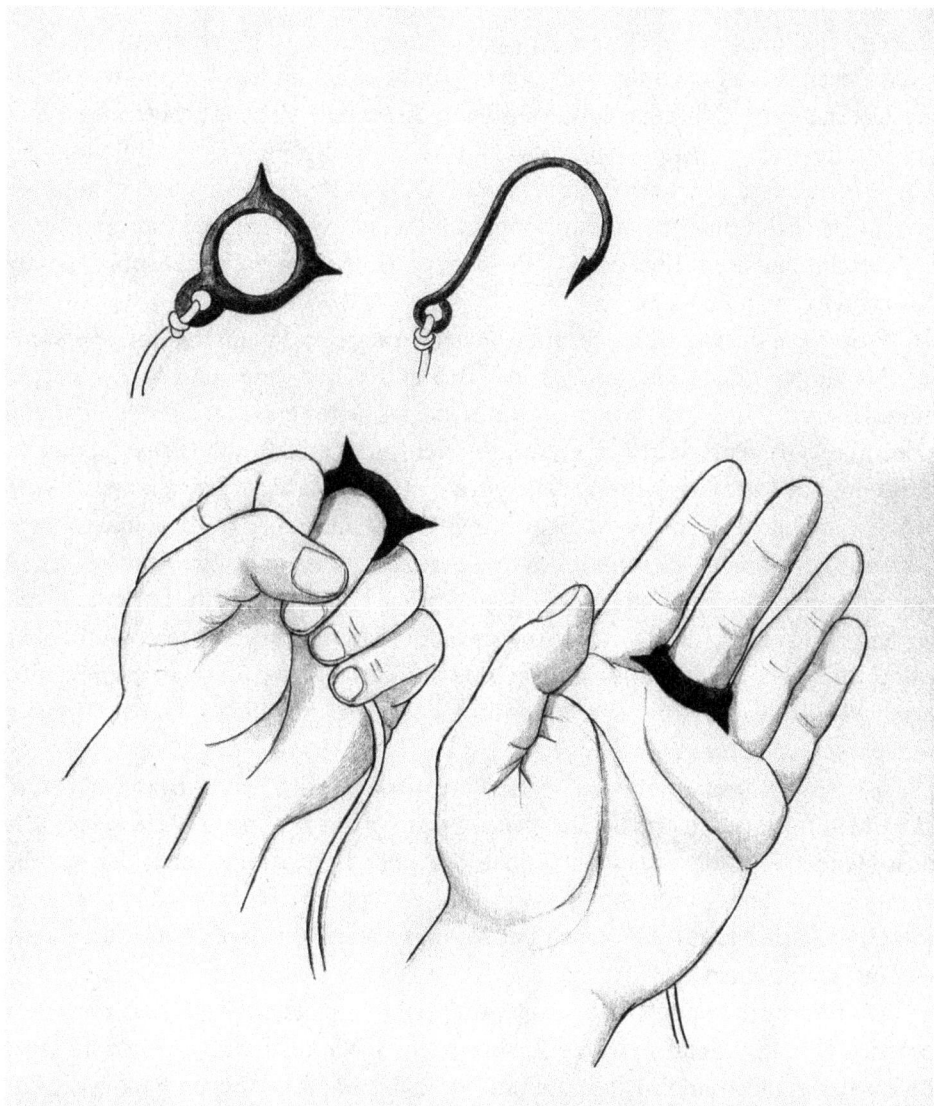

Fig. 45: Kakushi or kakute, one version, where the points are at off angles, so as to fit snugly into the fingers when not in use. The points can be oriented in nearly any direction with this type, making them more versatile. The kaginawa is presented for comparison.

capability combines features of the shuko with those of the kaginawa. When attached to a rope the kakushi could be swung like any other flexible weapon in order to facilitate ensnaring, but it packed little substantial capability to injure on impact even if the blow might stun or be painful. Though this weapon was by no means exclusive to Ninjutsu, it was used and associated with the art because it met the criteria of easy concealment, portability and effectiveness in the purposes for which it was used. Even when used in a street fight, if a witness wasn't able to see the nature of the ring, the amount of pain inflicted would appear disproportional to the technique used. The bearer of the kakushi would therefore appear immensely powerful to any onlookers.

We believe the kakushi to be quite ancient and we are taught that early versions were made of bone, antler and wood. Bone and antler were actually a preferred material even though they were nowhere near as strong as steel. Since the bone kakushi was used primarily for grasping softer things and on soft tissue in combat, it did not need to be that strong. There were other advantages as well. Some types of bone are harder than wood, lighter than metal and more comfortable to wear because they rapidly acquired body temperature. Bone and wood do not make the same noise as metal when clashing with hard objects. Finally, bone does not expand and contract in the same way metal does under different temperatures or wood when wet or dry. Bone was also used to make a variety of other implements, especially for people working around water because it often floats, making it easier to retrieve and harder to lose.

It is our understanding that written records are said to confirm the arrival of kakushi techniques in the Samurai Bugei during the Edo period. However, it is possible that Samurai warriors who had this knowledge did not consider it to be of much significance until the Edo period when fighting styles started to change in ways that emphasized more individualized combat and the need to seize an enemy without killing them.

We believe that along with many other daily implements and tools the art or practice of using them may date further back in Ninjutsu, but we have no clear means to demonstrate this. The opinion for this is in part based on what we know Ninja did for a living for centuries before this knowledge was shared with other external sources.

In what regards kakushibuki in general, it is necessary to view them as a category with their own associated strategy and purpose. The art of forcing an enemy into submission is called *torite*, and it exists in many schools of classical jujutsu, WuShu and various modern budo. We also see that during the Edo period many martial styles were branching from one another. In order to keep track of where various schools gained their techniques and from what styles they may have improvised, better efforts were made to codify their teachings in writing.

A factor that seems to have contributed to the increased attention paid to small-concealed weapons, was that during the Edo period the caste system was more strongly enforced than in previous eras, dictating for instance the dress of the various social castes and guilds. Naturally, the weapons people were permitted to wear were also strictly coded, limiting the repertoire available to the common man and warrior alike. Concealed weapons would have presented certain advantages that were unlikely to have been anticipated by dress codes. Though we have no caste system now in most societies, and usually no code for dress except within certain milieu, weapons of any kind still draw significant attention from government authorities and there are regulations concerning what a person may carry openly that has potential as a weapon. This was likely the situation historically as well. So as interest grew in concealable weapons, martial artists started to get creative in developing their arsenal and abilities in this area. It's quite logical, then, that some of them would turn to Ninjutsu as a source of this kind of knowledge, and that others would adopt the use of daily implements as the Ninja had done for centuries before them. This subject matter, when explored, opens other important topics to be understood in the martial arts that are completely relevant to how we see martial arts functioning today.

One such area deals with the subject of origins and why they are important. Densho from Edo period schools of martial arts often cite the origins of their schools and these fall generally into documented lineages. One purpose of these documents is to demonstrate their lineage and the direct passage of teachings from founding schools or warriors. Where appropriate, this kind of document was like a deed to a school's teachings, and enhanced prestige where one could prove the connection to older and highly respected traditions and famous people. Noble or established professional warrior houses date from around the early Heian period. Warrior families vied with each other since that time to establish their respective reputations.

The transmission of writing in China occurred after the onset of the Iron Age, and began during the period of state formation during the second millennium BC. Early writing systems were used for keeping track of titles and stock items and soon, as the complexity increased, for expression of religion and history. It follows that those with the earliest documentation could make proven claims of legitimacy provided that the possibility of fakery was minimal. This dynamic was no different in early Japan. There was a vested interest in writing, keeping, guarding, selling, and even forging documents. Systems of military arts were considered by some to be a commodity or saleable service. They could be provided to the client who needed their men trained in order to achieve some political and/or financial goal.

Documents aged and needed to be periodically replaced. They were updated also as the arts changed. Having the oldest documents did not therefore mean one had the best, most comprehensive or most effective system; it was instead an issue of tracing "legitimate" claims and prestige.

If documents were secret, closely guarded and not shown to anyone except the next headmaster , a person stealing them would have to know that (or a similar) system beforehand and be able teach it to others in order for it to have any real value. A creative martial artist could fake the knowledge, as long as what they taught looked like a close approximation or an interpretation of what was in the document.

Today, many practitioners attempt to mix various arts together in a quest to develop the most comprehensive system they can. The Ninja had also done this, in the remote past. I have heard practitioners in martial arts society of Japanese origin question whether Ninjutsu is in fact a legitimate "fighting art." The most common activities for which Ninja were known did not necessarily involve fighting. It seems to be this issue that makes some people claim Ninja had no specific fighting art of their own. Yet Ninja are known to have participated in battles among and against Samurai warriors. Martial arts are part of Ninjutsu, but the reverse is not always so. When we speak of Ninja acquiring arts from other sources people may assume this to mean they do not have their own martial arts. Going back far enough all warrior societies developed curricula of fighting skills which came to be known as their own. As Ninja groups took in fighting arts, they adapted them to their needs, ultimately changing them and making them their own. They, as spies, have been doing this as long as they have existed. Spies in China and other parts of Asia undoubtedly had fighting skills as well. They routinely placed themselves in dangerous situations that at any moment might require the ability to fight and to do so in a manner different from their foes. Ninja fought to avoid capture, as well as to capture and assassinate others, thus specializing in techniques needed for these situations. Though Ninja regarded their mission as a higher priority than vanquishing some individual foe, they still needed to be able to defend themselves. For these reasons, our position is that asserting that Ninja possessed no martial art of their own is simply absurd.

A person may be tempted to conclude that the lack of direct information about fighting skills found in known historical written works on Ninjutsu is evidence that Ninja had no special combative arts. In fact, the lack of evidence of a fighting art is merely a lack of evidence, not proof that the arts didn't exist. Grandmaster Law has repeatedly stated that, to the Ninja, their fighting art was sacrosanct and never shared with outsiders. It does, however, seem to be the case that not all Ninja groups practiced the same martial arts. Some may have shared dojo with Samurai and non-Samurai alike and favored certain weapons that are seen in Samurai bugei to this day. That stated, there are similarities across the spectrum of Ninja groups, in large part due to the need to adapt the fighting skills to Ninja activities. There was no one "right" way to perform Ninja martial arts.

Taking these factors into account, we can make some sense of the sometimes confusing information that various people in the public media have put out on the subject of Ninjutsu and their martial arts. Like everything else the Ninja did, all elements of the arts were blended together. Tools and weapons were practiced under one core strategy, and not subject to hard and specific distinction. If the martial arts of the Ninja have varied origins according to the groups involved, the same can be said for their tools. With such a long history behind Ninja culture and activities, the tools would be expected to have different applications from group to group. It would be analogous to one group today saying that rakes are used primarily to spread cement, while others say they are used to rake leaves, a third group asserting they use them to harvest sea urchins and so on. They are all potentially true and yet divergent. The actual motion of using the rake in all these situations, however, will be similar. Just because a tradition says things were done a certain way in a certain text, does not mean that it was the only way to do it, nor that everyone did it that way, or even that the same group did it consistently the same way every time over generations.

The arts of Ninjutsu continue to evolve, and trying to encapsulate their ways according to some rigid system frozen in history is the work of museums. While studying the history of centuries old Ninjutsu is important and necessary for those trying to deepen their understanding, it in some ways detracts from learning the relevant things that a person involved in Ninjutsu should know today. The modern world has many things in it that didn't exist before, many of which have been incorporated into Ninjutsu. In this way, the kakushibuki remain as relevant and vital now as during the Edo period and before. Only now, there are many new ways in which to conceive them. Take for example bungee cords, as they are sold in hardware stores, we have trained with them. In what way is this tool a form of kakushibuki? This subject will be explored further below.

Modern Ninjutsu is distinguished by its focus on retaining skills that continue to have significant modern applications. Some Ninja skills, such as how to read lips at a distance for the purpose of spying remains a skill that is still useful today, only now it can be enhanced through the use of binoculars or supplanted by hi-tech microphones. Ninja society is, by its very definition, shadowy and deceptive. Even the techniques are not what they appear, and despite overlap with other arts and what others may state, Ninja do have techniques not found in other sources—again because the methods were adapted for their special needs.

The possession of Densho, even if legitimate in their origin and owned by a teacher of a system, does not necessarily mean that the teacher has the full ability to understand what is in them or the capability to accurately teach the content. Even if a person can read what is in the densho, they may not know how to interpret the content. To achieve the ability to teach the art using Densho they may have to learn old writing systems. It is far better when the master instructor already knows and understands the art so that the densho (if they exist for that art) become more of a symbolic part of their martial patrimony, and are not critical to transmission of knowledge. Densho continue to be duplicated and modernized for contemporary people to understand them. Some can even be purchased at auctions, antique markets and through the internet.

Grandmaster Law states that a master and instructor in Ninjutsu is a living scroll or densho. Ninja, as we have stated earlier, did not generally keep densho. Some of the extant materials contain only skeletal information and are of little value except in understanding some generalities about the historical Ninja. Grandmaster Law would liken this fact to keeping the hundred-dollar bill in your sock and the five-dollar bill in your wallet, thus when the thief or robber gets your wallet all he gets is five dollars. The scroll or densho is like the five-dollar bill. This is why, in the opinion of our group, the historical publications on Ninjutsu do not contain information about fighting skills. So someone getting such a document may feel that it is of immense value, but to those who composed it, it does not have the same value as understanding the living dynamics of Ninjutsu when taught personally by a master of the art.

All of these issues make determining the origins of various arts very difficult. It is easy to infer that some accounts are part fact and part fiction. Those who recorded the information in densho and historical accounts were free to include or leave out anything that they wished without third party validation. As it happens to be reported in Western media sources, many of the atrocities committed by the Japanese military in World War II have been altered or simply left out of the history books used to teach Japanese school children. The point is that, as time goes by, the shameful and/or unwanted parts of history can, as apparently hoped for by some, become forgotten after only a few generations.

Taking into account the process whereby parts of history are gradually forgotten and looking at remaining historical material through which people seek to revive information with the intent of influencing the present, represents one way in which cultures appear to preserve something from the past, but irrevocably alter it in doing so. Historical material has the potential to influence thought and decisions about current and future systems. The present interest in Ninjutsu has dramatically changed the nature of debate in martial art society and shifted how martial arts present and sell themselves to the public in the last three decades.

It is important to maintain a commonsense approach to the understanding of even the most historically documented and legitimate schools. The founder of a school may have been the first to formally bring an art to the Samurai class (who more assiduously kept records for the spiritual and commodity value of their martial systems), or the first to commit it to written account, but he may not have really been the one to "invent" it or even develop it. A case in point would be the Manriki-kusari of the Masaki Ryu. Though the founder of this art, to my knowledge, had never made the claim to be the first to use chains in combat; a person might naively assume this based on how sparsely documented the chain was prior to that. The chain had long been a ubiquitous tool, like the staff and the rope. While the founder was undoubtedly Masaki Toshimitsu, he was by no means the first to use chains as weapons. Chains are illustrated in older documents as being weapons and parts of weapons well before the Edo period when he founded his art. There is no reason to believe that chains alone or bearing weights (fundo) were not being used in earlier times. Masaki Toshimitsu should be respectfully credited with using the kusari (chain) in the form that we now commonly see illustrated in the Masaki Ryu, which was developed with a specific purpose and in a specific context. The history of Shurikenjutsu and many other arts can be similarly understood.

For many of the martial arts found outside the Far East, South East Asia, and even some that reside there now the subject of legitimacy has become hopelessly muddied. More importantly, spying, as it exists today, is not done by people who train in public schools of Ninjutsu. Most of the people seeking to develop an understanding of Ninjutsu even if they train in fighting arts associated with Ninjutsu are actually engaged in historical recreation unless the intent is to actually use the art. Their practice can be likened to the activities of people engaged in civil war re-enactments with added benefits of physical conditioning and other refinements that are part of any traditional martial art. In our tradition, while we realize the importance of understanding ancient weapons and how they were used, we feel it's better to focus on what they mean to us today, rather than trying to have a comprehensive, detailed and "historically correct" perception. Seeking a *working knowledge* of these historical tools makes them come alive as we see the analogous possibilities that exist all around us in the most mundane everyday things.

To illustrate further, among the kakushibuki of the Edo period, there was the conceptually and technically convergent practice of using ornamental hairpins or Kanzashi and needles and short small daggers called Kaiken by Samurai women and shuriken used generally by men. Does this convergence tell us something useful now? Is the gender distinction being made here of any importance? It is necessary to reflect on these questions as we move through the last chapter.

One other important issue to consider is that very little of the diverse types of kakushibuki, shuriken and shaken along with other Samurai and Ninja tools are known or available in the West. Very recent publications from Western authors have begun to show and explain these, also translations of Japanese historical works on these subjects are coming out that will lead to an exponential leap in understanding the historical Japanese warrior society and Ninjutsu by persons outside Japan.

Thus far we have seen that the Ninja methods, credo and origins were deeply woven into the culture in which they operated. The art adapted with all of the historical changes in the strategy of warfare and conflict in their broader sense. Being secretively cultivated among the common people and warrior society alike, the Ninja arts did not endorse the showy traditions associated with other warrior groups serving the aristocracy, the strongmen, daimyo and the bakufu. Consistent with this secrecy, when Samurai adopted some Ninja practices, they would not openly credit the Ninja as the source of the material.

Because of their unique attributes, Ninjutsu skills, strategy and thinking are still useful to the common man, soldier and spy of today. This contemporary martial relevance is in large part related to the fact that Ninja did not rely on the weaponry and armor of the Samurai to practice Ninjutsu. Ninja were therefore able to fight using all manner of movement that would not be possible in armored grappling and permitted the perpetuation of many unarmed combat skills that continue to be seen in a number of related Chinese martial arts and certain branches of jujutsu.

The observation made earlier that Ninja postures and stances or kamae are typically comfortable with a regular shoulder width gait unlike many of the postures of warriors using long weapons and body armor have limitations and there are exceptions. Many WuShu traditions utilize long and wide stances as part of their unarmed combat as well. It was also stated earlier that the refined rolling techniques of the Ninja cannot be easily or stealthily executed wearing armor and Ninja rolling techniques are deeply incorporated into the unarmed and close quarter combat system of Ninja taijutsu. Ninja taijutsu also utilizes body movement or *sabaki* that is extremely close to the enemy and requires the ability to sense the opponent's movement and intent through body contact without necessarily viewing them (as would be the case in darkness). This is difficult to do in armor, and also in arts that rely on long weapons and percussive techniques. Some of these elements of Ninja combative strategy while not categorical of their arts nevertheless show how they adapted techniques to suit their operative needs. These points were reviewed because they speak to what is relevant now, even the most well-equipped modern soldier wears body armor that is intended to interfere as little as possible with movement even if it is often combined with a lot of other heavy equipment. Wide stances and sweeping movement slow the fighter down and are frequently abandoned by those who know the realities of contemporary combat.

The socially low profile strategy of the Ninja remains appropriate today because any evidence of open public belligerence is not tolerated and leads to fairly rapid intervention by police. As there were few social constraints of tradition for Ninja, they were not obligated to respect the dress, behavior codes and methods of the increasingly specialized Samurai warriors. Ninja were free to continue to incorporate the weapons of both the professional warrior and the tools of the peasant as needed. This is similar to the free anonymity that the average person enjoys today, though they would not generally have access to more powerful military grade weapons. To the Ninja, the act of fighting was and is considered to be a necessity, to both protect immediate family and the interests of their community. These are all attributes that resonate well with how we can rationally justify training in combative skills now.

It should be understood that Ninja clothing and weapons were primarily utilitarian in nature. The intimidating appearance of the rarely donned shozoku was not coincidental and though of added benefit, the main purpose of its design was camouflage and protection. When seeking to instill fear, the Ninja sometimes used fearsome masks, magic combined with shamanistic type spells or incantations and displays of fireworks. These must have worked well among the more superstitious and less educated people they encountered. In the places and times prior to the arrival of scientific teachings, superstition was a more prevalent and powerful force.

Even in modern Western society, where people try to portray themselves as rational, most engage in superstitious beliefs and ceremonial activities based in myth. This phenomenon is not unique to lesser poverty stricken cultures, despite the common stereotype. Some of these superstitions are still exploited by some for a variety of reasons. It comes as no surprise that over the course of their history Ninja also exploited these systems as potential weaknesses in others. The relevance of these points should not be lost for martial artists today who are trying to have a rational and commonsense perspective about the meaning of their practice.

To understand the Ninja mind it is important to understand the way in which they used their weapons, their clothing and appearance and appreciate these as neither arbitrary nor idiosyncratic practices intended only to create drama and fear. In fact, this was no more the case than the intimidating appearance of the well-equipped and camouflaged 21st century commando prepped for warfare in the jungle. Ninja must certainly have appeared strange to others, and their ancient practices are often a source of derision and humor in modern times. They have become an endless source of amusement, generating comic book characters and both the heroes and villains of children's stories. But, just as during daylight hours we can laugh at that which really truly frightens us, at night, our primal fear of being hunted like an animal returns to remind us that the paradigm which existed during the time of the Ninja is with us still.

A large part of human civilization is predicated on the primitive need to control dangers and perceived threats. Our evolution and cultural history seems deeply influenced by our early collective experiences of being hunted by predators. One by one, they go extinct, but we have never been able to do away with our own predatory drives, behaviors and fears. The Ninja understood the role of primitive predatory and protective drives in the human social context. Expressions of these mental processes in the martial arts can cause those who do not understand them to be quite uncomfortable with the aggression involved and lead to unusual interpretations or rationalizations far removed from them to explain the purpose and spirit of martial practice. Indeed many martial artists prefer to explain their practice as a form of love, higher consciousness, or as being on some moral high ground. These interpretations now make up part of the new martial landscape and are important to bear in mind when examining reasons for practicing Ninjutsu combat systems and other martial arts today and these justifications for practicing martial arts came about because to many people these arts are simply unnecessary. A person can live a moral high ground or a life of love and deep devotion without ever giving martial arts a thought. But the question remains: is there a civilized rationale for feeling one's own predatory and protective drives?

What is a Modern Ninja?

It is our understanding that there exist Ninja families which continue to train in the arts while maintaining their anonymity from mainstream martial society. I have heard this believably affirmed by two trustworthy outside sources. These people have seemingly no interest in exposing their skills to the public and it appears that the secrecy is probably maintained as a matter of tradition. Given the unknown numbers of such groups and their respective skill sets, it can be legitimately asked what will become of them and their arts? Teaching these arts to outsiders may dilute their original content, yet keeping them within their families risks their eventual extinction should the family line die out. There is no doubt that many ancient methods are relics of the past and their place is in a museum, because they have become obsolete. A case can be made that teaching the arts to outsiders is one way to ensure their survival by introducing "new blood," as it were. This perhaps also amplifies the risk that the arts will be simplified, misrepresented, and copied by those who do not understand them. Nevertheless, it is no doubt inevitable that human curiosity will eventually lead to the exposure of the precious pearls within all cultures and societies. We are witnessing this unfolding in many domains of history and anthropology, all over the world, whether it is examining the evidence of genetics as it relates to the origins of populations or the study of linguistics.

Most traditions practiced by historical Ninja have lost the combative significance that they once had. Like so many other things, advances in the technology of combat and gathering intelligence have made many of these activities much safer for today's covert operator. Though the technology has advanced, the underlying concepts and strategy may not have. Satellites and various listening devices can now accomplish what once required stealth and a good deal of creativity and endurance. That said, many agencies cannot afford the modern ultra-high tech tools used by the governmental departments of the developed nations, and there are limitations in the quality of the intelligence gathered using these tools. Since the occurrence of the 9-11 terrorist attacks on New York City in 2001, American and other international intelligence and spy organizations have reiterated publically the special value of direct human intelligence that is gathered by an actual person who has infiltrated a target group. All intelligence gathering comes at a tremendously high cost and risk. Whether it is the equipment used, the training of the operatives, or the guaranteeing of their secrecy or integrity, the difficulty and price is high in resources, money and time. Of course, spies and their administrators are also at constant risk in the effort to provide intelligence. This point has been repeatedly made in the very high profile and risky investigations that have taken place and continue into organized crime.

Private investigators and police detectives will use the personal computer, data files, listening and video equipment as part of their job, but may not have all of that on hand at the moment when it is most needed. Methods of stealth, acting, hand-to-hand combat, covert communication, and above all the creative versatility found in the arts of the Ninjutsu remain completely relevant to people in such professions.

Even for the average person (if there really is such a thing), these arts are very relevant in the domain of self-defense or perhaps in the broader sense for self-preservation. This is not only the case with combat methods, but with other important elements of the arts, including things like stealth and evasion. Skills of this kind can be life-saving in dealing with highly dangerous situations in which the odds are unfavorable, such as surviving gang assaults, stalkers, abductors, and those who would invade our homes. When outnumbered, it is sound strategy to avoid a direct confrontation, and to use stealth and evasive tactics to escape assailants. There are many survivors of this sort of attack who can attest to the value of these training methods.

Other aspects like the utilitarian methods of rope tying, the shoge, the shuko, and shuriken are all useful survival implements in ways that would take many additional pages to explain. But to give examples: just as shuriken attached to a rope can be used to set traps for game, they can also be used to break a car window in case of emergency. Modern Ninjutsu practitioners often believe they are training for the kind of dangers that contemporary living can bring. This is true regarding the techniques that involve self-defense against knife and gun wielding attackers, gangs, car-jackers, rapists and other opportunistic criminals. Anything is possible regarding the degree of violence required to survive and prevail in a combative situation.

The justice system and other official government agencies spend time and effort defining justifiable self-defense. While this is understandable, if the law is to be fair to all it must then attempt to anticipate all the possible scenarios that could occur, which is impossible to do; thus, cases are tried on evidence, witness testimonials and individualized analyses on a case-by-case basis. Consideration is then made for the appropriate use of force for a particular situation. Evidence of this kind is based on the subjective perceptions of others, the study of which is an area of special attention in Ninjutsu.

How is the legal system to provide an appropriate response when the aggressor's intent is actually unknowable? When one person, or a group for that matter, attacks another, it is generally not possible to know if the intent is to kill or to leave the victim in some other state; therefore, it often cannot be determined whether the response given was adequate or excessive. In the practice of any martial art which teaches people to defend themselves, it is necessary to have an appreciation of this issue because it draws on the very real distinctions between the allowable options available for self-defense. Strategies like the use of a firearm or techniques that involve only hitting provide little alternative but total commitment to the offensive or counter-offensive. The person using these weapons and strategy cannot really employ them sparingly and be effective against a determined attacker. Take, for example, another situation where the law and ethics are likely to be unclear and perhaps even unhelpful. Many martial arts, including our own, employ the use of pinning techniques. If a competent martial artist pins an adversary, is s/he prepared to do what must be done to stop that adversary from struggling free if there is little possibility of help arriving? If the enemy calms down, should he then be released? What if he is released only to resume the attack? Would it have been wiser for the martial artist to break the pinned man's arm, to knock him out or even temporarily blind him?

The law says it is excessive force if the aggressor yields and the martial artist hurts him further. How long should the martial artist wait? If the aggressor has support coming, should he then be injured before being released? He might be emboldened and even more determined to exact revenge when his friends arrive. The martial artist cannot simply continue to pin a man while being attacked by others—that would severely reduce any chance of survival and success. Would being able to tie him up with his own clothes change the equation? It probably would. Just having the competence to pin an aggressive attacker in a fight can in itself be a real challenge, let alone having the skills to manage these additional problems.

Exploring these self-defense conundrums and what the martial needs are of both common people and those who deliberately place themselves in peril by choosing a high-risk line of work leads to the question of what an art like Ninjutsu has to offer. This question indicates a need to determine whether the niche of society into which Ninjutsu evolved still exists, albeit in a different form, and whether a so-called Ninja could still meaningfully exist today. Perhaps it would be helpful to reframe the question: what was it about Ninjutsu that made it suitable for the people who used it, and which skills did the Ninja use that remain relevant for us today?

Ninja evolved in a context that was not as different as we might think from that experienced in many parts of the world today, including parts of Western and more developed nations. Though there is peace in most of Western and Far Eastern society and the overwhelming majority of people can live quite comfortably without learning any fighting skills, the interconnectedness of the modern world brings us closer to elements both within our society and others for whom the resolution of conflict through violence is common.

In this manner we can speak of military, paramilitary, and non-military or civilian forms of conflict. Despite the portrayals in the media, modern military conflict is still significantly dependent on basic weapons that are held in the hands of the soldier and not just the high-tech machines and computer-guided systems seen on television. Though guided missiles and drones are used fairly regularly to take out targets that are not easily accessed by ground forces, those areas will eventually come to be monitored by soldiers until the situation is rendered peaceful enough for them to leave. Soldiers have always needed combative techniques for hand-to-hand fighting. Due to the nature of their training and deployment such training rarely takes them to a level that would be considered mastery of more than a few basic techniques needed for survival in the most common situations. The more specialized the needs of the operative, the greater the importance of more comprehensive training. Thus, the hand-to-hand combat training of Special Forces is more complete than that of an infantryman. Specialized combatants are expected to need this kind of skill due to the nature of their work, which is likely to bring them at some point into direct personal contact with the enemy.

Ninjutsu was adapted and refined for special purposes. It therefore may seem paradoxical that Ninja were, for the most part, martial generalists. Grandmaster Law has always emphasized that training in Ninjutsu should avoid spending a great deal of time perfecting any special category of techniques. The idea is to avoid becoming hyper-specialized and predictable. In order to develop versatility that can be spontaneously expressed in combat it is necessary to continuously vary the training. So we can say that if Ninja specialized in anything, it was in being versatile.

Ninja engaged in activities that can be easily defined and categorized, but the commission of those activities had to stand the test of unpredictable field circumstances. Hence the need to maintain what Grandmaster Law calls a "neutral" state of mind. This means keeping a mind that is calm, receptive and observant. A mind that is focused only on doing something specific will not be receptive and instantly loses the capacity to be versatile.

When performing from a neutral state, it feels like fighting with the subconscious mind. When this happens to a novice, he will typically report having engaged in combat with another person without realizing the result until it was over. When I have observed this, they are seen to act with surprise at the way the technique "seemed to come from nowhere" and at how quickly it worked. To a more advanced fighter, the feeling will be more like the quasi-automated feeling we have when setting up the dinner table; we can do it conscientiously while having a conversation with someone and still achieve a good result.

The reason this occurs has to do with the way the brain functions. This is a very complex area of psychology, but suffice it to say that martial arts practiced on a live opponent, with emphasis on sensing the movement and intent of an enemy with whom you are in direct *physical* contact, does employ some of the same areas of the brain or pathways used to learn through memorization of sequences of movement, but adds a layer of complexity not present in sequenced movement alone. That added complexity involves other brain areas that are activated in actual combat. If the martial artists are not accustomed to the experience of using these additional brain structures in actual practice, they will experience an unsettling unfamiliarity during combat that will impair confidence and competent execution of technique. They will often state that they were unprepared for what happened. In fact, some of the structures alluded to here *directly impact* feelings of anxiety and areas governing the "fight or flight" response. These areas of the brain can be trained to handle stress and rapidly changing situations, as would occur in a fight, such that they will not be overwhelmed and the person can respond with what they have learned.

I once asked Grandmaster Law during dinner what he felt like in the middle of combat and he answered with the question, "What does it feel like eating your dinner?" I realized he was identifying it as essentially the same state of mind. I wasn't necessarily thinking about which item I was going to pick up off my plate next, I just took what was there based on how I felt. Thinking about it, a lot of the things we do every day are like this, so the feeling is already familiar to us. Most people are not used to feeling this way while fighting unless they have extensive training that really approximates actual fighting stress. Our training and the expression of what we have learned in martial arts should "feel" like an everyday activity.

It follows from the discussion above that training should, as closely as possible, approximate the fighting conditions likely to be encountered in our lives. How is this concept important to what constitutes a so-called "Ninja" in the modern world? Is it necessary to change how we define a Ninja? Or should it remain a purely historical construct? I would stress that when we talk about Ninja, that we are, in fact, discussing the historical persons who used the art of Ninjutsu in the commission of acts that were traditionally performed by Ninja and for which the art prepared them. Any person who might fit that description today could fairly consider themselves Ninja. Persons who are spies, scouts, assassins, saboteurs and even military or paramilitary combatants and advisors who use this art as the basis of their strategy and methodology would be "Ninja." Others, even if engaged in similar professions, who are not intimately tied to the art or who have limited training in it probably should not consider themselves to be Ninja. Civilians who study these arts who have expertise, either through research or direct training and do not use the art professionally do not fit this description. The question remains as to whether a person competent in the Ninja arts and who teaches it in a professional or semi-professional capacity to people who use the art is, in fact, a Ninja? We would consider that person a Ninja. The people we would thus consider actual "Ninja" would not constitute the bulk of those interested in the art. The majority who are interested are either those who try to maintain an approximate historical construct of the art by practicing it with ancient weapons; the other group is largely composed of those interested in learning the art for self-preservation because they regard it as superior in a variety of ways for that purpose.

The position held within our school is that Ninjutsu must continue to evolve. In order to do so it must remain combatively relevant. It must by definition prepare the practitioner for actual contemporary combat. The actual techniques can be quite ancient, but the tool/weapon used would not necessarily be so. Given that the average civilian has little actual time available to devote to learning the martial arts, if the goal is, indeed, self-preservation, they should not spend much time working with swords, spears, naginata and training in samurai armor. Arts that emphasize this sort of training, while perfectly valid in their own right, and while still conferring indirect combative benefit, do not follow the core values of Ninjutsu as held by our group. Naturally, many of these schools do not train only with medieval weapons, and they do spend time on self-defense and combat, but it is the proportion and degree of importance attached to those arts that matters most, in addition to the actual effectiveness of the skills.

It might seem rather pointless to discuss what specifications are necessary to have someone more or less legitimately consider him- or herself to be a Ninja. For most persons interested in the arts of Ninjutsu, it really is of no importance. The more important question is: how can Ninjutsu benefit a person who decides to train in it, and how should we contrast this and situate it amongst the choices people have in selecting a martial art? It is equally pointless to try to engage in some sort of debate about which martial arts are "the best" or, for that matter, the most effective. The point made earlier about the frame of mind a person should ideally have in a combative situation gets to the heart of the matter in what regards combative effectiveness in all martial arts, including Ninjutsu, as long as the skills are there to handle the task.

Aside from those specifically seeking out Ninjutsu, the majority of people seeking any kind of martial arts training, at least in the initial stages, justify their interest along two basic lines: self-defense and the need to improve health or fitness. The need to be able to competently defend yourself will depend on many factors both intrinsic and extrinsic. *Intrinsic factors* are typically things like natural ability and, by corollary, limitations caused by disability, whether physical, psychological, personality-based, or due to age. Some personal factors such as race and gender are also influences because they can affect choices about with whom a person may feel comfortable training. In principle, most of these things should not matter too much, although they exert effects on individuals as it pertains to their perspective and experience with training.

Extrinsic factors consist of things like the type of people or situations the martial artist expects to encounter and to have to defend against. Other extrinsic factors are important, like profession: working in law enforcement, prisons, healthcare, security, bodyguard, military, secret services, real estate, cab driver, store clerk, social work or just the demographic of working in economically impoverished and crime-ridden areas—each of these professions has an effect on how the need is perceived. Then there are the usual constraints that affect us all: What training can you afford? Is the training you would like available in your area, or would it require a life-altering plan like living in Japan or China?

For many, after all, the ability to remain calm and competent in any high stress situation is one of the desired effects of training in martial arts. Although it may seem fairly obvious why this is sought after, it is important to be clear as to how and why this helps. It has nothing to do with being cold hearted, stoic, or tough, and has everything to do with being prepared. Take any text on survival, whether it is on street survival, wilderness or extreme emergency situations, and the first and most important point to be made is to remain calm; the next is to be prepared. For the average person, a violent confrontation is well outside of their "comfort zone." It seems like a tall order to expect such a person to remain calm, even with a fair bit of training.

What kind of training would you have to have in order to be prepared for a violent confrontation? Can a martial art prepare a person to feel like they're enjoying a meal in the middle of combat? Bearing in mind all the intrinsic and extrinsic factors that you as an individual carry to this equation, it then becomes meaningful to understand why you wish to train in martial arts. That will help you decide which martial arts to train in as it becomes clear that to make such a choice a person has to know the specific characteristics of the arts available.

Anyone advertising to teach the arts of Ninjutsu and who has opened a dojo or accepted students is probably familiar with the visits, phone calls, and emails from people (typically young males), who think it would be "cool" to be a Ninja. They bring with them all the fantasies about what they will do with their newly acquired skills. Should these people be turned away as being too immature and ignorant to be taught? Indeed, some such persons are so eager to attach themselves to anyone purporting to teach Ninjutsu that they are easily mislead and will pursue charlatans, devoting their time and money in their pursuit of Ninja recognition. Such persons can also be easily persuaded to act as lackeys and engage in malevolent behavior in the belief that they are helping the cause of their teacher or school.

I would submit that such vulnerable individuals have as much a right to train in these arts as anyone else. It is important, however, to be very clear with them what the training will prepare them for and to provide guidance in finding their own true rationale for training. In general, people with a superficial understanding and reason for studying will not persist when confronted with the workouts and pain involved.

After taking stock of the situation, we can look at what Ninjutsu offers. The art teaches a set of skills, both cognitive and physical, that are exactly relevant to any person feeling a need to learn self-defense. In fact, the more a person trains in these skills, the more prepared they are to handle dangerous adversaries. It seems like overkill for a person to learn the methods of a secret society engaged in espionage or guerilla warfare and activities like assassination just so that they can defend themselves. But people who train in Ninjutsu today do not usually learn all the skills that a Ninja needed to do their work. They only need to learn a subset of the skills in order to meet this requirement. Most other martial arts also have dimensions that are not particularly relevant to people who wish only to have a self-defense system. These aspects of the arts can provide a cultural experience in addition to other indirect benefits. Training halls that spend a lot of time on sword skills and glaive type weapons like the naginata are clearly not focused primarily on self-defense. If the goal is self-defense, then it is important to think about the probability that the skills being taught will be used in an actual confrontation. If that probability is low, consider training in other aspects of the same art or in another art entirely.

Another thing to consider is whether using what you are being taught will get you in trouble with law enforcement. Training in nunchaku is actually very enjoyable and somewhat challenging, but nunchaku are illegal in most places and carrying them, let alone using them, can lead to charges and a criminal record. Many of the skills learned in Ninjutsu are of this kind; it is necessary to make sure that students are not misled into thinking that training with shuriken and shaken is something that can be readily employed on the street. This is to a significant degree why the focus of this work has been on the improvisational thinking Ninja had about weapons and tools as a matter of practicality and survival.

The historical Ninja had a number of things in common with the average person today. They lived in a society where the potential for violence was frequently present. Like us, they were forbidden from carrying weapons openly that could be used for self-defense. When travelling under an assumed civilian identity, they were for all intents and purposes common civilians dependent on the forces of social order for protection. What was not average about Ninja was their knowledge. Governments have a tough time outlawing knowledge, but they do restrict access to information. They cannot, however, restrict a fundamental and creative way of thinking about weapons and how to use them. Unless a person works in a profession that permits them to carry arms, they are left with common everyday tools.

It isn't sufficient to be able to imagine how to use a hammer or hatchet for self-defense. To be truly capable of using implements and their derivatives it is necessary to actually train in methods that permit them to be used effectively. To acquire such skills, a martial art is required. Criminals who use weapons on civilians are not as concerned with the law and are willing to risk the consequences of carrying illegal weapons. Most ordinary citizens and would-be victims will not take these risks and instead try to avoid the dangerous criminal elements of society. The only options available to a civilian in violent confrontational situations are to allow themselves to be victimized or to resist.

Resisting comes at a significant risk that can only be reduced by increasing competence in fighting skills and/or the use of effective weapons. Weapons can dramatically improve the chances of success in fighting back, so any art that teaches the effective use of legal and common implements has a more realistic focus on self-defense. Many tools and items that we use for gardening, construction, and in the office can be used for self-defense. Browsing down the aisles at any hardware store always reminds me of the tools I train with routinely in Ninjutsu. Rakes, shovels, clippers, hoes, weeders, ropes, chains, plumbs and bungee cords all come to mind.

The same kind of analysis regarding realistic application and practicality should be applied to the empty hand fighting skills taught by an art for self-defense. Considerations on how much ground fighting they practice, strategies for multiple attackers, required use of physical strength, actual effectiveness of the strikes used and so forth must all be looked at. Do the classes actually practice scenarios that a person is likely to encounter in everyday life and if so, is the training as close to reality as you can get? Another aspect that is not often raised is to determine, within a reasonable degree of accuracy, how much training is required in the art before a person can acquire an acceptable level of competence with it. Some arts are highly effective, but are not a practical choice because the investment in time, energy and, of course, money, may be too large for the average person. How this is figured will, of course, depend on what an individual thinks is an acceptable level of competence. This feeling of competence is highly subjective and is also influenced by any success or failures experienced in actual fighting.

Because of the pressures and demands that existed for historical Ninja, the martial arts employed by them were by necessity designed for dealing with unfavorable odds, and therefore had to be effective, direct, and not require extensive amounts of training to use, at least for self-defense. Above all else, the methods had to be versatile while maintaining advantage through the element of surprise by being unpredictable. These characteristics make Ninjutsu martial skills very useful to any person who is concerned with self-defense today.

Self-defense is part of the larger survival concept. Throughout the text we have seen how the tools and weapons employed by the Ninja were useful for the activities in which Ninja engaged: combat and both wilderness and emergency survival. The psychological training and physical training also focuses on these skills. Though these are not traditionally thought of as martial arts, they are considered by many to be complementary if not essential. In Ninjutsu society, this aspect of training is felt to be very helpful and advantageous.

Many people are drawn to martial arts because, in addition to concerns with the risk of victimization and violence, they appropriately understand that martial arts can be effective for neutralizing our own internal propensity towards violence. We have seen in the first chapter that the meaning of the words for martial arts in Chinese WuShu essentially means to "stop fighting." Although this is true in the literal sense, it is also true in the spiritual domain. The healthy and safe release of aggression, coupled with reduction in anxiety, leads to less aggressive reactions or the impulse to harm others. The exception being when the art is used for unethical purposes, in which case the violence can compound itself and cause a person to eventually destroy his own life and the lives of others (as will be discussed further below). This is why historically the culture of nearly all martial arts admonishes practitioners towards an ethic of humility and ethical use of the skills. It could be effectively argued that historical Ninjutsu was used unethically (or at least under a different set of values), but this in no way requires modern practitioners to adopt such an idea.

Numerous martial arts also have healing methods as part of their curricula; not all of these are truly realistic, but many are tried and true. These are areas in martial culture where it is important to be cautious. Many martial arts traditions are cashing in on "new age" trends of healing, taking advantage of the ignorance of people experiencing the usual and inevitable psychosomatic sensations brought on by stress, while offering nothing more than common sense practices to reduce it.

The same can be said of the so-called spiritual training in some places, and really it is up to individual students to be cautious about what they accept and believe. It is important to be critical in looking at whether the techniques taught really can be used in a peaceful manner. As previously stated, arts that teach primarily striking are not as well suited to the peaceful resolution of a fight as an art utilizing methods of submission. Imagine having to stop a loved one, who may be physically vulnerable and has lost control, from assaulting you or other family members, and all you have learned in martial arts is to kick and punch them? Or if it is your job to control people who are endangering themselves or others and you are not allowed to strike them or you will hurt them and subsequently lose your job? These situations call for submission holds and grappling methods. Arts that do not cover these fighting strategies do not offer all the needed methods of relatively peaceful conflict resolution.

Ninjutsu, through techniques of submission, offers a "life and limb" sparing alternative to total brutality. The Ninjutsu practitioner can mete out defense only to the degree necessary or as desired; this approach provides more potential control over the outcome. It is this principle that reveals and makes clear that training in an art that gives a person options and choice is the more compassionate way. A martial art of this kind is consistent with the moral practice of martial arts as informed by Buddhism and its "eight-fold path," including "right action," in that, as a person exercises intent, they do so in a manner inflicting the least overall harm. The moment exists when that intent is an expression of what that person sees as justified, and it is an opportunity for them to pay attention to and to improve Karma through peaceful action. To some, that is a spiritual teaching; to another it might be common sense, or perhaps both.

Opportunities such as these also satisfy the concerns a person may have in training in the martial arts regarding the potential for excessive violence that can occur in combative situations. In other words, effective methods executed properly will typically de-escalate most individuals. Some people "black out" in a fight and fight with extreme brutality that stops only when their adversary is well beyond the ability to voluntarily submit. Such people are extremely dangerous and capable of manslaughter. Persons of this kind can only be stopped either by escape or by inflicting serious injury. Hopefully, it is obvious that escape is always the preferable option as long as no loved ones are left behind to face the situation. In Ninjutsu, emphasis is placed on preparing for realistic scenarios in order to stand a chance against some of the frightening savagery one may encounter. Above and beyond the situations that can be resolved peacefully, a person also has to have the capability to engage in mortal combat should the need arise and be able to do so with minimal risk to their integrity. Suffering crippling injury is little solace for having leveled the playing field with the adversary or having fought for a reason that retrospectively was in defense of an immature ego.

Training in Ninjutsu improves physical fitness, as do most martial arts. Nearly all martial arts, practical or not, improve concentration, mood and confidence. Ninjutsu, when practiced close to its original form, is actually very harsh and difficult, taking the level of fitness to the extreme. I have found through personal experience that this training does not appeal to most people. They find it to be too harsh and not in line with the more humble and less painful goals they have in mind. Even a significantly reduced Ninjutsu exercise regimen is perceived as "hard." Also, the vast majority of schools do not train in real endurance of cold, fatigue, hunger and methods causing psychological stress, due to the liability of training people who are not born or obligated to do these things when all they are looking for is self-defense. Nor do most of us have time for this level of training. Nevertheless, the knowledge of how to train in these things and when it is appropriate is good to have, should the need ever arise. It should be stated, however, that training of this kind, especially early in life, makes a person more mentally resilient, probably increases longevity, and improves healing and immunity by reducing the overall threshold for the experience of stress. Fortunately, a person does not have to be at peak physical condition to perform most of the combative techniques in the art; therefore, people training in Ninjutsu can start learning self-defense before their overall condition has improved. It also means that the fighting skills remain accessible as a person ages.

There are acrobatics in the art, which serve a variety of purposes, not all of which are combative. These are not truly needed for a person learning the self-defense methods. The oldest and most experienced practitioners are, in fact, more effective at performing the techniques and can easily handle beginners like a cat toying with a mouse.

Some of the methods described in this book might be viewed as cruel. The historical Ninja lived in a context that required many of them to be able to cripple, torture, and kill others. In many parts of the world people have the same freedom in acting with whatever level of force or violence they think is justified. The Ninja perspective is that any potentially lethal physical conflict is a situation in which things have broken down to the point where all that matters is survival. The honor is in the survival itself, because it is one's own life and family that is sacred. Cruelty in the conventional sense was, at times, needed to serve a greater objective (as in the case of torture). The Ninja only considered it cruel to use their methods unnecessarily or gratuitously. Ninjutsu practitioners were and are taught to refrain from such excesses for many reasons. Gratuitous use of violence is a fast track to self-destruction. Keeping the perspective contextual helps us to understand also that what was at one time an acceptable practice of cruel behavior and punishment is usually no longer defensible; in the same way most parts of our society no longer condone vigilante hangings or the burning of witches, for example.

Ninja placed great importance on having a proper frame of mind and a non-egotistical approach to their arts and lifestyle. The use of the arts for destructive and selfish purposes is fraught with the same risks as any other such endeavors. While the arts can confer a technical advantage over others, the underlying feelings of greed, jealousy, and hatred will ultimately cause the individual in question to become alienated from society and experience the souring of their relationships. In such individuals, nefarious acts do not impart any true satisfaction or contentment because they are based in narcissism, and materialism, which are by nature lonely and empty. The rewards will eventually feel insufficient and unsatisfying, and the individuals will ultimately extenuate themselves because materialism in the service of narcissism will never allow a person to possess enough to satisfy. The inescapable internal state of agitation will cause people of this kind to increase risk unwisely and push themselves to the point of provoking their own technical failures, eventual captures, and resultant punishments; or they will destroy themselves and any chance of experiencing happiness; or both. The only other option for people trapped in such egocentric pursuits is to come to a realization of their folly (usually brought on by suffering loss), and to choose a different and healthier way to live. It should be remembered that the forces of social order generally have the financial resources and time to outstrip even very clever criminals, especially where the exploitation of an individual's weaknesses and need for human relationships are concerned.

The Ninja often laid down their lives for their lords, their families, and just causes. Sometimes they were on the losing side or a less than honorable side of a battle. Even in the service of a leader who is immoral, the soldier and operative can still be honorable in their service. Persons interested in martial arts need not look for opportunities to engage in heroics, but it is good to remember those who had such an ethic in history because they guide us in having an analogous modern perspective on the meaning of martial arts today. It does not matter anymore that the historical Ninja could not be openly credited for their achievements, or even recognized today as being important in a lot of ways. As persons interested in Ninjutsu or martial arts in the broader sense, it is enough to take home with us the lessons taught by the Ninja's methods. Many of the things that intimidate and limit us in daily life are just the kind of things that a martial arts mindset can help us overcome. There is no need to be engaged in or swayed by historical dogma.

That said, the history and traditions can still fill our practice with meaning and impart a sense of belonging, as well as help us contextualize our modern practice. The history of Ninjutsu is a testament to the creativity and genius of mankind. It also brings to light humankind's greatest tragedy—our inability to cease being our own most dangerous adversary. In other words, humanity's inability to rid itself of conflict means the continued need for the tools of conflict resolution.

When that conflict has escalated to the point of imminent danger, the art can be used to resolve it to whatever end is required. The use of martial arts is the only practice combining physical and psychological elements available to help people manage the risks of physical combat. Hopefully this exploration into the practical-mindedness of Ninjutsu and how it manifests contextually, both historically and currently, will help people interested in martial arts and self-defense to think in a manner that improves their chances of success. There is much about Ninjutsu that can entertain and challenge anyone interested in this field, although much of it will have to be explored in other works. For those engaged in one or more of the many other martial arts, we hope that this work has improved appreciation for the different ways in which the use of martial arts acquires meaning and enriches our lives through deepening our knowledge.

Finally, on a philosophical note; training in Ninjutsu imparts to practitioners an acute sense of how frail and impermanent life is. This understanding induces most practitioners to avoid conflict and the behaviors that precipitate it. At the same time, this approach lessens the fear and apprehension associated with that vulnerability. The feeling of freedom from the anxieties that cage our minds helps practitioners realize their potential and carve out their own destinies. They also learn that the nature of causality means that one's destiny is only something that can be influenced, not controlled, and that it is unwise to contribute to our own destruction by harming the community of living beings with whom we share our lives.

Glossary

AIKIDO: A Japanese martial art founded by the legendary master, *Morihei Ueshiba*. The practical aim of the art is at once self-defense and the neutralization of the opponent's violence. It shares some similarities to certain aspects of taijutsu and jujutsu. Ueshiba developed Aikido through several influences, the most prominent of which was Daito-Ryu Aikijujutsu, which he learned from *Sokaku Takeda* in the early 20th century. Ueshiba was also a deeply spiritual and religious man who saw Aikido as a vehicle to teach the universal principle of Ki which practitioners cultivate. This cultivation is used to become in harmony with oneself and nature, thus removing obstacles to the experience of universal love and compassion.

ATEMI and ATEMIJUTSU: The art of striking, which also involves finding vital points while fighting.

BAKUFU: The first formal military government established in Japan by *Minamoto no Yoritomo* in 1185 AD at the end of the *Gempei* war. The word *Bakufu* translates as "tent government"; this expression is meant to convey that it was a warrior government, since, by necessity or tradition, warriors held their conferences in tents on the battlefield. At its head was a *Shogun*, or supreme general, a term that had been used for centuries for generals leading campaigns and administrating regions in conflict. Yoritomo was the first Shogun of the Bakufu. It was an administration composed of warriors of the Samurai class; initially its alleged charge was to maintain peace and social order in the country while serving the aristocracy. It functioned, however, with increasing independence from the system of administrators and governors that ruled social order in the previously established system under the Emperor and the aristocracy and gradually assumed greater administrative leverage of its own internal workings and the expression of executive power in political spheres. The Imperial court repeatedly attempted to restore its own authority without success until 1868 when the Shogunate, the Bakufu, and the Samurai class (along with the caste system) were finally abolished. Hence the term "restoration" used to describe this change.

BA QUA CHANG (also written as Ba Kwa): A form of Chinese Wu Shu. Ba Qua Chang appears related to a form of Shaolin fighting but became known independently in the 19th century. The name translates as "Eight trigrams palm (or fist)," as it was inherited from the Shaolin style of that name, but the modern form has been changed through outside influences. It is said to emphasize stealth and deception over raw power, using an ever-changing pattern of hard and soft techniques, and to be so diverse that no one has mastered the entire system. The early masters of this art did not give ranks or belts.

BUDDHISM: A religion originating in India and dating back to approximately 600 BC. It is highly intellectual, philosophical and spiritual. Buddhism began with the experience of *Sidartha Gautama*, a prince who, upon discovering the nature of suffering, entered into a quest to reveal the roots of suffering and, through attaining insight, develop a method for how to end it. He engaged in years of ascetic practices with Yogis. Although recognizing these practices as helpful, he ultimately decided they were not necessary to achieve enlightenment. The term *Buddha* means "enlightened one," and the Buddha is believed to have freed himself from all attachments of the Ego, the mind, and the cycle of suffering or *Samsara*. Buddhism spread all over Central and Eastern Asia, and at one time was a dominant religion in the world. It has been of great influence on Eastern thought and more recently in modern Western thinking. In particular, some of its paradigms have helped develop healing psychological therapies.

BUDO: Over the centuries, the word "budo" has meant different things associated with the culture of the warrior and the ministrations of government. It can imply a certain underlying martial philosophy and associated etiquette. In common usage today the term is intended to distinguish martial arts that are based in a spiritual and more philosophical ideology from those of the classical bujutsu. They are conventionally defined as "martial ways," as "do" means "way" or "path," in a manner similar to the spiritual path undertaken by a monk; they seek to define through action the expression of higher values and the state of "mu" or "no mind" considered essential to attaining enlightenment. It would require an entire text to properly define the budo and such scholarly works are available. There are further distinctions regarding "ko budo" and the modern budo, where the former collectively refers to the classical bujutsu and budo. Modern budo or shin budo include arts such as Iaido, Kendo, Judo, and Kyudo among others. Note that the term ko budo is also used to refer to ancient Okinawan arts, that differ from classical Japanese martial arts in a number of important ways (4).

BUGEI: General term used to refer to entirety of traditional Japanese martial arts and their traditions.

BUJUTSU: A term used for traditional or classical martial art systems. It translates as "warrior methods" but is used in conversation as "martial arts" (14).

BUNRAKU: An ancient form of puppetry from Japan, which became crystallized as a tradition with some final modifications during the 18th century. The puppets can be large and complex and are handled by puppeteers donning black kimono similar in appearance to the shozoku of the Ninja, blending with a black backdrop to obscure their visibility.

BUSHI: A general term referring to a warrior. This term predates the rise of the Samurai class.

BUSHIDO: The so-called "Way of the Warrior" was an ethical code for Samurai warriors. It was developed gradually from the 11th to the 14th centuries. It was strongly influenced by Confucius (and his student Mencius), Shintoism and Zen Buddhism. Bushido admonished warriors to study not only martial arts but literature and etiquette. Some of the core values included filial piety, service to one's lord, frugality, mastery of the martial arts, and the acceptance of death. The "no mind" approach of Zen, or "mu," was the state of mind sought at all times but especially in battle; detachment from worldly desires and life in the pursuit of duty were areas where Bhuddhist values were followed. Under Bushido the rite of *seppuku* (ritual suicide) was considered a way of regaining lost honor. The seven virtues of Bushido are "Gi" (rectitude), "Yu" (courage), "Jin" (benevolence), "Rei" (respect), "Makoto" (honesty), "Meiyo" (honor), and "Chuugi" (loyalty). (http://en.wikipedia.org/wiki/Bushido)

CONFUCIANISM: A philosophical and ethical system of thought originating in China and developed by Confucius, who lived from 551-478 BC. It is held to the same level of reverence in the Far East as Major theistic religions are in the rest of the world. The system and its doctrines were further developed by Confucius' student Mencius. It encompasses moral, ethical, political and philosophical thinking. The philosophical domain speaks to metaphysical problems dealt with by other religious doctrines. The pursuit of Confucianism has man strive to achieve moral perfection in all domains of life. This philosophy is consistent with the Buddhist doctrines of right action, right thought, right speech, and the remainder of the eight-fold path, which if adhered to is believed to lead to facilitate enlightenment by the extinction of repeated cycles of Karma expressed through rebirth. It has influenced all cultures of the Far East and their ethical and religious systems.

Different schools of Confucianism subsequently appeared. Confucianism was used by Han Wudi (156-87 BC) as a political system to govern the state. Despite a loss of influence during the Tang Dynasty, Confucianism remained a mainstream Chinese orthodoxy for two millennia until the beginning of the 20th century, when Chinese Communism vigorously repressed it. Neo-Confucianism is now a combination of Taoist and Buddhist ideas with existing Confucian ideas to create a more complete metaphysics than had existed before. Today's Confucianism is primarily a creation of Zhu Xi (1130-1200 AD) and the other Neo-Confucians. Confucianism is at the philosophical core of Bushido. (http://en.wikipedia.org/wiki/confucianism)

DAIMYO: A term that eventually became a title for a feudal lord. It literally means "Great Name." Daimyo started as a title for a regional strongman or warrior commander who was either a professional warrior himself, or a warrior-administrator at the command of one or more armies. From the Kamakura period and into the later eras of near constant warfare of the Sengoku Jidai, this title came to denote the grander feudal lords who presided over ever larger domains. The title was hereditary when firmly established for generations. Daimyo came to be governed, at least in name, by the Shogun after the installment of the Kamakura Bakufu in 1185. The Shoguns themselves arose from the ranks of Daimyo. The Daimyo developed their own quasi-aristocratic organizations after the fall of the Shogunate in 1868, and continued to exert influence as important political families and significant wealthy landowners.

EDO: A city in the Kanto region that became the capital of Japan after the rise of the Shogun *Tokugawa Ieyasu*, in 1603 where Edo castle was situated. The previous capital and seat of the Emperor was Kyoto. Edo rapidly grew in population and infrastructure over the years, becoming a center of great wealth and power. After the collapse of the Shogunate, its name was changed to Tokyo and it was established formally as the capital city of Japan.

ETA: A term used to designate one of the lowest social classes in the Japanese caste system. The Eta, literally meaning "full of filth," now called "*burakumin*" (community people) or "hisabetsu buraku" (discriminated communities"), handled trades thought to be unworthy of the classes above them, such as slaughtering animals, handling hides and meat, and other jobs that involve getting dirty and working in hard labor. Discrimination against these people, though disappearing, persists in some places and ways to this day, in a manner not too dissimilar from that of the "untouchables" in India. (ref: http://en.wikipedia.org/wiki/Burakumin)

FUDO-MYO-O: The central Buddhist deity of the five great celestial kings of light. Also known as *Acala*. He is depicted with an angry expression; he has a seven knot braid (indicating that he is a servant of the Buddha), a sword in his right hand and a rope in his left. Purifying fire surrounds him; he is blue in color and has many other meaningful stigmata. He is one of the deities worshipped by warriors, including Ninja. The name and character of Fudo appears in some myths of the origins of some Japanese martial arts and even in the names of the arts themselves.

GETA: This is the term for a Japanese form of raised wooden sandal. They are worn today with traditional Japanese clothing such as kimono or yukata. There are several different styles of geta. The style most familiar to Westerners consists of an unfinished wooden board called a *dai* (stand) on which the foot rests, with a cloth thong which passes between the first and second toes. The two supporting pieces below the base, called *ha* (teeth), are also made of wood, and make a distinctive "clacking" sound while walking. Some geta have a rounded *dai* while others have a rectangular *dai*. Ninja were known to use modified Geta as aquatic footwear and for other improvised purposes.

GOKENIN: Term used to refer to a household retainer serving directly under the service of a Daimyo or Shogun (22).This term has changed in meaning over time. It was considered a social status prior to the Edo period. In the Edo period, they were the lowest ranking direct retainers to the Shogun and were not allowed direct audience to the Shogun.

HAN: Term used in reference to a territory under the rule of a Daimyo. These are outside the Kanto plain and differ from a Tenryo (see below) (25).

HATAMOTO: A term meaning "standard bearer" or "banner men"; direct Samurai retainers to the Shogun. They ranged in rank from very lowly and nearly impoverished Samurai who administrated social order, to administrators of major government offices under the *Roju* and the *Wakadoriyoshi*, which were governing councils made up of feudal Daimyo under the Shogun. Hatamoto were allowed direct audience with the Shogun (25). (http://en.wikipedia.org/wiki/ hatamoto)

HEIAN: Usually refers to the Heian Period (794 to 1185), the last period of classical Japanese history to be directly governed by the aristocratic Imperial system before the Kamakura Bakufu (see above) began its official rule during the so-called Kamakura period. The Heian period is considered the peak of the Japanese Imperial culture and is now celebrated for its art, especially poetry and literature. The name Heian is a word that means "peace" in Japanese. It is also important due to the rise of Buddhism to a prominent place in Japanese society during this time.

HEIHO: Generally, "martial principles"; more specifically, Heiho is thought of as a strategy that expresses itself within the actual practice of technique and on the battlefield. Each traditional martial discipline has a heiho that is particular to its school (14).

HOJOJUTSU: A martial art that is combined with taijutsu and other arts which involve grappling such as *kumiuchi*. Hojojutsu consists of ways to bind enemies with ropes or appropriate substitutes for rope. Methods range from simple to very complex. It is an art that is disappearing, but continues to be practiced in the Samurai bugei and in Ninjutsu.

IGA: The name of a province in Japan, and also the name of one of the most famous historical Ninja clans who lived there. This clan was known for having extensive operations and alliances throughout the 17th century political infrastructure.

INUIT: The aboriginal people of the arctic and part of the sub-arctic regions of the Northern Hemisphere. They subsisted in the past primarily as a hunter-gatherer and nomadic culture, which they still practice to some extent today. They have specialized skills and adaptations for living in the harsh arctic climate.

JOMON: A term used to define a particular time period and its people. The Jomon period dates from 10,000BC to 300BC. It is likely that a number of tribes or populations and related cultures existed in Japan during that time. Human populations are generally thought to have existed in Japan at least as far back as 40,000 years ago, when glaciation had lowered sea levels enough to connect it with the mainland. Stone tools and fossils indicate a hunter-gatherer culture during these early times. The word Jomon means "cord marked"; this refers to patterns on pottery impressed by a cord into clay. Evidence of human activity increases after 10,000BC for this period characterized as either Mesolithic or Neolithic. Rudimentary agriculture began during this time to supplement hunting, fishing and coastal gathering, leading to a semi-sedentary lifestyle. Before it ended the Jomon culture elaborated considerably, including in its agricultural practices. It is believed that the migration of Northern Asian people, mostly Manchurian, to the Islands was in part a catalyst for these changes. The subsequent Yayoi period is when large open migrations of Northern Asian people from the continent colonized the islands and dramatically changed the region's culture and way of life, forming what was to become modern Japanese culture.

JUJUTSU: This is not a single martial art, but rather a collective group of arts for which there are many schools. *Classical jujutsu* is a term used to describe older styles that were used by Samurai or by groups who were their contemporaries. The popular martial art/sport, judo, is derived from several styles of classical jujutsu pared down to a narrower curriculum. Jujutsu arose from the various older schools of kumiuchi, and shows influences from Chinese grappling, striking, atemi, and joint-locking methods. Although nearly all the classical schools of jujutsu incorporate the use of weapons both concealed and non-, it later emphasized the unarmed combat for which it is now best known. Modern derivative styles of jujutsu are widely practiced today and are frequently the basis of "self-defense" styles for close quarter engagement, some originating from non-warrior groups such as the *shomen yawara* or "commoners yawara (jujutsu)" (5). The different styles emphasize joint-locks, atemi systems, throws, grappling, striking, and weapons to different degrees, along with the use of smaller weapons that blend well with grappling. Much of the modern "mixed martial arts," or MMA, are strongly influenced by the grappling techniques of jujutsu and judo.

JUTTE: An iron truncheon or baton (boshin) fitted with a hook (kagi) emanating from the handle (tsuka), and bearing a pommel at the base of the handle (kikuza) used for striking, to which a colored cord could be affixed for use in hojojutsu. It was used in general as a non-lethal arresting tool. In some arts the hook was used for trapping blades (25, 21).

KAMAKURA: An ancient city in Kanagawa prefecture, Japan. It is the site of a famous giant Buddha sculpture, called the "*Daibutsu*," that marks it as a place where early Japanese Buddhism exerted influence on nobles. It is also the name of the first Shogunate or Japanese military regime called the Kamakura Bakufu (see above) and the historical period that it defined. Kamakura was taken as the city where Minamoto no Yoritomo launched his operations against the Taira before becoming the first Shogun presiding over most of Japan. He maintained the seat of power in Kamakura for governance by the Bakufu after consolidation of power. This time and place has enormous historical significance in the cultural and political history of the country.

KARMA: One of the three fundamental beliefs in Hinduism; karma has found its way into many other philosophical and modern systems of thought and is fundamental to Buddhism. It goes hand in hand with reincarnation, in that it posits a natural spiritual law wherein a soul, through multiple lives, experiences the effects of all prior actions taken. In a way, it is a form of cause and effect that places the individual in the position of being responsible for what happens to him in subsequent lives. In this system of thought, our actions are said to leave marks on the soul that remains and exert influence until reversed and the soul is freed from the cycle of reincarnation and duality. In Buddhism, only intentional actions are Karmic. Karma itself is neutral; the effects are experienced by the individual with either gratification or suffering. It is a concept that continues to influence Eastern and Western thought. (http://en.wikipedia.org/wiki/Karma)

KATA: A Japanese term for a prearranged set of techniques. In classical martial arts, "kata" are always practiced with a partner, an attacker (uke) and a defender (tori). In modern competition-oriented martial sports, and in some types of Kung Fu, they are performed alone. In the latter instance, kata are used more as a way for the individual to develop their style and form rather than for any substantial combative ability. Kata are found in nearly all martial arts and distinguish the prearranged and instructive from of learning from the "free" form, as would be represented in practices such as randori and kumite which are a form of spontaneous sparring (14).

KINAI: is a Japanese term that refers to the central provinces of Japan. It is an ancient designation centered on the ancient capital of Nara and Heian-kyo. It includes the provinces of Omi, Yamato, Kii, Izumi, Kawachi, and Settsu (24).
Koga/Koka: Name of one of the major Ninja clans, under which there is reported to be approximately 50 subgroups or families.

KORYU: This is a term that is made up of two other characters: "ko" (old) and "ryu" (flow), which in this case speaks to styles, schools, or traditions. Although the term can be used to refer to traditions outside the martial arts, in this text it exclusively has this meaning. It is generally accepted that koryu can trace their lineage with documentation prior to the Meiji restoration of 1868. In this sense, they are classical arts that were concerned with combat effectiveness as it was defined in the pre-reformation era, along with other attributes essential to being a warrior. They are to be distinguished from the budo arts of the modern era which are more concerned with certain aspects of spiritual refinement and less with combat readiness; these include Judo, Kendo, Iaido and Aikido (14).

KUGUTSU: Literally "puppet" in Japanese, the word also refers to people who lived a Gypsy lifestyle. They were skilled entertainers, particularly as acrobats and puppeteers. They are believed by some to have mysterious links to Ninjutsu and other significant areas of Japanese culture and history (15).

KUJIKIRI: Literally "nine syllables cutting," these are a series of esoteric hand signs accompanied by prayers or incantations that were employed by various people, including both Ninja and Samurai. The symbols were part of specific spiritual practices that were believed to impart various benefits, such as protection from calamity and evil, as well as courage, determination, perception, and invisibility of intent. It is sometimes called kuji for short, referring to the number nine.

KUMIUCHI: This is a term used to refer to grappling. It has two major variants. The first is grappling in armor, known as yoroi kumiuchi or katchu kumiuchi; the second form, without armor, is called heifuku kumiuchi or suhada kumiuchi. The terms have been used in combination with other terms such as yawara (see below) according to the preferences of the schools' leadership and conceptualization of the terms (5).

KUNG FU: Translating from Chinese as "hard work" or "to expend energy doing something," *Kung Fu* is phrase used by the Chinese and by Westerners colloquially to refer to Chinese martial arts in general. Chinese martial arts are more correctly called Wu Shu (see below). People knowledgeable about Chinese martial arts will usually refer to their individual arts by name.

KURAMA (Mountain): A mountain proximal to the old Japanese capital, which was first known as Heian-Kyo, then as Kyoto. The mountain is a holy site for Yamabushi, practitioners of Shugen. It has a Buddhist temple, hot springs and was an ancient stronghold for the training and spiritual development. In myth, it is where the Tengu and their king, Sojobo, trained Yoshitsune no Minamoto in their martial arts. It is now a popular tourist attraction where festivals (matsuri) and religious rites continue to be practiced.

KWAN DAO: A Chinese pole-arm, with a long shaft usually made of wood, with a broad flat and curved blade on one end and a pointed metal cap or ring on the other. The broad blade sometimes also had a secondary blade or saw teeth running off its back which could be used in a hook-like fashion to stop other blades, entangle clothing or armor and hook the limbs of the enemy. It is still practiced in Shaolin

Wu Shu and other styles. It is popularly depicted in paintings and sculpture as being wielded by the fierce armored general Kwan Yu, a hero who may have created it and after whom it was named. It is the most likely predecessor to the Japanese Naginata.

KYUDO: A form of budo for the practice of archery, it has both classical and modern representations.

KYUJUTSU: The classical martial art of archery. It is the actual art that was used to prepare warriors for combat using the bow, as opposed to Kyudo.

KYUSHO and KYUSHOJUTSU: The art of using vulnerable anatomical points of the body. It involves understanding all the varieties of such points (bone, nerve, blood vessel, etc.), learning to protect one's own vulnerable points, and the art of conditioning one's own body to attack these points in an enemy.

MARISHITEN: The Buddhist patron goddess of the warrior. She continues to be worshiped by various people such as military personnel, police officers, sumo wrestlers, members of the classical martial traditions, and other religious practitioners. She is believed to bestow various benefits to her followers, including invisibility; inscrutability to one's enemies; clarity of mind; enhanced intuition; imperturbability; and both selflessness and compassion. There is an extensive mythology associated with this goddess and she is sometimes represented as a man. Illustrations of Marishiten often show her riding on the back of a boar and fiercely wielding a bow, sword and spear (14).

METSUKE: These were Samurai whose role it was to oversee and inspect matters of law and order for the retainers of a Daimyo. It is a post that became formalized during the Tokugawa Shogunate. Ronin came under the jurisdiction of law enforcement of the town or city, the "Machi Bugyo." Outside the jurisdiction and range of influence of the Bugyo law enforcement was pursued by local organizations, some of which later became Yakuza. O-Metsuke were like their lower counterparts, but worked under the Shogun, investigating and spying on the activities of Daimyo within the capital and outside it as well. They were known to have employed Ninja to perform duties unsuitable for Samurai due to etiquette, or their known presence in the organization. Although Metsuke concerned themselves primarily with internal matters, they paid close attention to Bugyo activities as happenings there also influenced their retainers (25).

MINAMOTO NO YORITOMO: One of the most important historical Japanese figures. He is known as the first *Shogun*, or supreme general, over the new *Kamakura Bakufu*, which marked the beginning of the Kamakura period. He was born to a partially aristocratic lineage by marriage to the Fujiwara family. His grandfather and father, as well as a number of his direct family, were executed in the aftermath of a series of rebellions for the throne of Emperor. He and his half-brother Minamoto no Yoshitsune were exiled. Yoritomo was sent to Izu; he later married into the Hojo Clan and was eventually able to establish a military position at Kamakura. Due to severe oppression by the Taira Clan then exercising power, the Minamoto revolted and definitively routed the Taira by 1185. They then established Go-Toba as the new Emperor and reigned as the dominant military power in the land after that point. He eventually took the full title of Shogun in 1192. (http://en.wikipedia.org/wiki/Minamoto no Yoritomo)

MINAMOTO NO YOSHITSUNE: The half-brother of Minamoto no Yoritomo. He was exiled like Yoritomo after the Taira seized executive power in the capital in 1160 with the Heiji rebellion, "*Heiji no Ran*." While Yoritomo was sent to Izu, Yoshitsune, at approximately one year old, was sent to live in a monastery at the Kurama Temple. It is there that the legendary and mythological training in the martial arts began under Sojobo, king of the Tengu and the Yamabushi. Yoshitsune and Minamoto no Noriyori were later credited with winning several critical battles against the Taira, including strong participation at Dan no Ura which facilitated Yoritomo's ascension to power. In one such battle he killed his own cousin and brother's rival Minamoto no Yoshinaka. After the Taira defeat, he sided with the cloistered Emperor Go-Shirakawa against Yoritomo. He was relentlessly pursued by Yoritomo and ultimately was obligated to commit seppuku after betrayal by Fujiwara no Hidehira, and defeat by Fujiwara no Yasuhira, Hidehira's son. (http://en.wikipedia.org/wiki/Minamoto no Yoshitsune)

NIHON SHOKI: A book that was written in 720 AD during the Tempyo era (720-794) in the Nara period by Imperial court member Fujiwara no Fuhito. It was written under the direction of Nagayao, the grandson of emperor Temmu, with the guidance of a monk called Doji who had returned from study in Tang China. The Nihon-Shoki is the source of the myth and cult of Shotoku Taishi, a god-like Imperial saint of the Asuka period. It is important, as it is cited as the second oldest text of Japan after the Kojiki (written in 712 AD) and often credited as a source of valuable archeological and anthropological information on ancient Japan. Among the many implications of these texts was the intent that they would establish the

Imperial line as divine and establish its perpetuation on a Chinese model (Note: this account may be challenged by others) (18).

NINGU: Also known as "Ninja tools." These are an array of tools that Ninja usually carried on their persons. These practical items served multiple purposes applied to various Ninja activities, and could even be used as weapons when necessary.

OKHOTSK: A small town at the mouth of the Okhotsk River where it reaches the sea of Okhotsk in Russia. The actual town was established in 1647. In this text, it is used as the name given to the aboriginal people in this region who have a unique language and are believed to be related to early aboriginal peoples of the Japanese archipelago.

OMATSURI: A word meaning "Grand festival" as opposed to *Matsuri*, meaning festival.

SABAKI: Evasive body movement used in combat for both offensive and defensive purposes. There are many types of sabaki movements. Their primary strategy is to infiltrate the movement of the enemy and provide physical advantage.

Samurai: Later designation for a warrior having become a social class and institution as expressed in the military government under the Shogunate.

SEPPUKU: Correct term for ritual suicide as performed by the Samurai (as opposed by the more vulgar term "hara-kiri") as a means of preserving their honor and the honor of the family. It was performed to either atone for a wrong done or to prevent disgrace at the hands of an enemy. It entailed the cutting open of one's own lower abdomen with the Wakizashi or Tanto followed by decapitation performed typically by a respected ally or peer, termed a Kaishaku.

SHAOLIN: Translated as: "Young Forest Temple," and it is the name of an order of Chinese Buddhist Monasteries associated with Chan Buddhism. They are well known in the West due to their martial arts, which was first popularized in the US in a series called "Kung Fu." The first monastery of the order was built in Henan during the Wei Dynasty. Its monks practiced Buddhism without martial arts until after the arrival of Bodhidharma (who, in Chinese, is called Tamo) in the 5th or 6th century. He is thought to have been Persian or South Asian. The name bears a resemblance to the Persian name "Taymoore." He came to teach Buddhism, but was originally refused entrance. He is said to have meditated facing a wall in a nearby cave for 9 years. After finally being admitted he found the monks to be in poor physical condition, so he taught them exercises which became incorporated with martial arts. The monks eventually developed their martial skills to a high level to repel those who raided the monasteries, for physical health, and as a form of discipline. Many of the martial arts are thought to have come from warriors retiring into monastic life and sometimes seeking safe haven. The monks eventually became militarized and between 600 and 1644 even fought in campaigns against rebellions and Japanese bandits. By the end of this period they had developed their own unique martial arts. The temples were repeatedly destroyed and rebuilt. They were ultimately dispersed by the communist government in China only to be popularly restored in 1982. Shao-lin enjoys a healthy and highly respected reputation in the world of martial arts today. (http://wikipedia.org/wiki/shaolin)

SHAOLIN CHIN NA: One of the many styles practiced at the Shao-lin temple and which has many techniques that bear a strong resemblance to many (though not all) techniques found in Taijutsu.

SHINOBI: Name used synonymously to refer to the Ninja.

SHINOBI-IRI: The art practiced by Ninja for the penetration of buildings. It involves the combination of many skills such as stealth, climbing, picking through locks, acrobatics, and even contortion.

SHOGUN: A term, meaning supreme general, that was applied to military generals leading campaigns before the Kamakura period. After the establishment of the Kamakura Bakufu the term was given to its leader and essentially reserved for that post. The first recognized Shogun was Minamoto no Yoritomo. He granted himself the title "Sei I Tai Shogun," translating as "barbarian conquering supreme general," after the defeat of the Taira clan in 1185 at the battle of Dan no Ura when his ascension to power actually took place. Shogun thereafter were Samurai and military dictators who eventually came to rule over the majority of the Japanese archipelago and its major military families through the control of territorial warlords called Daimyo. They ruled by succession and overthrow from 1192 A.D. to 1868 A.D. The Shogun claimed loyalty and subordination to the Emperor, but this was not exercised in reality.

SHOGUNATE: A word used in western texts for the government headed by a supreme military dictator known as the Shogun.

SHUGEN-(Do): Religious practices of the Yamabushi. "Shu" refers to ascetic practices and "Gen" to natural divine powers. (ref : http://members.shaw.ca/shugendo/intro.html) These are ancient practices that incorporate some Buddhist, Taoist and old Shinto ways and concepts. Shugen is, however, a unique and distinct religion from those that have influenced it. It continues to be practiced today in sacred mountain regions throughout Japan.

SOHEI: Literally, "warrior monk," from "so," a designation for monk, and "hei," meaning warrior. The term probably dates from the early17th or late 16th century but is used to describe warriors in the service of the powerful monastic communities of the Kinai region that exerted their influence starting in the later part of the 6th century. The important distinction to be made is that only a subset of these warriors were actually monks, even if they lived on monastic domains and worked for the Buddhist (and in some cases Shinto) clerical communities. Many were bushi who served the temples, and accompanied nobles ordained into the priesthood to their new residence and life. The decline in their power began with seizing of power by the first Shogun and the Samurai class. They continued to maintain their forces until they were attacked by the forces of Oda Nobunaga (who destroyed the Enryakuji) and their ultimate destruction later under Toyotomi Hideyoshi in 1585 (Adolphson).

SOJOBO: The mythical Tengu King of Mount Kurama. He is a Yamabushi Tengu most popularly depicted teaching the boy Minamoto no Yoshitsune the art of Kenjutsu in the 12th century.

TAIHOJUTSU: Term referring to the arts and methods used for apprehending and arresting people. It involves the techniques of toritejutsu which encompasses seizing, immobilizing, and capturing people.

TENGU: Mythical creatures that are part of Japanese folklore, literature, and art. They are associated with the culture of the Yamabushi or Yamahoshii. Among the places they are said to dwell is Mount Kurama, with their leader *Sojobo*. They are reputed to be accomplished warriors and have a penchant for purveying justice through mischievous acts played against those who disrespect the Dharma and those who violate virtue through greed, grandiosity and the misuse of knowledge. They come in two forms: the *Karasu Tengu*, which are crow-like, and the *Yamabushi*

Tengu which are more humanoid. They have special powers, such as shape shifting, changing form from human to animal and back, telepathy, and space-time travel. They appear in Japanese culture around the 6th to 7th century and are probably related to Far Eastern and South Asian myths of the Hindu and Buddhist deity *Garuda* and the Chinese Mountain God *Tiangou*. Their name translates in Japanese as "Heavenly Dog," even though they bear no resemblance to dogs. Perhaps this name implies one of their favored transformations, that of turning into a fox.

TENRYO: A territory managed by a governor appointed by the Shogunate.

TOKUGAWA: Either the last and most enduring Shogunate, or the name given to a particular era. Tokugawa Ieyasu was the first Shogun of his line, one which spanned 250 years. He became Shogun in 1603 after the death of Toyotomi Hideyoshi and the following war of succession. The nation was essentially at peace during this era (also called the Edo period), although this is not to say that there weren't political crises. This regime was known to have a rigidly imposed caste system and to practice corrupt acquisitions of the lesser land holdings of Daimyo that fell out of favor with its administration. Over time it became increasingly corrupt and bureaucratic, until it was abolished in 1868 with the Samurai class and the caste system. There is an abundant documentation of the flowering of the arts in this era and the rise of the merchant class and the decline of the Samurai in popular literature, film and in historical records.

TORIMONO-SANDOGU: These are the special weapons used to apprehend criminals. They are fierce pole-arms with thorny metal barbs designed to entangle the weapons, clothing, or, worse, the skin of the victim. They come in three major types. They are best known as part of the Taihojutsu arsenal used by Japanese feudal law enforcement.

TOYOTOMI HIDEYOSHI (1536-1598): He was one of the most enigmatic leaders in feudal Japan. He was born a peasant. It is reputed that, through a combination of cunning, charm, talent, determination, and an undoubtedly high IQ, met with unparalleled opportunity and success. He served under Oda Nobunaga for years and acquired tremendous military experience through a series of conflicts and negotiations, which ultimately (after the assassination of Oda Nobunaga) led to the unification of Japan under his rule. He was awarded a title by the Imperial court that previously had only been awarded to the Fujiwara. He is famous for building the administrative foundation for the Shogunate, which followed his rule. He divided the social caste of Bushi from peasant and other commoners and conducted a nationwide sword hunt to disarm the population and reduce the risk of popular rebellion. He began the formal persecution of Christians in Japan. He invaded Korea at the end of his reign. This was a bloody and brutal campaign that eventually failed to yield the grand results of domination in Asia which he sought. His reign ended with his death from illness. A war of succession followed, with Tokugawa Ieyasu acquiring total rule over the nation as Shogun in 1603. Hideyoshi's heir and wife committed suicide in 1615 after two sieges of Osaka castle, eliminating all doubt of Tokugawa supremacy. (www.samurai-archives.com/hideyoshi.html)

TSUBO GIRI: A boring tool with a two-pointed head. It is similar in shape to a wrench, with a shaft handle and usually a ring at the other end.

UKEMI: The term "Uke" meaning to receive and "mi" the ground. The Uke is the person in martial practice who performs the attack so that the "Tori," the person performing the technique, may practice. Thus Ukemi has come to mean the art of falling and receiving technique without incurring injury.

WAKIZASHI: The short sword worn by Samurai as part of their two-sword retinue, the longer sword is called a "Katana" and the two swords combined are called a "Daisho."

WuShu: The Mandarin Chinese word for martial arts.

YABUSAME: An ancient art that was highly developed in Samurai culture. It was used in battle for centuries and continues to be popular today as a competition sport in Japan. It is often depicted to Westerners taking place at matsuri. In this art, horsemen shoot at targets with the bow while the horse is in full gallop.

YADOMEJUTSU: A rarely seen art, practiced mostly in the Samurai Bugei and reportedly in a number of Ninjutsu traditions. It consists of deflecting and capturing projectiles and arrows in particular. It involves doing so with or without a weapon.

YAKUZA: Collective name for traditional organized crime groups in Japan. Their name comes from the worst hand one can be dealt in the card game of Hanafuda. This hand includes an eight, a nine and a three, calling them Ya, Ku and Sa. Another name they go by is the *Gokudo.* Their origin is complex and includes participation of the historical *Kabukimono*, the *Hatamoto yakko*, the *Tekiya* and the *Bakuto*. They really came into being during the Edo period. The Kabukimono and Hatamoto Yakko dressed flamboyantly and were often Ronin (Masterless Samurai) who lived in the larger towns gambling, pursuing entertainment, drinking, and otherwise showing their obvious displacement in an ordered society. The Tekiya were peddlers who eventually became an organized force of people making their living on the street. The Bakuto were gamblers, and it is from this group that many Yakuza traditions come. These include the tattoos, *irezumi*, greetings and finger cutting as penance. They control criminal trades like the protection racket, which probably started as a form of legitimate protection in areas where there were no police. They also control prostitution, gambling and corporate skimming. They became more deeply political in the 19th century and some modern Yakuza are members of ultra-nationalist movements including the *Kokuryu-Kai* or Black Dragon Society. The Yakuza continue to exist today; they are largely tolerated and even seen as necessary semi-public organizations in Japan. (http://en.wikipedia.org/wiki/Yakuza)

YAMABUSHI: Although this term sounds like it should mean "mountain warrior" , it in fact means "mountain priest" . Another word for Yamabushi is Yamahoshii. Perhaps the choice of the term bushi in the name is intentional, because Yamabushi are known to have practiced various martial arts – including, for some, the arts of Ninjutsu. It's a sect and community of ascetics inhabiting sacred mountain areas of Japan. To the Yamabushi, mountains are natural Mandalas. They practice *Shugen(-Do)*, which is a religion that is native to Japan and influenced most heavily by esoteric Buddhism, Shintoism and Shamanism. Their culture probably dates back to before the 10th century, by which time they appear more frequently in records. Their martial skills seem to originate with ancient Chinese martial arts, mystical ascetic practices and a profound link to the Shinobi.

YAWARA: The term "Ju" from jujutsu reads also as *yawaragu* (or *yawara* after the "gu" was later dropped). Conceptually it means to "soften." The term yawarajutsu was later replaced in popular culture with jujutsu (Serge Mol Classical fighting arts). For some, the concept is based in the idea of Chinese origin that softness can conquer hardness, and thus the warrior makes himself soft in order to defeat his foe. Another conceptualization is that the technique "softens" the enemy, either softening his will to fight or physically depleting and impairing him. The term has also been interchangeably used to refer to a small, concealed short stick-like weapon made of wood, iron or bone that is held in the palm with either end protruding. It can have a ring piece around the finger, which is attached to the shaft, the common iron version of this weapon being called a *suntetsu* or a *tenouchi*, which is a variant with a longer rope attached that can be used for binding the enemy in classical Jujutsu fighting systems. It is used for close quarter engagement, with particular attention to koppojutsu and atemi.

YAYOI: An era in Japan from 300 BC to 250 AD, followed by the Kofun period and preceded by the Jomon. It is named after a section of Tokyo where the first excavations dating to this period took place. The first organized cultivation of rice in paddies is believed to have taken place in this era as did the evolution of new forms of pottery and other arts. There was a tremendous increase in the population during this time. Evidence from linguistic studies give mixed evidence that this was due to Manchurian and Korean (at that time *Koguryo* and *Paekche*) immigration even if genetically the populations are very close. There was significant cultural expansion during this time, as demonstrated in various arts such as ceramics, tools and weapons made with iron; agriculture; clothing; architecture; and social stratification. There is noted to have been strong cultural influence from China and Korea, consistent with a theory of immigration. Shinto originated during this period, which is of particular relevance as it is tied so closely to the identity of the Japanese people.(http://en.wikipedia.org/wiki/Yayoi)

ZEN: The continuation of Chan Buddhism in Japan. It tends to be less inclined toward the devotional prayer style of practice and more towards the experiential. Its main practice is meditation; Zen uses *Koan* (a short verse) and metaphor to express the inexpressible non-duality of enlightenment, or "*Satori*" as it is called in Japanese Zen. It has become very popular in the West.

References/Sources

1. *The Art of War*, By Sun Tze, Translation by Thomas Cleary. Shambhala 2009

2. *The Book of the Samurai, the Warrior Class of Japan*, by Stephen R Turnbull Ch 1, Copyright 1982 Bison Books

3. *Chosakushu* Vol 3 *Zukai Shurikenjutsu*, Vol1 *Hojojutsu* by Fujita Seiko

4. *Classical Budo: The Martial Arts and Ways of Japan*, Vol 2 by Donn F. Draeger. Weatherhill Publishing 1973.

5. *Classical Fighting Arts of Japan—A Complete Guide to Koryu Jujutsu* by Serge Mol. Kodansha International 2001.

6. *Classical Weaponry of Japan—Special Weapons and Tactics of the Martial Arts* by Serge Mol. Kodansha International 2003.

7. *Comprehensive Asian Fighting Arts* by Donn F. Draeger and Robert W. Smith. Kodansha International 1980.

8. *The Essence of Shaolin White Crane-Martial Power and Qigong* by Dr. Yang, Jwing-Ming. YMAA Publication Center 1996.

9. *Feudal Architecture of Japan* by Kiyoshi Hirai, Heibonsha survey of Japanese Art Vol 13, Weatherhill Press 1973

10. *Fujita Seiko The Last Koga Ninja* by Phillip T. Hevener, Copyright 2008, Xlibris

11. *Guns, Germs and Steel* by Jared Diamond, *The Fates of Human Societies* Copyright 1999, Norton Press

12. *Heavenly Warriors—The evolution of Japan's Military, 500-1300* by William Wayne Farris. Harvard University Press 1992.

13. *Japanese Throwing Weapons: Mastering Shuriken Throwing Techniques* by Daniel

Fletcher. Tuttle Publishing 2011.

14. *Koryu Bujutsu: Classical Warrior Traditions of Japan* Edited by Diane Skoss. Koryu Books 1997.

15. *Kugutsu Mawashi no Ki* by Oe Masafusa 1041–1111

16. *Ninja—The True Story of Japan's Secret Warrior Cult* by Stephen Turnbull. The Caxton Publishing Group 1991.

17. *Ninjutsu* by Tsuneyoshi Matsuno, Copyright 1991. Translation of original work by Kensai Buyouken, Copyright 1916.

18. *The Prince and The Monk, Shotoku Worship in Shinran's Buddhism*, by Kenneth Doo Young Lee Copyright 2007, State University of New York Press.

19. *Samurai: An Illustrated History* by Mitsuo Kure, Tuttle Publishing 2002.

20. *Secrets of the Ninja: Their training, tools and techniques* by Hiromitsu Kuroi, Cocoro Books, Copyright 2002

21. *Secret Weapons of Jujutsu* by Don Cunningham, Budo Kai Ltd 2000.

22. *Shoninki: The secret teachings of the Ninja, the 17th century manual of the art of concealment by Master Natori Masazumi with commentaries by Axel Mazuer Translated* by Jon E. Graham. Destiny Books 2009.

23. *Soldiers of the Dragon-Chinese Armies 1500 BC-AD 1840* by C.J. Peers. Osprey Publishing 2006.

24. *The Teeth and Claws of the Buddha-Monastic Warriors and Sohei in Japanese History* by Mikael S Adolphson. University of Hawaii Press 2007.

25. *Taiho-Jutsu: Law and Order in the Age of the Samurai* by Don Cunningham. Tuttle Publishing 2004.

Internet Resources

Note this list is only used when the actual website does not appear directly in the text.

Ir-1:
www.go-star.com/antiquing/puzzleboxes.htm (pg 41)

Ir-2:
http://www.dougukan.jp/contents-en/ (pg 50)

Ir-3: www.heritageofjapan.wordpress.com (pg 81, 89)

Ir-4:
http://genderaquafish.files.wordpress.com/2011/04/11-c-lim-braving-the-sea.pdf (pg 113)

Ir-5:
http://www.nms.ac.uk/collections/details.php?item_id=330698&terms=Living%20Lands&key=location.entry_3&offset=272 (pg 93)

Ir-6:
http://cabinetmagazine.org/issues/26/foer.php (mizugumo and ukidaru as in the bansenshukai) (pg 96)

About the Author

Michel Farivar is a Board Certified psychiatrist born and raised in Toronto, Canada, who studied Medicine at the University of Brussels in Belgium and trained in both Internal Medicine and Psychiatry in Cleveland, Ohio. He met Grandmaster Robert Law in 1982 in Toronto. At that time he was actively training in Tae Kwon Do and had a 1st Dan black belt from Park Brothers, learning from Sam Park.

Life was about to change:

I was invited to join Grandmaster Laws' class by a friend of mine in high school, ostensibly to learn a different and unorthodox form of self-defense. By a strange coincidence, as we were strolling down Yonge street and she was telling me about him and his classes, we practically tripped over Grandmaster Law himself out shopping with his family.

Back then we called him "Sensei," and he had not told us anything about where his methods came from, or what they were.

I was the first to arrive for the next class, curious to learn about this strange "new" martial art. Grandmaster Law bluntly asked me if I could defend myself with Tae Kwon Do, against a knife, a stick, or any other weapon. I truthfully answered that I really wasn't sure.

He told me to attack him with full intent after assuring me I would not be harmed. Grandmaster Law is not a tall man, and I fancied myself to be good with my feet, so I tried a quick roundhouse kick to the head. I felt my foot graze the stubble on his cheek. Next thing I know, I'm on the floor, hands and legs entwined behind me and I cannot move—as promised, totally unharmed. Grandmaster Law was sitting on me, chuckling, "Must have been luck! Want to try that again?"

"Sure!" I said, wanting to know how he did that. Needless to say, the result was essentially the same the second time. I was hooked.

After that I trained eighteen months straight with him before starting university. Unbeknownst to me, I had been selected among about 20 others to be his Uke and assist him in teaching the art.

It was around 1983-4, that Grandmaster Law was encouraged by a friend of his to go public with Ninjutsu and it was just before then that he had revealed it to me. The schools to which he has title as headmaster are Yoshin Miji and Geijin Kasuga Ryu. The latter being the main art taught.

I have been training with him ever since then, though there were years when I had to be away at school, and returning only in summer to receive instruction.

During absences I always practiced, found people to teach and deepened my knowledge.

I received my license to teach core techniques in 1986, my Master title in 1999 and succession to the art in 2009. In spite of meeting these goals, I consider myself still very much a student in the art.

I wrote this book for several reasons. One was to give a voice to the complexity and wonder of this martial art, and the never-ending intrigue I experience with its effectiveness and almost terrifying efficiency. Another reason was to express the grass roots of Ninjutsu and show that it is not an art based on the sword, like so many of its contemporaries. Most importantly, I wanted to honor Grandmaster Law, who taught me personally and at no monetary cost, and to thank him for believing in me.

About Grandmaster Robert Law

Grandmaster Robert Law was born into a Ninja family. He is half Japanese. His Aunt and Uncle (who were Japanese on his mother's side) trained him and spared no hardship in preparing him. This regimen began for him at age 5 or 6 and continued relentlessly for many years away in isolated areas on the Japanese islands and eventually in North America.

He is keenly aware of how hard earned his training was and of the admonishments of his teachers to keep certain areas of the art hidden. As a result, he only reveals more in depth teachings to those whom he feels have earned it. Grandmaster Law does not feel that it is worthwhile to exploit his Ninja lineage for fame or recognition.

He has lived in many countries and taught the art to all kinds of people, many of who did not know that they were learning the Ninja arts. His students include military personnel, law enforcement officers, and even special groups like those in rape crisis centers. He has over 50 years of teaching experience.

He has confided that his reasons for going partially public are to help repair some of the unpleasant stereotypes and myths regarding the Ninja. He also wants people to be aware that the Ninja continue to exist and practice their arts, and that they are not in fact represented by a single individual or group as some would have us believe.

Some will take the obscurity of this art and its practitioners as license to conjecture. Even if the schools over which he presides go fully public, this would remain the case. Hence the Grandmaster will continue to teach and reveal only those aspects of his art that he is comfortable releasing.

The Grandmaster also feels that the public is now more receptive to a serious exploration of Ninjutsu. It is entirely within the Ninja tradition to break new ground and to adapt to the modernization of the world in which they live. Grandmaster Law does not desire that his art be relegated to the status of a historical anecdote or an item of mention in a museum. More importantly, the art no longer knows the boundaries of borders and race.

The following is a list of some (but not all) of the arts the Grandmaster teaches to the public as Grandmaster to the Geijin Ryu, Yoshin-Miji Ryu:

Nin-Po Taijutsu (Ninja Hand to Hand Combat)
Taihenjutsu (Art of Body Movement)
Dakentaijutsu (Art of Body Striking)
Jutaijutsu (Art of Grappling and Ground fighting)
Bojutsu (Art of the Full Staff)
Hanbojutsu (Art of the Half-Staff)
Ninja Ken-Po (Art of Swordsmanship)
Kenjutsu (Art of Sword fighting)
Tantojutsu (Art of the Tanto (Knife))
Shurikenjutsu (Art of Using and Throwing Shuriken)
Kusarijutsu (Art of the Chain and Rope)
Kyoketsu Shoge (Art of the Kyoketsu Shoge)
Kusarigama (Art of the Kusarigama)
Te'ppo (Art of Guns)
Ninki (Art of Ninja Tools and Small Weapons)

Fukiya (Art of the Blowgun)
Heiho (Art of Martial Principles)
Gotonpo (Art of Escape)
Nin-Po Nikkyo (Art of Spiritual Development)
Yarijutsu (Art of the Spear (also Sojutsu)
Naginatajutsu (Art of the Naginata)
Bajutsu (Art of Horsemanship)
Sui-ren (Art of Water Combat)
Shinobi-iri (Art of Penetrating Structures)
Hensojutsu (Art of Disguise and Impersonation)
Cho-ho (Art of Espionage)
Bo-ryaku (Art of Strategy)
Intonjutsu (Art of Concealment and Camouflage)
Hojojutsu (Art of Rope Tying, Knots and Binding)

www.ingramcontent.com/pod-product-compliance
Lightning Source LLC
Chambersburg PA
CBHW031156270326
41931CB00006B/299